The Sex Myth

THE GAP BETWEEN OUR FANTASIES AND REALITY

Rachel Hills

Simon & Schuster Paperbacks

New York   London   Toronto   Sydney   New Delhi

Simon & Schuster Paperbacks
An Imprint of Simon & Schuster, Inc.
1230 Avenue of the Americas
New York, NY 10020

First Simon & Schuster trade paperback edition August 2015

SIMON & SCHUSTER PAPERBACKS and colophon are registered trademarks of Simon & Schuster, Inc.

For information about special discounts for bulk purchases, please contact Simon & Schuster Special Sales at 1-866-506-1949 or business@simonandschuster.com.

The Simon & Schuster Speakers Bureau can bring authors to your live event. For more information or to book an event, contact the Simon & Schuster Speakers Bureau at 1-866-248-3049 or visit our website at www.simonspeakers.com.

Manufactured in the United States of America

3   5   7   9   10   8   6   4

Library of Congress Cataloging-in-Publication Data

Hills, Rachel.
The sex myth : the gap between our fantasies and reality / Rachel Hills.
        pages cm
1. Sex customs. 2. Sex (Psychology)—Social aspects.
3. Identity (Psychology). 4. Sex in popular culture. 5. Feminism.
6. Feminist Theory. I. Title.
HQ21.H4565 2015
306.7—dc23
2015003770

ISBN 978-1-4516-8578-7
ISBN 978-1-4516-8580-0 (ebook)

Note to readers: Some names and identifying details of people portrayed in this book have been changed.

For Monica

The most toxic formulas in our cultures are not passed down in political practice, they're passed down in mundane narratives.

—Junot Díaz

My point is not that everything is bad, but that everything is dangerous.

—Michel Foucault

Contents

Introduction

When I was in my late teens and early twenties, I was consumed by sex. Not by the physical urge to have it, although I had my share of crushes and unfulfilled desires. Nor was I overly concerned with the particulars of how I might go about it, although I studiously read *Cosmopolitan* each month so that I would know what to do when the occasion arose. My obsession was more esoteric than that. I was consumed by the *idea* of sex—by what it meant and by what it might reveal about who I was.

If I didn't have sex, did that make me frigid or a loser? If I did do it, but with someone I didn't love—or worse, with someone who didn't love me—would I regret the decision later? What if *Cosmo*'s thirty-six hot new sex positions failed me in practice? (Friends had reported that some of them were tricky to pull off.)

I had grown up on a diet of teen magazines that treated sex with cautious reverence, followed by women's magazines that celebrated it as a symbol of female empowerment. In the sitcoms I watched on TV, the single characters dated (and by implication, slept with) new people each week. In the conversations I had with acquaintances, sex was at once a subject of nervous excitement and an unspoken assumption—something it was expected that *everyone* was doing. I, meanwhile, had made it not only through high school a virgin, but through four years of college as well.

This was not an outcome of my own design, and it was not something that most people would have guessed about me. From the outside, I looked like a normal girl—or at least I hoped I did. I did "normal girl" things like go to parties, flirt, and exchange dirty jokes with my friends. In some arenas, I even fared a little better than normal. I didn't just go to the occasional party; I was a veritable social butterfly. I didn't just try to make myself look "presentable" for class; I got up an extra forty-five minutes early to wash, dry, and straighten my hair. But beneath the facade, I felt unattractive in the most literal sense of the word: incapable of attracting anyone I was interested in, regardless of how many friends I had or how much I manipulated my appearance to match what I thought I was supposed to look like.

These two states—"girl about town" and "secret sexual loser"— seemed irreconcilable to me, each one canceling out the other. My lack of a sex life felt like a mark of failed moral character, the physical manifestation of every flaw I had ever suspected I had and of every defect I feared that the people around me were all too aware of but were too polite to mention out loud. Why else would I be uniquely incapable of an act that everyone else appeared to navigate with ease?

In an era in which most of what we hear and read about sex tends toward the sensational, my story might seem unusual. But my concerns weren't unique to me at all. To the contrary, they were a reflection of broader social and political trends. They were a product of a culture that tells us that we must be sexy, sexually active, and skilled in bed in order to be adequate human beings—and that teaches us that the truth of who we are can be found in our sex lives.

Sex is an act bound up in the body, but the way that each of us experiences it is driven by more than just biology. Everything about sex—from the stories we choose to share with our friends to the people we choose to do it with to the remarkably standardized sexual playbook that starts with kissing, followed by touching, and finally penetration—is influenced by social and cultural forces. Sex is not just physical but symbolic, employed as a barometer of the success of our relationships and the degree to which other people want to be intimate with us. It serves as a proxy for our physical attractiveness and how well we fit in with the people around us.

What each of us believes about sex is a product of our particular time and place. The second-century theologian Clement of Alexandria advised Christians not only against engaging in nonreproductive sexual acts such as oral and anal sex but also against having sex at especially pleasurable times of day—such as the morning, the daytime, or after dinner (that is to say, at virtually any time of the day). The Victorians delighted in cataloging every variety of possible deviance: from bondage to bestiality to having sex from behind rather than face-to-face. Even the ancient Greeks, regularly praised for their open-minded approach to carnal matters, operated within a complex and contradictory code of sexual ethics, in which sexual relationships between boys and men were treated as a rite of passage into adulthood, but it was considered demeaning for a man to be penetrated by a man of the same age and social status.

But despite our long-standing preoccupation with sexuality, most people know surprisingly little about the sex lives of others. One result of this information gap is that, like I did, many people assume that others are having better sex, and more of it, than they actually are. While researching his book *Guyland: The Perilous World in Which Boys Become Men*, sociologist Michael Kimmel asked male college students across the United States what proportion of their classmates they believed had sex on any given weekend. The average answer they gave was about 80 percent. In fact, according to the Online College Social Life Survey, a cross-campus study of more than 24,000 American university students, 80 percent is the proportion of college seniors who have *ever* had sex. Writes Kimmel: "The actual percentage [who have sex] on any given weekend is closer to 5 to 10 percent." Kathleen Bogle, another American sociologist whose research focuses on young people and casual sex, has made similar observations: no matter how much sex the students she interviewed were having, most of them assumed that other young people were having even more.

Even when I felt most isolated and insecure, I knew that many people had sexual histories that were less perfect—or at least more complex—than they let on in public. Most of the conversations I participated in about sex were at once embellished and notably lacking in detail: designed to convey an impression of experience and sophistication while giving away as little information as possible. But the wall wasn't always up. I would drop my guard around my closest friends, and they would drop theirs around me. The issues they were dealing with were often different from my own, but they were enough to suggest that others too may have covered up any cracks in their sexual facade with a metaphorical layer of paint.

It wasn't until shortly before my twenty-fifth birthday, however, that I began to realize how thinly that coat of paint might be applied. This book is dedicated to my good friend Monica, a vivacious ball of energy I met through a youth arts organization we both worked at in our early twenties, and with whom I fell in swift platonic love when I read her witty, self-reflective blogs and zines, in which she chronicled everything from the guys she was crushing on to her work as a bartender.

Monica represented everything I thought a young woman should be, and everything I aspired to be myself. She was confident and friendly and adventurous, and one of the smartest, most insightful people I knew. She was *fun*—the kind of person who always stayed out late, because you never knew how the night would end if you went out, but you always knew what would happen if you stayed home. This was a woman who, only a couple of years before, had crafted badges reading "five-dollar kiss" and worn them out to clubs. In other words, she was about as far from the stereotype of the uptight wallflower as you could get.

Then one summer evening, when we were walking to our respective public transport hubs after a party, she turned to me and declared, in the same careless-yet-dramatic manner in which she might have told me about a new band she had discovered, "You know, next month it will be two years since I've had sex. And I haven't kissed anyone in a year."

I tried not to show it at the time, but I was floored. That my own sexual history fell short of the benchmarks that had been set out for me, I knew very well. But to realize that one of my most brilliant, gregarious friends might be in the same boat was a revelation. If someone as outgoing and seemingly sexually confident as Monica was not sexually active, then maybe sex wasn't so ubiquitous—or its absence such a mark of failure—after all.

My curiosity piqued, I decided to find out what my peers were really experiencing, with a view to writing an article about my observations. I set up an online survey and distributed the call-out to my friends and acquaintances—all strictly anonymous, of course—asking them how many people they'd had sex with and what kinds of relationships they'd had. One guy, in his late twenties, confessed that after losing his virginity a decade earlier, he didn't have sex again for two years. "I wasn't particularly interested in it," he wrote. "I would pick up girls in bars but didn't want to take things any further than second or third base." He told me that he had laughed when he saw *40 Days and 40 Nights*, the early-00s comedy depicting teen heartthrob Josh Hartnett's struggle to stay celibate for a month. One thirtysomething colleague revealed that she hadn't had sex in more than ten years, since her last relationship had ended.

The responses weren't all about not getting laid. One man, in his early thirties, divulged that he'd had over one hundred sexual partners. Another friend, a gay man then in his early twenties, told me over dinner that he'd had more than three hundred partners (two years later, when we revisited the conversation, he was up to almost five hundred). But they were even greater exceptions than I was. At the same time that I was starting to ask myself these questions, academics like Kimmel, Bogle, and New York University's Paula England were beginning to conduct broad-scale quantitative surveys of young adults' sexual behavior. Like my own informal surveys, their results suggested that my generation's sex and social lives weren't the booze-soaked, wet-T-shirt-clad perma-party they were increasingly being portrayed as in the media.

Even more interesting than the survey results were the conversations my investigation sparked with the people I encountered in my day-to-day life. As soon as people knew I was writing about sex, they wanted to talk to me about it—and not just in the usual exchange of repartee or relationship troubleshooting that I was accustomed to. They wanted to talk about their insecurities and uncertainties, about those aspects of their sexual histories they had never quite been able to make sense of or were too embarrassed to tell other people about. Everyone, it seemed, had a story to tell, and most of them felt like they were falling short of the ideal in some way.

The more of these conversations I had, the more I realized that we needed a new way of speaking about sex: one that not only encompassed a broader array of experiences but that treated sex as a social act as much as a biological one. It was time to go beyond the usual conversations about the battle of the sexes, hookup culture, and the effects of Internet pornography to look more deeply at the assumptions we hold about sexuality and why we believe them to be true. In other words, it was time to formalize my investigation.

So I went to the library and picked up every book I could find on the subject, along with hundreds of academic journal articles across the fields of sociology, psychology, and medical science. I wanted to educate myself on everything from campus casual sex cultures to how norms are created and upheld to the way that our perceptions of sexual dysfunction have evolved over time. I continued to read the same magazines and watch the same TV shows that had fueled my insecurities about my own sexual history, but instead of looking to them for guidance on the ways of the world, I studied their content with a critical eye, interrogating the assumptions they made about their readers and the surprisingly subtle ways in which they communicated what kind of behavior was acceptable and expected.

Along the way, I traveled across the United States, Canada, Australia, and the UK to speak with more than two hundred people about their sex lives, and was contacted by hundreds more. Most of them, like me, were members of the generation popularly known as Millennials—those born between the early 1980s and the mid-1990s. They were men and women, gay and straight, white, black,

Asian, and Latino. But for all their differences, they were united by a sense that there was something wrong with the stories we tell about sex, and most of all, with the way that our culture alternately elevates and demonizes sexuality.

I began to realize that we were in the grip of a Sex Myth, which regulated our sexual behavior even as on the surface we appeared to be more free than we had ever been before. The first layer of the Sex Myth was the most obvious: the media myth of a hypersexual society, visible in everything from moral panics over wayward youth to the saturation of sexual content in popular culture to the idea that to be sexually liberated—to be confident, free, and, above all, true to ourselves—meant being sexual in one very particular way.

The second, less obvious, dimension of the Sex Myth was the cultural and emotional value invested in sex: the belief that sex was more special, more significant, a source of greater thrills and more perfect pleasure than any other activity humans engage in. I didn't feel unattractive and inadequate just because I wasn't having sex. I felt that way because I lived in a culture that told me that my sex life was one of the most defining qualities of who I was. It wasn't sex that was the problem, but the importance that I, and so many others, had attached to it.

In this book, I will make visible some of the building blocks upon which our assumptions about sex are grounded: our beliefs about what is normal and desirable, how it is appropriate for a man or a woman to behave, and what makes a person good in bed. I will chart how we have moved from a culture that told us we were dirty if we did have sex to one that tells us we are defective if we do not do it enough—and how these seemingly conflicting ideas have more in common than we tend to think. Most crucially, I will show how the

Sex Myth has made sex the bedrock of our morals and identity, and how this link between sex and self is used to shape our behavior and even our desires.

Finally, I will consider what life might look like beyond the Sex Myth. What would it take to live in a society that respects difference in all its forms? How can we create a culture that privileges more than just a facade of sexual freedom? Is it possible to drain sex of its grand significance, and is that something we should even aspire to do?

This book probably won't demolish our existing beliefs about sex completely, and it probably won't usher us into a new sexual utopia. But I believe that the first step to solving a problem is to name it, and I hope that in naming the Sex Myth, we can begin to move toward a way of thinking about sex that is less fraught, more honest, and ultimately more free for everyone.

1

This Is Not What Liberation Looks Like

The first episode of the British teen drama *Skins* began with a cacophony of phone calls. Tony Stonem, the show's charismatic alpha-male lead, was on a mission: to help his best friend, the hapless but lovable nerd Sid, lose his virginity before his seventeenth birthday. And the key to achieving this goal? "We go to a party and get some girl raucously spliffed," joked Tony. "In her confused state, she comes to believe—momentarily, of course—that you're attractive. And then she bangs your brains out."

As plotlines go, virginity-loss quests like this one are a standard coming-of-age trope. Think of the pact between four friends to get laid before senior prom in *American Pie*, or Blair Waldorf's increasingly frenzied attempts to seduce her reluctant high school sweetheart Nate in the first season of *Gossip Girl*. But when *Skins* launched in the United States at the beginning of 2011, the notoriously conservative Parents Television Council declared it "the most dangerous show for children we have ever seen."

The reaction may have been over the top, but it wasn't surprising. *Skins*, after all, was a show about young people writ wild that, in the words of PTC president Tim Winter, "[made] light of lying to parents" and showed "all manner of harmful, irresponsible, illegal, and adult-themed behavior"—much of it sexual. And there is little that simultaneously terrifies and titillates more than the spectacle of youth out of control.

Skins, to its credit, took the allure of the out-of-control teenager to a less glamorous place than many of its counterparts. Where the high school juniors on *Gossip Girl* had earth-shattering orgasms in the backseats of limousines, their counterparts in *Skins* got it on in bathroom stalls, their adolescent butt cheeks awkwardly on display. Where the teenage cast of the CW's *90210* sipped on cocktails in upscale Mexican resorts without so much as a request for an ID, their equivalents on *Skins* got wasted at seedy outdoor raves.

But just because *Skins* employed a grittier brand of hedonism than other teenage dramas doesn't mean that it revealed an unspoken truth of young adult life. To the contrary, shows like *Skins* tell us exactly what we want to hear: that young people today are more shameless, wanton, and darkly glamorous than any generation before them. They don't challenge our preconceptions of sex so much as they affirm them, while wrapping up our voyeurism with a bow of rebellion. In other words, shows like *Skins* feed directly into the first layer of the Sex Myth: that our culture has never been more sexually debauched, and that this debauchery is alternately the source of our downfall and our freedom.

Millennials Gone Wild

Older people have wrung their hands over young people's bad behavior since Plato complained about youth disrespecting their parents and rioting in the streets in the fourth century BC. And as signs of aging go, that first moment of horror at what the next generation might be doing with their genitals ranks up there with sprouting your first gray hair or hanging up your dancing shoes in favor of a night in with Netflix. But at some point in the mid-'00s, anxieties about teens, twentysomethings, and sex began to hit a fever pitch.

Part of it was a product of popular culture. The first half of the '00s saw the rise of *Girls Gone Wild*, which enticed young women to take off their tops and perform on camera in exchange for *GGW*-branded hats and T-shirts. It saw Britney Spears and Christina Aguilera (and later Hilary Duff, Selena Gomez, and Miley Cyrus) go from artificially chaste Disney stars to artificially sexy pop starlets in the blink of a music video. Paris Hilton and Kim Kardashian parlayed homemade sex tapes into international media empires encompassing jewelry, nightclubs, music, multiple reality TV shows, and more. *Playboy* went from a soft-core porn magazine to an aspirational pop culture brand, and Victoria's Secret went from a staid underwear retailer to a family-friendly peep show starring some of the world's most beautiful women.

Where the 1980s had been dominated by antiporn crusaders such as radical feminist Andrea Dworkin and legal scholar Catharine MacKinnon, by the beginning of the twenty-first century, the cultural pendulum had swung in a more libertarian direction. The "sex wars," which had pitted feminists against one another on the integrity of everything from sex work to BDSM to having sex with men, had been won, and the winning position was that sexual imagery didn't have to be degrading or objectifying. To the contrary: eroticism could be a source of power.

And increasingly, for younger women especially, sexuality had become a key arena in which power was exercised, whether it was

books such as *The Ethical Slut* or *The Happy Hook-Up*, which promoted the invigorating possibilities of casual sex, or dynamic, successful women such as singer Beyoncé, Olympic swimmer Amanda
Beard, and would-be lawyers taking off their clothes for soft-core
men's magazines like *Maxim* and *FHM*.

Enter Ariel Levy, whose 2005 book, *Female Chauvinist Pigs*,
flipped the prevailing story about sex and popular culture on its
head. Levy's concern wasn't about the proliferation of sex but its
representation, and the way that sex and female empowerment had
become entwined in a manner that was both ubiquitous and compulsory. "What we once regarded as a *kind* of sexual expression we
now view *as* sexuality," she wrote. But the success of *Female Chauvinist Pigs* also provided a platform for a number of unarticulated
anxieties that had been brewing just beneath the surface of public
debate, and the news media and commentariat enthusiastically
latched on to the idea that young people today—and young women
in particular—were more sexually precocious than any generation
that had come before them.

On NPR, sex educator Deborah Roffman worried that casual
sex was robbing twentysomethings of their capacity to form intimate relationships, while Christian sociologist Mark Regnerus argued in *Slate* that hooking up tipped the scales of sexual power too
far in men's favor, labeling it a matter of "sexual economics." In Brit-
ain's *Daily Mail*, filmmaker Olivia Lichtenstein reported breathlessly
on the "deeply disturbing . . . generation SEX." In my home country
of Australia, the newspapers told stories of ten-year-olds smeared
with too much lipstick and twentysomethings dropping their pants
to shake their buttocks "like G-stringed baboons in oestrus." As one
article said, salivating, "They're here, they're mostly bare, and they
don't care who's looking."

This wasn't the first time there had been widespread alarm about the sexual habits of the young and single. In his 1920 novel *This Side of Paradise*, F. Scott Fitzgerald told tales of Victorian mothers startled by "how casually their daughters were accustomed to being kissed." When the oral contraceptive pill made its debut in the early 1960s, *US News & World Report* worried that it would "lead to sexual anarchy." A 1964 cover story for *Time* despaired the dawn of "champagne parties for teenagers, padded brassieres for twelve-year-olds, and going 'steady' at ever younger ages." The magazine recalled the Orgone Box, a closet-shaped device popularized by Austrian psychoanalyst and sex liberationist Wilhelm Reich in the 1940s, which claimed to unleash the sexual energy of the person inside it. "Now," the anonymous editorial lamented, "it sometimes seems that all America is one big Orgone Box."

But although teenagers and twentysomethings were the subject of much of this moralizing, the real anxiety wasn't about young people—not really. They were just a lightning rod for a broader set of concerns about a sexual culture that was changing then and is still doing so now, in ways both real and imagined.

And a lot has changed. Over the past half century, the way we form our families has diversified from the cookie-cutter nuclear model that wallpapered popular culture in the 1950s and 1960s to encompass same-sex couples, single parents, blended families, and more. We are marrying later and in smaller numbers—in 2013, 28 percent of American adults had never married, up from just 15 percent in 1960. In the space of fifty years, sex has gone from being permitted only within marriage to being accepted within a monogamous relationship to being embraced—in some circles, at least—outside the framework of any ongoing relationship at all. And with the rise of new online and mobile dating technologies such as Tinder and OkCupid, if you're looking for no-strings-attached sex, it is easier to find now than ever before.

More than an anxiety about young people in particular, the hysteria over teen and twentysomething sex that emerged in the '00s was rooted in a fear that, in an attempt to create a sexually liberated society, we had accidentally unleashed more freedom than we could handle. As Australian newspaper the *Age* warned in 2009: "[m]any teenagers and young adults have turned the free-sex mantra of the 1970s into a lifestyle, and older generations simply don't have a clue."

When I first began to notice these articles in my early twenties, I was skeptical of how accurate they were. For my own twenty-second birthday party, I had asked my friends to dress up as hotel heiresses Paris and Nicky Hilton, famous for their fortune and their skimpy clothes, for a night at a downtown Sydney club. It seemed fun, theatrical, and mildly humorous, an act of performance and satire. We applied the same tongue-in-cheek humor a few months later when the Tina Fey–penned *Mean Girls* was released in cinemas, heading out to a college party in sky-high heels and thigh-skimming skirts. To a casual observer on the street, we probably looked like the very image of "raunch culture," but in our minds, we were making fun of the stereotype.

The hypersexualized *Girls Gone Wild* story that was dominating the media didn't fit with anything I'd seen or experienced. I had spent most of the first half of my twenties convinced that everyone was getting laid more than I was, but not once had I imagined it manifesting as a row of naked buttocks convulsing like "baboons in oestrus." It was less in-your-face than that. It was in the sigh one friend let out a few days after breaking up with her long-term boyfriend. "How *do* you do it?" she asked me, driving her fork into the college cafeteria table in an effort to diffuse her sexual frustration. It was in the grin on another friend's face as he pointed to the car seat on which he'd had his first one-night stand. Most of what we knew about each other's sex lives was communicated through inference. You told people about the three weekends during which you did hook up, not the forty-nine during which you didn't.

Like most college students, most of my friends had had sex at some point, whether it was with a high school sweetheart, a one-night stand, or a first love they had met on campus. Some of them had had casual sex, or had hooked up in relationships that petered out before either party had a chance to define them. But the sex my friends were having didn't look like the scandalous descriptions in the newspapers or the aspirational hedonism in the magazines we read.

It wasn't just our experiences that diverged from the media stereotypes. The Online College Social Life Survey found that 72 percent of college students engage in some kind of hookup at least once by their senior year, but it also found that most of them don't do it all that often, with 40 percent of those surveyed hooking up with three or fewer people over the course of their college career. Nor did "hooking up" necessarily translate to the type of sexual activity that most people who write about its dangers might imagine. Only one-third of students had engaged in intercourse during their most recent hookup. Even more telling, one in five students hadn't hooked up at all.

These statistics were echoed in stories I heard from young people across the English-speaking world. "A lot of people say that college is so full of sex," reported Shannon, a pretty freshman with long limbs and strawberry-blond hair. "And it is a pretty party-hard environment in terms of drinking. It can be full-on. But sex? Not so much."

A nineteen-year-old communications student at an East Coast liberal arts university, Shannon is smart, articulate, and sexually confident. She first had sex three years ago, with her high school boyfriend. "For me, sex was a really big deal," she recalls as we sit cross-legged on the floor of her dorm room. "I was really adamant that we had to wait at least six months before we did it." When Shannon and her boyfriend did have sex, she didn't feel pressured at all. "We'd been fooling around for an hour or so already and I was so turned on, there was absolutely no pain at all. Quite the opposite, in fact." After that, they had sex any chance they could, in ways that were generous and playful. "It set me up to expect men to take care of my needs," she explains.

Shannon and her boyfriend were very serious about each other—they dated for almost three years and had talked about getting married—but split up at the end of high school, when Shannon "just felt that [she] needed to be single." In the nine months since their breakup, Shannon has slept with six men—one a vacation romance in South America, some guys she knows from school, and a couple more she met in bars and clubs. "I have definitely slept with more people now than I ever thought I would," she says. Shannon's positive experiences with her ex have proved helpful when it comes to negotiating casual hookups. "I am very much aware of what I should expect from guys, in terms of how I am treated," she asserts. "I can tell if a guy has had a girlfriend before. If they've only really [had sex] casually, then they don't have a clue what to do apart from the basics. So I can tell if they've had a girl give them some instruction."

She tells me about a friend she hooked up with a month or two ago, who asked her to go down on him but refused to kiss her after. "I told him he was never getting in my bed again," she recalls with anger. "That was the only time I felt bad about a sexual choice I had made, and I hated that he had made me feel like that." They're still friends, and "he thinks it's going to happen again, but it's not," she says. "Most of the guys I've been with have been really lovely, though," she clarifies. "I've been lucky that way."

But Shannon is an exception among the people she knows. Most of her friends in high school were virgins, and a lot of the girls she knows at college are, too. "I am probably the most sexually active of all my friends," she says.

Shannon tells me about a drinking game she played with some of the girls in her dorm recently—"Never Have I Ever," in which each person declares something they have "never" done, and anyone who *has* done the act in question has to take a drink. "One of the girls said she had never taken anyone home," she recalls, "and I said I had." Even though it had happened a few times, she told them she'd only done it once to soften the blow. "And they were still shocked!" she exclaims. "I thought to myself, if a reporter was here, in this big group of fifteen girls, and only one of us had in two months taken one person home, they wouldn't believe it."

Footloose and Fancy Free: Sex without Limits

Even the most flimsy media portrayals don't grow out of thin air, and the myth of our hypersexual culture is no different. Ethan, a twenty-four-year-old aspiring screenwriter living in East LA, is caustic and contrarian. He reads *Vanity Fair* and the *Economist*, and likes to think of himself as a young Ernest Hemingway or Christopher Hitchens—provocative, hard drinking, and hard living. Tall and slender, with blue eyes and a smattering of dark brown stubble on his chin, Ethan is confident in his intellect but less so in his physical appearance. "I know that I am not what most people think of as handsome, chiseled, or toned," he says self-deprecatingly, taking a sip of his cheap beer. "I scrub up okay in a suit, but I'm not someone who will walk into a room and make heads turn."

Ethan is equally critical of the images of female "sexiness" that pervade popular culture. "It's completely different from what most women look like," he says. On the question of casual sex, he is ambivalent. Until recently, he used to worry that he was inexperienced compared with other men his age. He didn't have sex until college, and he spent most of those years in a long-term relationship. But since graduating and moving to LA, he has encountered the opposite problem; instead of feeling embarrassed by the sex he is not having, he has begun to feel an unexpected shame about all the sex he *is* having.

When Ethan arrived in LA last year, he had been with two women. In the past fourteen months, he has slept with five more: an old acquaintance from high school, a close friend, his housemate, and a couple of girls he met around town. "For a long while, I thought I was doing something really self-destructive by having sex with people I didn't have feelings for," he says. He doesn't think so anymore. "I think it was more just a slow admission to myself that I like to have sex. And I don't need to be in a relationship to enjoy it, so long as both parties are aware that those are the terms."

Ethan may have come to terms with casual sex now, but he is still cynical about the role he believes popular culture plays in promoting an illusion of sexual excess. We might respond to Katy Perry's whipped-cream bikinis and Robin Thicke's music-video boasts of sexual prowess with amusement or derision, but in an attention economy, any form of recognition is a form of validation—intended or not. And it has an impact, says Ethan. "Even when it is presented in a condemning light, the fact that we broadcast it doesn't validate it exactly, but it certainly says that it's interesting. That it's something you should want to know about."

In the fifty years since the sexual revolution, there have been concrete changes in what we know about sex and the scope of the behaviors we engage in. But the most significant transformations in the way that we engage with sexuality have taken place inside our heads. They are less about what we do than they are about the way we *think* about sex—about the types of behavior we celebrate and those we condemn. We have moved from a culture that demanded we keep sexuality hidden from view to one that demands we speak it out loud in the name of liberation.

The sexual revolution of the 1960s wasn't just a product of medical innovations such as penicillin and the Pill; it was a public rejection of the old rules that had governed sex and relationships. That sex should only happen within marriage. That its primary aim should be reproduction. That it was a necessary evil rather than a source of pleasure and joy. And if reining sex in was oppressive, it followed that reversing the rules would set sex free—and set the people free in the process.

Sex wasn't just personal but political, and the ramifications of what you did with your body had the potential to transform society. As author Linda Grant recalls in her book *Sexing the Millennium: A Political History of the Sexual Revolution*: "At the time, to fuck was in and of itself a form of liberation. It was hip to be promiscuous and square not to be, it was a defying of convention. . . . The implications went far beyond whether or not you were getting laid or if you were enjoying the sex you were having."

Grant's words still ring true today. Sex may no longer be viewed as an explicit act of transgression—at least, not if you're heterosexual—but for many of us, sexuality is still intimately entwined with questions of freedom and resistance.

Partly, this is because the ways in which we are sexual *are* still limited by culture and politics—especially for those of us who are women, gay or lesbian, or transgender, or whose sexual expression falls outside the continuum of what is considered to be "normal" or desirable. But there is another reason we are able to hold two seemingly contradictory positions—the feeling of being unprecedentedly free and that of being unfairly oppressed—at the same time. And that's because there is something kind of *sexy* about the idea that our sexuality is being repressed.

If sexuality is being inhibited by some external force, then having sex—or even talking about it—feels like an act of defiance, which in turn makes sex more exciting and more pleasurable. As the French philosopher Michel Foucault wrote in his book *The History of Sexuality*, "What sustains our eagerness to speak of sex in terms of repression is doubtless this opportunity to speak out against the powers that be, to utter truths and promise bliss."

Tullia, twenty-six, is soft-spoken and philosophical; her sharply cut bob and elegant posture reflect her job in the fashion industry. She admires the unstudied sensuality of women such as actress Scarlett Johansson and Victoria's Secret model Miranda Kerr, and seeks to emulate their blend of confidence and femininity in her own life. For Tullia, sex is a profoundly intimate, almost meditative experience, during which the rest of the world falls away. It is also a source of excitement, a taste of rebellion and living on the edge. She tells me how, while in Catholic high school, she would sneak out of the house to go clubbing with friends, armed with black eyeliner and a fake ID in her purse. "I was very curious to experience life. I wanted to party. I wanted to meet guys," she recalls. "Basically, I wanted to do everything that my parents and teachers thought I shouldn't be doing."

Tullia's high school high jinks were ultimately short-lived, and she spent most of her college years in a steady relationship. But she looks back on her experiences as life-affirming and empowering. She perceives her more recent casual encounters the same way. "I love the thrill of a new body," she says. "You put your most into the experience and let go of your fear."

But as life-affirming as Tullia's sexual experiences have been, she is mindful that they also serve another purpose. Learning how to apply makeup and going to clubs while in high school, for instance, wasn't just a means of enticing boys. It was also a vehicle for becoming more interesting to other girls. "I went to a Catholic girls' school, so I didn't wear my skirt short to attract boys. I did it to attract girls— to be accepted into the cool girls, as one of the pretty girls."

Similarly, playing the role of the sexually liberated young woman as an adult isn't just a matter of the sex Tullia does or doesn't have. It's about how she presents herself, how she interacts with people, the products she consumes, and the lifestyle she pursues. As she describes it: "You're going to music festivals, you're regularly getting a bikini wax and pedicure. You're dining out with your friends and meeting new people. Even if you've got a boyfriend, the lifestyle doesn't change all that much. You're still out there, still part of the scene." To be sexually "free" is not just a question of doing as you please but a public display of self: an identity that is contemporary, cultured, and financially secure.

The shift from sexual restraint to liberalism that has taken place in Western culture over the last half century reflects more than just a rejection of the perceived repressions of our forebears, argues British cultural theorist Mark Jancovich. It has also coincided with a transformation of the types of people and occupations that are classified as middle-class, as the "craftsmen and small shopkeepers" who made up the old petite bourgeoisie have been replaced by a new bourgeoisie comprised of people working in sales, marketing, advertising, fashion, and the creative industries.

To be middle-class, Jancovich argues, is to be defined as much by what you are *not*—economically and culturally—as by what you are. The small-business owners who formed the original middle classes in the eighteenth and nineteenth centuries stood out because they defied the categorizations of their day. They were neither landed aristocrats nor working poor. Instead, they occupied the middle: wealthy enough to own their own businesses and earn money off other people's labor, but lacking the institutional privilege of the old nobility.

The middle class of this era sought to distinguish themselves in other ways, too: rebelling against the marriages of convenience and sexual hypocrisy they associated with the upper classes, and developing their own set of ethics that valorized moderation, purity, and romantic love instead. As Canadian sociologists Erin Connell and Alan Hunt explain it: "While sexual passion could drag the individual down, romantic love, linked with reverence and devotion, could lift the married couple to the gates of heaven."

In the same way, the philosophy of freedom and fun favored by the educated middle classes today serves to identify this group as *not* repressed and *not* moralizing—and therefore distinguish them from less savvy outsiders.

The other quality that defines the middle class, according to Jancovich, is the desire not to be judged. For the old petite bourgeoisie, this aim was achieved through the creation of a strict moral code of "respectability and restraint," which, if followed to the letter, left no loopholes through which one could be found wanting.

Today, we seek the same judgment-free state by attempting to demolish the rules by which we might be evaluated altogether. In place of these, Jancovich argues, we have adopted "an ethic of fun, which is defined as 'modern' and sophisticated." But in turning fun into a virtue, we have also made it yet another benchmark on which we can be deemed inadequate.

"You Have to Go Crazy Now, Because You Can't Later"

For no demographic group is the link between sex, fun, and freedom more powerful than it is for the young and single. We expect young adults to experiment sexually not only because they are physically mature humans with adult desires, but also because of the broader fantasy of youth as a time of unfettered independence, ripe with possibilities that have not yet been diminished by the weight of responsibility or convention.

The assumption that teens and twentysomethings are uncontrollably sexed serves as the mirror of the drab but "respectable" married couple who no longer have any sex at all. As Noah, a twenty-two-year-old trans man living in Seattle, describes it dryly, "You have to go crazy now, because you can't later. So you've gotta fuck everyone while you still can." He wonders if there might be less pressure for young queer people to "get it out of their systems" in their twenties, because there isn't the same expectation that their period of freedom will end. "You go somewhere like [Seattle gay bars] Pony or the Wildrose, and you see people my parents' age and, like, I know that they're still getting it on. It's still an accepted part of the community." He laughs. "Oh god, the sagging Prince Alberts I've seen!"

Seattle gay bars aside, the perception is that young people have more sexual opportunity than other groups—and that they ought to be taking advantage of those opportunities while they last. Witness the *New York Observer*'s shock in 2011 when, at the end of one Manhattan house party, not one of the twentysomething revelers went home with anyone. "Young New Yorkers no longer care about having sex," the paper announced dramatically. The young adults in question were of the same creative-class ilk that Jancovich describes—"day laborers in film, public relations, media, fashion"— but although they were fashionable, successful, and attractive, sex was not their Friday-night priority.

The *Observer* argued that desire had been replaced with narcissism, fornicating with Twitter followers. "Sex is antithetical to the way [young people] socialize, disruptive to the larger plan, a gateway to chaos in a digitally ordered world," theorized journalist Nate Freeman. The hours they worked were too long, their social circles too interwoven to accommodate the fallout of failed intimacy. "It's harder to go home with someone knowing that you'll be seeing their avatar the next morning and every morning after that."

It wasn't conceivable that the people at the party might not have met anyone they were attracted to on that particular night, or that they might have met someone they liked but weren't in the right frame of mind to make a move. The fact that no one, at least as far as Freeman knew, got laid meant that there must be something wrong—not only with the young people at the party, but with their entire generation.

For most twentysomethings, *not* taking a stranger home at the end of a party is more typical than picking someone up. But for young people whose experiences don't fit the fun, free ideal, there can be a sense that they are missing out on an essential part of their youth. Sarah, twenty-five, hasn't had sex in four years, and not because she is morally or even personally opposed to it. She says, "It just literally has not happened. Like, I have not been in a situation where sex has even been a possibility."

Sarah is attractive and outgoing, with long dark hair and slim hips. Two years ago, she packed her bags and moved from her native Melbourne to live and work in Beijing, where she is studying Mandarin. During her university years, Sarah channeled some of her thirst for excitement into her sex life, sleeping with guys she met at house parties and in her local theater scene. She is yet to have a serious boyfriend, but she had her first threesome the same year she lost her virginity. Then, all of a sudden, she stopped hooking up entirely.

Officially, it was a one-night stand gone wrong that caused her to take pause. She had met a guy at a house party, and at the end of the night they went up to his room to have sex. "I wasn't really planning it, I was just such a go-with-the-flow kind of person back then," she explains. After it was over, they went back downstairs and he showed her out. It had been nice meeting her, he said. And then he shut the door.

Sarah had had one-night stands before—in fact, they were the only type of sex that she'd had. But this felt different from all the times before. "I think with the others, there was at least some pretense that they would call," she says. And Sarah always wanted them to call. On reflection, she concedes that most of the guys she slept with weren't great matches for her anyway. "I never stopped to think if we got along. It was just all being young and wanting to love life and have these exciting hookups. And yes," she admits sheepishly, "wanting them to call."

After that night, Sarah didn't just stop hooking up with strangers. She stopped having sex altogether. At first it was intentional, a bid to regain control over her body and emotions. Ten months later, when she emerged from her period of self-enforced celibacy, it became circumstantial. Sarah didn't want to avoid sex, but the opportunities no longer presented themselves the way they used to. Where once the parties and shows she attended had seemed ripe with sexual potential, now the people who set her loins ablaze were few and far between. Those who did were often unattainable—already in a relationship or just too cool to connect with her on the level that she desired.

Now Sarah channels her thirst for excitement into nonsexual aspects of her life—travel, activism, friends, her blog. But she admits that she sometimes feels like she is missing out. "I have this angst, this feeling that now is the youngest and hottest I'm ever going to be," she says. "I feel like I should be 'out there' more. I mean, sex is *fun*, and relationships are fun. I get jealous hearing about other people's interesting love lives, and feeling like I'm missing out on that."

Like Tullia, Sarah views sex as a marker of being engaged with the world around you. "Everything in media, literature, popular culture points to sex," she says. "If you're not married or in a relationship, it's expected that you'll be hooking up with people and dating. That's just what you *do*. You have a love life and that's what you talk about with your girlfriends or whatever. You talk about whatever the latest chapter is. And it's only recently that I've thought that maybe it's okay not to do that. That it's fine, I don't have to constantly be on the search for my next boyfriend or hookup."

If sex is an expression of freedom, it is a freedom that is dependent on the ability to exercise autonomy in other areas: financially, from parental surveillance, and from the demands of a committed relationship. If you are bound by any of these restrictions, your capacity to be sexually liberated—at least in the format that liberation is usually sold to us—diminishes accordingly. "Freedom" becomes a source of risk instead.

I meet Lauren, a gregarious high school senior with a passion for performing, at a surburban strip-mall Starbucks an hour or so south of Los Angeles. Lauren hopes to study musical theater after she graduates. If she does, she will be the first member of her family to go to college. She is passionate about gay rights and is a member of her local Gay-Straight Alliance. She is also a virgin, as are most of the girls she is friends with at school.

Lauren grew up in a Catholic Hispanic family, where most of her older female relatives became mothers before they finished high school. Her parents expected that she would follow the same path. "My goals are not taken very seriously in my family," she tells me. "All of my aunts on both sides of the family got pregnant when they were teenagers, and everyone thinks that the same thing is going to happen to me. That that's just the way Latinas are: we stay home, we have kids, we take care of our husbands. But I'm not like that. I want to have a career."

For Lauren and her friends, sex is an obstacle to future success. When everyone in your family and community expects you to be sexually active, *not* having sex becomes the transgressive thing to do. It's also the safer option. "So many women in my friends' families had to drop out of high school because they got pregnant. They couldn't continue on to college," Lauren says. "So there's a feeling that if we have sex, or even if we think about it too much, those doors will close to us."

She doesn't think it should have to be that way. "Being sexually active shouldn't change anything about you," she says. "If you were a successful student before you had sex, you should be a successful student after as well. If I got pregnant, I would still find a way to continue my education." But she also suspects she won't be having sex anytime soon, and that's not just a matter of avoiding pregnancy. "There aren't many guys at my school who I'd really date. It's hard because everyone knows each other, so I know that if I started getting involved with a guy he would tell his friends, and it would get back to my friends and it would be really complicated. As much as I'd like to change perceptions, it's still high school." For now, Lauren's sexual liberation will have to wait.

From Sexual Liberation to Great Sexpectations

But a sexual culture that trumpets freedom from the rooftops is not the same thing as a sexual culture that is truly free. And in practice, today's "open-minded" and educated middle classes have not eluded judgment so much as we have changed the terms upon which we are judged.

Where once we were condemned for being *too* sexual, today we are admonished for not being sexual enough. Where it was considered perverse to engage in any activity more adventurous than the missionary position, today you risk being labeled boring if you don't. In our attempt to overturn the rules that once governed our sexuality, we have replaced one brand of regulation with another.

Foucault believed that his late-twentieth-century contemporaries were wrong to dismiss their Victorian predecessors as buttoned-up and repressed. The culture they lived in may have been tightly controlled, but it was a control that was imposed not by making sex invisible but by continually invoking it: through heated discussions about the birth rate, the proper age for marriage, how often couples should have sex, and more. Similarly, the omnipresence of sex in media and popular culture today—and the particular types of sexual expression we celebrate and condemn—are not the revolutionary break from an oppressive past they might at first seem. Rather, they are a continuation of a fixation on sexuality that reaches back to the dawn of Western civilization.

And if the words we speak about sex have been used to convey the limits of acceptable and unacceptable behavior for thousands of years, it stands to reason that the multitudes of conversations we engage in about sex now—in the media, in popular culture, and with each other—might serve the same function. In other words, the compulsion to appear "liberated" is a form of regulation of its own.

We won't achieve sexual freedom simply by replacing an oppressive set of rules with its opposite. It is true that being told that the only "good" sex is that which occurs within marriage and produces children is harmful to many people. But just as our predecessors were stigmatized for failing to achieve the old benchmarks of sexual purity, so too are many people today suffering for their struggle to meet the new standards of sexual "freedom." Recent studies of sexual attitudes in Finland, for example, show that as public appreciation of the importance of sex has increased, dissatisfaction with individual sex lives has also grown.

None of this is to suggest that things aren't better now than they were before. We may have grander expectations of what our sex lives should look and feel like, but we also have more information about how our bodies work and the pleasure possibilities available to us. We may be surrounded by images that objectify and sexualize women, but we have also raised a generation of young women who are more comfortable with pursuing the people and pleasures they desire than those who came before them. Young men too are challenging traditional gender roles, showing a greater willingness to confront and acknowledge their vulnerabilities.

But as we have stripped away some of the old taboos around sex and pleasure, we have replaced them with new anxieties around performance, desirability, and what it means to be "normal." As Leonore Tiefer, a psychologist at New York University, writes in her book *Sex Is Not a Natural Act and Other Essays*, "It used to be that sex was so secret, so hidden, and so private that people felt completely unprepared and anxious that they wouldn't know what to do and would somehow do it wrong. Now, sex is so not-secret, so not-hidden, and so not-private that people feel anxious that they can't possibly measure up to what they think is the 'normal' standard of sexual life." Our shift from a sexual culture that privileges respectability and restraint to one that privileges freedom has also been accompanied by an increased emphasis on sex as a path to status, self-expression, and personal fulfillment.

The old sexual regime was repressive because it narrowed people's options in a manner that was both painful and psychologically unsustainable. If you were gay, you weren't allowed to be with the person you loved. If you were a woman, sex was fraught with risk and stigma. But it wasn't just the terms of the regime that needed to be dismantled. It was the very fact that there was a regime at all.

Power isn't just exercised from above, imposed by government legislation, corporations, or religious dictate. It is also present in the stories we tell about our lives, the ways in which we choose to interact with other people, and the assumptions that we leave unquestioned. Often, power is most present in the forums we *don't* immediately recognize as political: in truisms such as "women want love, men want sex," in the assumption that everyone is heterosexual until otherwise stated, and in the sex advice proffered in glossy magazines.

Nor is power purely oppressive, designed only to censor and to silence. It is also a generative force that carves out new rules and possibilities at the same time as it demolishes old ones. At their most effective, the forces that shape our behavior draw us in so that we don't just passively accept the parameters they set out for us, but so that we participate in their creation.

All this is to say that sex doesn't need to be actively suppressed in order to be controlled. Just because the current sexual ideal promotes fun, freedom, and pleasure doesn't mean that it isn't still an ideal upon which we are expected to model our behavior. And it does not mean that our sexuality isn't still being influenced by social and cultural forces.

If we are to be truly sexually free, we need to do more than just celebrate sex. We must understand why sex has been sold to us as the key not only to our freedom but to who we are and how we engage with the world. We need to look more deeply into how sex is regulated today, starting with the source of that regulation itself: the Sex Myth.

2

Sex: An Act Unlike Any Other

At the heart of the Sex Myth lies the idea that sex is unlike any other facet of human life: that it is more powerful, more transcendent, and an expression of a more authentic truth than any other activity we engage in. In contemporary Western culture, sex is more than a matter of reproduction, or even recreation. It is the arena in which the self is formed and the ground on which we are presumed to build our most profound intimacies. You might have strong relationships with your family, your friends, or the people you work with, but it is the person with whom you have sex who is considered to be your "significant other."

We are taught that sex is the ultimate source of pleasure—that it is, as Woody Allen once put it, "the most fun you can have without laughing." But we are also taught to fear sex as a source of corruption and moral decay—especially if you have the wrong kind of sex or do it with too many people.

What ties all these beliefs together is the idea that in sex we will find our truth: not just of who we are as individuals, but of how we are faring as a society. British sociologist Ken Plummer argues that sex "has become the Big Story," the part of our existence that we are compelled to confess and dissect more than any other. And it is this link between sex and self that sits at the root of how sex is regulated in our culture, more than any individual rule or whim of cultural fashion.

I meet Sofia, a glamorous young executive, at a bar in Beverly Hills. A vivacious twenty-six-year-old with a curvy figure and a great job, Sofia looks like the image of the modern, liberated woman. Her black leather skirt is cut to midthigh, and her makeup is immaculately applied. She is groomed to draw stares, and she succeeds. But there is an undercurrent of insecurity beneath her polished self-assurance.

Sofia is someone who puts a lot of stock in her sexuality. It is important to her that men find her attractive, and she has strong ideas about what a good relationship should look like. "You need to have passion, otherwise the relationship will die and you will drift apart," she tells me. For Sofia, sex is a reflection of how the rest of the world perceives her, an unbiased barometer of her attractiveness and her social desirability. But for all of her ideals about what a successful relationship should look like, those standards are not reflected in her own romantic life.

Sofia has been dating the same man for six years, the first two of which they didn't have sex at all—and not for a lack of trying on Sofia's part. Their make-out sessions rarely got past second base, limited to quick, platonic pecks on the mouth. "I felt like I wasn't attractive," she recalls. "[Not having sex] made me feel like I was worthless." These days, Sofia and her boyfriend do have sex, but it happens less frequently than she would like, and it lacks the rip-your-clothes-off passion she believes it ought to have. "You go to clubs and see people grinding on the dance floor, and hooking up in bathrooms at parties," she says. "Sometimes I wish I had that, too."

Sofia doesn't usually talk about her sex life this directly, and it shows. She speaks softly, glancing around furtively to check that no one is listening. She apologizes for herself often—when she swears, when she spills some of her soft drink on our table, and when she occasionally trips over her words. When she tries to describe how she feels about her relationship, she vacillates, contradicting herself within a single sentence: "It could be better, but I'm happy with it," or, "It's mediocre, but it's better than it used to be."

Sofia fears that if people knew she had to beg for two years to persuade her boyfriend to have sex with her—or that he needed "persuading" at all—they wouldn't think she was so desirable anymore. She worries that if they knew her sex life wasn't up to scratch, they would think that meant there was something wrong with her as well. Or worse still, that they might think there was something wrong with her boyfriend.

Part of Sofia's dissatisfaction is situational, a product of a relationship that isn't meeting her physical or emotional needs. She feels torn between her longing for what she perceives as a "normal" relationship—that is to say, one that includes lots of intense, exciting sex—and her desire for safety and stability. "Sometimes I wish that I could be single and just go out and party and take guys home and fuck them and then dump them," she says. "But if I did that, I wouldn't have my boyfriend anymore." But Sofia's anxiety is also a reflection of her belief that her value lies in her sexual desirability. "Every so often I wonder, *Why am I not having more sex?*" she tells me. "It comes from a feeling that if I'm not doing certain things, then I'm not normal."

It is fashionable these days to argue that we treat sex more lightly than we once did. That in laying sexuality bare and stripping it of mystery, we have drained it of its significance, and accordingly of its magic. But even the most casual sexual encounters still come with emotional strings attached, if not within the relationships in which they take place, then in their implications for how we perceive ourselves.

Sofia may aspire to an active, liberated sex life, but her approach to sex is far from carefree. To the contrary, sex is a matter of serious emotional significance for her, which goes far beyond her individual inability to live up to social expectations. It is a reaction to a culture that has taught her—and all of us—that sex is a matter of grave importance, which is central to her value as a woman and as a human being. It is a response, in other words, to the Sex Myth.

The Best (and Worst) Damn Thing

The belief that sex is uniquely powerful and important has deep roots in Western culture. The Christian priests of medieval Europe recorded all manner of sins, but they paid special attention to how and with whom their congregations had sex. Those who found pleasure in the "wrong" ways were forced to publicly atone for their bad behavior: dressed in sacks, starved of food, and excluded from the church until they had served their penance. The Victorians of the 1800s fretted about the dangers of unrestrained reproduction among the poor and the risks of not procreating enough among the middle and upper classes. They viewed sex as a degenerate, animal force, one that was necessary for the continuation of the species but also needed "to be brought under conscious control."

Fears about the dangers of unrestrained sexuality persist today. They're visible in concerns about the corrupting influence of pornography as an architect of sexual taste, or that same-sex marriage will lead to an increase in "gender and sexuality disorders" among children. In a 2011 essay for the *Atlantic,* journalist Natasha Vargas-Cooper claimed that Internet porn had "allowed many people to flirt openly with practices that may have always been desired, but had been deeply buried under social restraint"—among them anal sex, "first date doggy-style encounters," and simulated incest. Pornography, she argued, offered "an unvarnished (albeit partial) view of male sexuality as an often dark force streaked with aggression," revealing the "uncomfortable truth" that sex was neither neutral nor equal—that in fact it could be "a bitter, crushing experience, no matter how much power you think you have."

But our belief in the extraordinary powers of sexuality is not just apparent in our fears of how it might destroy us. It is also present in the ways we revel in its magic. We can see the Sex Myth in the emotive, larger-than-life language of glossy magazine covers—*explosive, amazing, crave, #BestNightEver*—and in the use of sex in advertising to render everything from burgers to toilet paper more exciting. The Sex Myth is visible in the worshipping of sex as an act of freedom and defiance, and in the belief that having sex is the act that transforms us from adolescents into adults.

Evan, a slight seventeen-year-old from Florida, describes what he perceives as the dividing line between those who have had sex and those who haven't. "I can't really put my finger on it, because I've never had sex," he says. "But the way people make it sound, once you cross that line the entire world is opened up, as far as getting close to people and relationships go." Greta, a twenty-five-year-old fashion blogger from Sydney, agrees. "I was eighteen when I lost my virginity, and I had built it up as this very big thing in my head," she recalls. "You're supposed to glow, or feel like a 'woman.' Then, when it happened, I was just like, 'Oh, it just feels like there's something in my vagina.' I'd had fingers and toys up there already, but I still thought that a penis was going to feel different, just because it's 'sex.' "

Whether it is feared or venerated, sex is always special, and the ways that we engage with it are always steeped in culture and symbolism. Sex is seen as the key to our vitality: the strongest of all human desires and the most profound act of intimacy we can achieve with another person. Representations of sex in media and popular culture tend to use what linguists David Machin and Joanna Thornborrow call "low modality" images: those whose larger-than-life colors, stylized locations, and exaggerated lighting place sex in a fantasy space where everything is bigger, bolder, and more emotionally evocative. In contrast, images of people who are *not* sexually active—whether they are virgins, asexual, or in a sexless relationship—are drained of color and emotion, which, according to Canadian researcher Ela Przybylo, suggests "not only melancholy but also a boring life, caused by an 'absence' of something, an absence of '*the thing.*' "

Some believe that sex is *so* important, in fact, that it is the reason for almost everything we do—that we diet, buy makeup, fight, compete, create, and earn money all in the pursuit of getting laid and passing on our DNA. But American sociologists John Gagnon and William Simon argue that for most people, the desire for sex is weaker—or at least more variable—than its omnipresence in our culture might have you think. In their influential 1973 book *Sexual Conduct: The Social Sources of Human Sexuality*, they argue that the human desire for sex is strongest at particular points in the life cycle: adolescence and early adulthood, the early years of marriage, and during extramarital affairs.

The rest of the time, they write, "sex is a relatively docile beast" that occupies "very little of most people's time and energy." Rather than repressing sexuality, they contend, we have exaggerated its importance. Michel Foucault makes a similar claim in *The History of Sexuality*, arguing that far from being buried, sex is spoken about constantly. "It may well be that we talk about sex more than anything else," he writes. This belief in the "special" powers of sexuality means that everything we do when it comes to sex is infused with significance, with a profound impact on our understanding of who we are and how we measure up. With so much riding on how we conduct our sex lives, sex doesn't need to be regulated externally: rather, we internalize the standards and implement them ourselves.

It's Only Natural: The Science of the Sex Myth

If we believe that sex is more significant than other things, that is partly a reflection of the physical pleasures and ramifications of the act. Sex between a man and a woman, at least, has the potential to produce children, a consequence that has inspired awe, joy, and terror throughout human history. Sex can also be a source of sublime pleasure, releasing a cocktail of happy hormones such as dopamine, oxytocin, and testosterone, which simultaneously satiate us and make us thirst for another hit.

These qualities mean that sex is often viewed as an activity that is driven purely by biology, untouched by social or cultural forces. We can civilize every other aspect of human life—how we dress, what we eat, how we engage with one another in social settings— but in matters of sex, our true animal nature cannot help but make itself known. Sex is believed to be uniquely untouched by external influences—a characteristic thought to make it both more dangerous and a more authentic expression of the human condition.

This belief that the biological aspects of sex reveal hidden truths about human nature is present in many popular accounts of sexuality: from the view that women are attracted to men who are in relationships because their "cavegirl brains" identify them as good providers to the notion that men are attracted to younger women because they are more fertile. These explanations resonate because they offer "a 'scientific' account" of our behavior, "both at the species and the individual level," contend York University academics Stevi Jackson and Amanda Rees. They argue that "in a world where many still take 'scientific' to be synonymous with 'true' . . . [these stories have] undoubted appeal."

But to speak about sex solely in terms of biology implies that what we currently believe to be true, desirable, or deviant has always been as such and always will be, with little room for debate. It is no coincidence that the behaviors and traits we most frequently draw upon biology to explain are those that we are most invested in believing to be true. So-called scientific accounts of sexuality rarely challenge our expectations of how sex works or how men and women behave. To the contrary: they almost always confirm them.

Biological accounts of sexuality are also used to make sense of individuals, positioning sex not as something that a person *does*, but as an act inherent and fundamental to who or what they *are*. For gay and lesbian people, for example, the idea that sexual orientation is biologically fixed has been central to achieving mainstream legitimacy. If sexuality is a choice, it is one that can be undone. If a person is "born this way," on the other hand, it is unchangeable and must be accepted.

But while sexual orientation might not be something we *choose*, it isn't solely biologically determined, either. Like other aspects of human physiology, our sexual preferences are a product of a combination of biology, environment, and social conditioning. Height, for example, is genetic, but good nutrition makes us taller. Similarly, evidence suggests that humans have a biological inclination to be attracted to one gender or both, which is influenced by a mix of prenatal hormonal and genetic factors. But the degree to which we express those preferences will depend on the environment we find ourselves in.

In the most extreme cases, this might manifest itself in people who are deeply attracted to people of their own gender but who are forced to bury those desires for fear of violence or social stigma, like the stoic cowboys in *Brokeback Mountain*. But social factors can influence the way we experience sexual orientation in more subtle ways, too. A 2014 study published in the *Journal of Sexual Medicine* found that 45.2 percent of men and 36.9 percent of women have fantasized about being with someone of the same sex. But only 2.3 percent of Americans identify as gay, lesbian, or bisexual. This is not to say that most straight people are secretly "bi," or that gay and lesbian people could be straight if only they chose to be. But it does suggest that our sexual desires are more complex than the labels we use to describe them.

Even the most physical aspects of sex are shaped by culture, right down to the question of what qualifies as "sex" in the first place. Not even the kiss, the cornerstone of Western romance, is universally erotic. In her book *Sex Is Not a Natural Act*, Leonore Tiefer shares the story of a couple she worked with as a sex therapist, both middle-class and in their midthirties. The man was Italian-American, and had come of age in a culture that considered deep kissing to be "highly intimate and erotic," an expected part of any loving relationship. The woman, who had grown up in Myanmar in Southeast Asia, thought kissing was "dirty, dangerous, and disgusting ... akin to sticking one's tongue in another's nose and wiggling it around."

The man feared that his wife didn't love him because she wasn't more "passionate" in foreplay, and she worried he didn't love her because he couldn't accept that she didn't want to kiss him in the manner he desired. But the problem wasn't that they didn't love each other. It was that they had different expectations of what a loving sexual relationship looked like. And if even something as fundamental as how we want to touch and be touched by our partners is influenced by our environment, it stands to reason that sex isn't so immune to social influence after all.

Up Close and Very, Very Personal: How What You "Do" Became Who You Are

Under the Sex Myth, sex isn't just a window into the truth of who we are as a species. It is a window into the truth of who we are as individuals. "When you get with someone, you're making a statement about yourself," says Yusuf, a smart, analytical twenty-four-year-old gay man with dark hair and eyes. "You're good enough for me, or I'm good enough for you." When Yusuf hooks up with a guy he finds attractive, it is an affirmation of his own attractiveness. When he is rejected, he falls into a tailspin of insecurity. "I'll think of another guy, one who is really good-looking, and think to myself, 'That guy would never be rejected.'" Sometimes, Yusuf will even have sex with someone he's not attracted to, just to prove that he can. It's gross, he admits with a smile, but says, "I enjoy the sex anyway, even if I'm not really into them."

To understand how sex became entwined with the self, we need to go back five hundred years, to the dawn of the period historians refer to as modernity. This was an era of enormous social and economic change in what we now call the West, which had a profound impact on the way people perceived themselves in relation to others—and, in turn, a powerful effect on the way we thought about sex.

At the beginning of this period, in the early 1500s, most Europeans lived in small, feudal farming communities, with high mortality and few opportunities for social advancement. Who you were and who you were allowed to be was a matter of class hierarchy, determined at birth and enforced by a community you would know for your entire life. By the mid-1600s, the transition to an industrial society was in full swing, and people were increasingly living in cities, surrounded by strangers. Now one's identity was not fixed but could be shaped by hard work and sheer force of will—at least in theory.

The transition from an agrarian to an industrial society created the need for a new interdependence and awareness of the self as distinct from other people. In cities, survival meant learning to get along not just with people you knew well but with people you might never see again. This demanded an increased attentiveness to how your actions affected the people around you. The twentieth-century German social scientist Norbert Elias called this "the civilizing process," writing that "in order to be really courteous by the standards of *civilité* one is to some extent obliged to observe, to look about oneself and to pay attention to people and their motives." This awareness of others led to an increased awareness of the self, Elias argued, which in turn led individuals to modify their behavior to be more considerate of and appealing to others.

This period also saw the redrawing of the lines between private and public life. In the old feudal societies, decisions relating to politics and religion were made behind closed doors, away from the eyes and influence of ordinary people. The domestic sphere, by comparison, was largely public. It was not uncommon to share a bed with a stranger of the opposite sex at an inn, for example, or to sleep naked when you did so. But the modern age turned these old divisions on their heads, as politics became a matter of public interest and acts related to the body—from sex to sleep to bathing and using the toilet—became private, and in some cases taboo.

This new sense of mystery surrounding the body infused sex with an unprecedented intimacy. If sexuality was a secret, then knowing the details of another person's sex life meant understanding them in a way that others did not. Combined with the increased emphasis on individual identity and interpersonal etiquette in this era, sex began to take on a new importance.

These days, sex is as much a topic of public conversation as politics, but it continues to be treated as an act of profound personal significance. There is a sense that sex is uniquely revealing: that if someone has a certain type of sex, they must be a certain corresponding type of person. Or more precisely, that certain types of (good or bad) people engage in particular sexual activities.

Most of us wouldn't radically change our opinion of our friends if we learned that they were bisexual, or into BDSM, or that they hadn't had sex in three years. We might be surprised—especially if it didn't fit with our existing beliefs about who that person was—but any new information about their sex life would be incorporated as one thread of a larger story, alongside their temperament, their taste in music, what makes them laugh, where they grew up, or the way they dress. That is to say, Sofia's fears that her friends would think less of her if they knew the truth about her relationship are probably misplaced.

But although we might be loath to judge individuals whom we know and love on the basis of their sex lives, we are far more willing to make such evaluations in the abstract. Plenty of people who wouldn't look down on a friend who told them they had never had sex still think of "virgins" as a category, as uptight, unattractive, or socially inept. The same people who would respond with nonchalance or inquisitive enthusiasm if someone they knew told them they were kinky still think of "kinky people" as strange, intimidating, or oversexed.

Like Norbert Elias's civilizing process, the link between sex and self usually manifests itself not externally, through an explicit condemnation of undesirable behaviors, but internally, as we carefully monitor what others say and do about their sex lives, and modify our own self-presentation accordingly. Sofia may not be able to create the sex life she would like to have, but she can influence the assumptions that people make about her through the way she dresses and the stories she chooses to share (and not to share) about her relationship. She might not feel sexy on the inside, but it matters a little less so long as she looks the part.

But looking the part only takes us so far. Identity isn't just built on the basis of what we like, do, and believe, but on our ability to create a cohesive story about who we are. And whether that "story" looks consistent from the outside or not, when it fails to align on the inside, we are left with a sense of discomfort at best, and at worst, a deep sense of shame.

Like Sofia, Greta doesn't have as much sex as most of her friends—although she does have as much sex as *she* wants to have. A self-possessed and outgoing twenty-five-year-old fashion blogger, with curly dark hair and a bold, colorful sense of style, Greta has been with the same guy since she was eighteen years old. When they first got together, they went through a "honeymoon period of ripping each other's clothes off," but in recent years, they've regularly gone weeks—or even months—without having sex. "I have a sluggish sex drive," she says with a shrug.

Where Sofia feels anxious about her desirability, Greta is confident about the state of her relationship. "We talk a lot. We play. We're really quite silly together, which I love. We kiss every day. We're quite physically affectionate with each other, always touching and holding hands and running our hands through each other's hair," she explains. The source of Greta's discomfort is that her sex life doesn't fit her identity as a progressive and powerful young woman. It's not just the amount of sex she has; it's the fact that she has only ever done it with one person. "I had this fear when I was about twenty-one that I was missing out on all these great dicks by staying with one man," she jokes. She talked it through with her boyfriend for a month or two before she came to the conclusion that "he was the person [she] wanted to be with," she recalls. "I realized that I don't need a lot of bad sex with a lot of different people."

Still, Greta admits she often feels like her sex life doesn't reflect her politics. "I feel like it should be more radical," she says. "It always comes as a bit of a shock to people when they find out I only have one notch on my bedpost, and that he and I have been together for such a long time, at such a young age. Paul is pretty much my first boyfriend, and certainly my first serious boyfriend. He's the only person I've had sex with, and he may end up being the only person I *ever* have sex with."

A sporadic sex life doesn't cause Greta the distress it does Sofia, but it is a source of disquiet nonetheless. "It doesn't mesh with my idea of myself," she reflects. "Intellectually, I know that there is no normal, and that the only thing you should be worried about when it comes to sex is if it makes you feel uncomfortable or if it's having a negative impact on your life. But still," she adds knowingly, "it's different when it happens to me."

Consumer Sex:
We Get What We Pay For

If the emergence of the self-made individual allowed the Sex Myth to flourish, the rise of consumer culture over the past fifty years has sent it into overdrive. Today, the question of who we are and how we are perceived by others is answered not just through what we do and how we interact with other people, but through the things we consume. And just as the clothes we wear, the cars we drive, and the food we eat have all become symbols of our values and identity, our relationship to sex has followed suit.

Of all the dreams today's young Westerners are sold about what our lives could look like, the biggest is that we have limitless opportunities, that we are free to pursue whatever work, relationships, and ways of being we like. And while sex isn't central to every young person's perception of what it means to be free, it is a key part of how that freedom is sold to us.

The old adage that "sex sells" is as true today as it ever was, and the exhilarating, "special" qualities of sex are used to market everything from fashion to popular culture to beauty products. But these products don't just promise sex. They also use sexuality to suggest other emotions and desires. Advertisements for perfume and high-end alcohol feature beautiful models to connote not just sexual desirability but wealth, distinction, and glamour. When pop stars like Miley Cyrus, Lady Gaga, or Rihanna dance onstage in skintight costumes, thrusting and grabbing at their groins, they do it not just to titillate their audiences but to intimidate them—and to position themselves as powerful, edgy, and transgressive in the process. Magazine covers plastered with promises to reignite our sex lives aren't just promising orgasms but also to make us more confident, self-actualized, and even more lovable.

Despite its reputation, consumer culture is neither inherently shallow nor meaningless. To the contrary, it facilitates desire by infusing everything it encounters with meaning. The right pair of shoes doesn't just protect your feet; it is a passport into the life of someone richer, more attractive, and more fashionable. A well-stocked iTunes library reveals more than just a love for music; it is a mark of taste and cultural savvy. And an active sex life doesn't only satisfy us erotically; it represents desirability, self-agency, and charisma. If consumer culture trades on the promise that we will find ourselves through the items we purchase, consumer *sex* promises that we will discover ourselves through sex. Who we sleep with, what we desire, and the acts we engage in are all part of a broader expression of personal taste.

In *Guyland*, Michael Kimmel quotes Jeff, a fraternity member at the University of Northern Iowa, who tells him that "the girls you hook up with, they're, like, a way of showing off to other guys. I mean, you tell your friends you hooked up with Melissa, and they're like, 'Whoa, dude, you are one stud.' So, I'm into Melissa because my guy friends think she is so hot, and now they think more of me because of it. It's a total guy thing." Jeff may be genuinely attracted to Melissa, but part of her appeal is what his desire for her reveals about his good taste, and about his own desirability and skill with women.

This "consumer" approach to sex isn't just visible in what we do. It is also present in how we frame our experiences in everyday life. Rebecca, a nineteen-year-old college sophomore, has yet to have sex, but that doesn't mean she isn't sexual. "Just because somebody isn't sexually active doesn't mean they're not thinking about it," she says. "I've got a libido, and it's quite heated. I don't feel the way a virgin is 'supposed' to feel. [I don't feel] chaste and self-censored."

Rebecca is quiet but opinionated, a close observer of the people around her. Her best friends know she is a virgin, but most people she meets assume that she is not. "I'm not a huge social character, but I am quite independent, and I think people imagine that confidence goes hand in hand with sexual availability. I go out and I drink and I've kissed boys, and people think that naturally there would have been an occasion when that would have led to me sleeping with one of them." But she hasn't—mostly because she has yet to meet somebody she *wants* to sleep with. "It doesn't have to be on a bed of roses or anything, I just want it to be something kind of nice."

Rebecca also pays attention to the assumptions she sees her classmates making about each other's sex lives. She tells me about a conversation she overheard recently, in a campus computer lab around exam time. "One of the girls was stressing out about the paper she was working on, and this other girl piped up and told her, 'You just really need to get laid. Go out and get some sex.'"

It was a casual remark, probably intended as a joke, but Rebecca saw something more in it: a desire to communicate a particular type of sexual experience. "To me, a comment like that says that she's sexually active, and that she assumes that everyone else is, too," Rebecca explains. "And the thing is, both of those girls could be virgins for all we know. Because they're not really directly saying, 'Hey, I'm having sex.' But their conversation is designed to make people think they are." The subtext, she says, is that sex is important to them, "and it should be to you, too."

Consumer sex isn't about pleasure or a desire to connect with other people. It is inward looking, a matter of proving something to yourself and to others. And contrary to what Jeff says, it's not just a "guy thing," either. In *Female Chauvinist Pigs*, Ariel Levy speaks with Annie, a "beautiful twenty-nine-year-old" who treats sex as "a kind of shopping." When Levy interviews her, Annie has had sex with thirty-five people, and her mission is to get her number up to one hundred. Many of her experiences, she tells Levy, have been "pretty fucking lame," but she is "willing to take that," because she wants to have sex with as many people as possible. "The thing about when you start accumulating sex for its own sake is that the exercise of it is not that sexual," Annie observes. "Sometimes having this kind of sex, this shopping kind of sex, is based on insecurities for me, am-I-attractive insecurities."

In their book *Sexual Conduct*, John Gagnon and William Simon hypothesize that rather than needing to "constrain severely the powerful sexual impulse in order to maintain social stability," earlier societies might have had to "*invent* an importance for sexuality." This, they argued, would not only "assure a high level of reproductive activity," but would provide a powerful incentive for conformity in other areas of life—and one unlimited by natural resources.

In today's consumer society, it's not hard to see how our special preoccupation with sex might be channeled into practices that are *very* useful from a political or economic perspective. In contemporary Western culture, desirability is strongly tied to what we consume, with women in particular encouraged to purchase products that promise to make them more sexually appealing, such as makeup, skin-care formulas, designer clothes, and cosmetic surgery. Increasingly, there is a market for products that allow men, too, to manipulate their appearance to become more attractive, with the men's grooming industry valued at $33 billion annually in 2011.

Sexual desirability is also connected to what we produce. Work is more than just a means to purchase products that promise to make us more attractive; it is also a source of attractiveness in its own right, as men and women who are "successful" in the ways that matter to the people around them—be that money, power, or cultural cachet—are considered more attractive sexual partners. Even reproduction itself is an economic good, as governments in France, Germany, Estonia, and Australia have proved with their appeals to young couples to have more children—and create a workforce to pay for their future pensions.

None of this is to imply that if sex were not so important, or so central to our sense of personal value, people wouldn't still go on diets, purchase beauty products, or turn up to work on Monday morning. But promoting sex as a path to status and self-worth, and suggesting that if we produce and consume in the right ways we will get more access to it, certainly encourages behavior that is economically desirable. In the next chapter, we will begin to look more closely at what those desirable behaviors are and how they are upheld, starting with the need to be "normal."

3

Freaks and Geeks:
The Trouble with "Normal"

If the Sex Myth teaches us that sex reveals the essence of who we are, normality is the barometer by which we come to understand how "who we are" is valued by other people. To be "normal" is to be embraced, accepted, one of the gang. To be "abnormal," on the other hand, is to mark yourself out as different, deviant, and in some way deficient. But in the early twenty-first century, a time when most of us pride ourselves on our open-mindedness, what does it mean to be normal?

Michael identifies as straight but has kissed guys and watched gay porn. His father is a cross-dresser. Now thirty-two, he has been married for four years to a woman with whom he has been in a relationship since he was twenty-five. It is not technically "open," but they have flirted with the idea of hooking up with other people. Once, on a drunken night not long after they married, his wife and one of her friends teased him with the possibility of a threesome—a promise Michael was only too keen to take them up on. "It ended up with us just talking," he admits sheepishly. So it is no surprise, then, that I receive a quizzical look when I ask him what's considered "normal" these days when it comes to sex. "Nothing," he says. "It all depends on what is normal to you."

We are sitting in London's Victoria train station on a rainy Friday afternoon, all grand red brick and polished archways on the outside, a miniature city of chain coffee stores and mass-market retailers bathed in fluorescent light inside. Bright-eyed and well-built, with reddish-brown stubble and a sleeve of tattoos down each arm, Michael is eager to share his experiences, speaking candidly about everything from his insecurities (height, masculinity, perversity) to his "obsession" with breasts. "I am the biggest boob fan you'll ever meet," he says with a grin.

Growing up in the working-class outer suburbs of London, Michael didn't feel like he fit in with other guys, and he didn't think girls were attracted to him. He had long hair and bad acne, and listened to heavy rock in a community where alternative music wasn't cool. When Michael was sixteen, a group of guys he knew went through his bags and found a letter he had written to a friend, pondering whether he might be gay. They later took him down to a local park and "beat the shit out of" him. Experiences like these might explain why he is so fervently opposed to the idea that some ways of being sexual might be more acceptable or desirable than others. "Nothing should be seen as alien or should be looked down upon as wrong," he says forcefully.

Michael's attitudes toward sexual norms are typical of people his age. "I don't know what normal is," Faith, a bohemian twenty-three-year-old American working as an English teacher in Spain, tells me over Skype. "In my experience, pretty much everything is normal," says Max, a lanky frat boy from Ohio. "What I like about now is that everything is considered normal," says Nicole, a

Vancouver-based librarian with sci-fi-inspired gold eyeliner and a bright streak through her jet-black hair.

Remarks like these are not surprising. Of all the convictions that govern sexual conduct in the secular West, perhaps the most important is that there *are* no longer any rules. To suggest otherwise is to challenge the very fabric of how we perceive ourselves: as free, self-actualized individuals carving out our destinies from a sea of limitless options and living in an open, laissez-faire culture in which almost anything is "okay" so long as all people involved consent to it. In an era that prides itself on pluralism, the idea that some ways of being sexual might be more "okay" than others is borderline offensive, a throwback to a less enlightened past.

If normality seems passé, it is partly because the lines between deviant and desirable sex no longer fall as decisively as they once did. Some people and practices that were considered dangerous have been brought into the mainstream—think same-sex relationships, oral sex, or masturbation—while other behaviors that once flew under the radar have been recast as undesirable, like the long-term heterosexual couple who only have sex in the missionary position.

But the borders between "normal" and "abnormal" sex haven't been erased completely. Another reason most people struggle to define what is normal is because normality is designed not to be noticed. The things that are most "normal" are often so seemingly ubiquitous that we don't usually bother to talk about them.

Many of the people I spoke with in the course of researching this book had difficulty articulating what was normal in their city, within their generation, or even within their group of friends. But most of them had no trouble listing a swath of things that were considered *abnormal*—and these were often contradictory: Having a high sex drive. Having a low sex drive. Abstaining from sex until marriage. Losing your virginity before your fifteenth birthday. Losing your virginity after your eighteenth birthday. Being gay, bisexual, or transgender. Bestiality. BDSM. Pubic hair on women. Not being able to orgasm. Not caring whether or not you have an orgasm. Being in a sexual relationship with more than one person at a time. Not having sex with anyone at all. There may be more than one way to pass as normal now, but there are even more ways to fail to make the grade.

They were more detailed still when it came to the times in their lives where they felt less than normal themselves, and the consequences of breaching this divide. Nicole was fiercely independent and confident in her choice to refrain from dating until very recently. But as a twenty-five-year-old virgin gearing up for the fourth date of her life, she still felt like a late bloomer. "My friends think it's hilarious because I'm usually the most self-assured of all of us, but here I'm wondering, *What do I do if he tries to hold my hand?*" Faith was a staunch political liberal, but admitted that questioning her sexual orientation over the past year had left her feeling "totally out at sea." She explained, "Most people think that either you're gay or you're not, or else you're bisexual and you're half-and-half. It feels like there's not really a place in between all those things, where you just don't know yet."

Whether we like it or not, norms still matter. In this chapter, we will look at how ideas of what is normal have changed over time and why being different scares us, and strip down the veneer of our laissez-faire culture to reveal the conventions and ideals that still lie beneath.

Normality Matters:
What's Normal and Why We Care

For a word that is so central to how we understand sex, what we consider to be normal is surprisingly amorphous. In its most literal sense, what's "normal" is a matter of statistics: an objective measure of how frequently a given experience, attitude, or behavior occurs within a population. In a medical setting, normality is synonymous with health and abnormality with disease and dysfunction. Culturally speaking, what qualifies as normal and what doesn't is a reflection of shared values and assumptions. People and practices that are held in high esteem are usually also labeled "normal," whether their experiences are common or not, while those that are regarded with suspicion and contempt are labeled "abnormal." Normality, in this social context, is a synonym for "okay," while abnormality is equated with perversion or defect.

Sex sits at the juncture of these three approaches. It is practiced through the body, and therefore prone to the same medical analysis as any other health issue. Having a "normal" sex life is treated as a matter of physical and mental well-being. Sex is also deeply cultural, a subject of endless scrutiny in the media and in the everyday discussions that shape our perceptions of the boundaries between acceptable and unacceptable behavior. And like most things that we collectively deem to be important, it is relentlessly measured, as experts scramble to inform us of what "really" goes on behind other people's closed doors.

Our beliefs about what it means to be sexually "normal" draw upon each of these frameworks—medical, cultural, and statistical. That some men ejaculate more quickly than others, for example, is a biological fact. But the way that we respond to that fact is cultural, changing throughout history to reflect the ideals and standards of the day. What constitutes "too soon" has changed over time, too.

The earliest known tales of premature ejaculation date back to ancient Greek mythology. Erichthonius, a mythical early ruler of ancient Athens, was said to have been conceived when Hephaestus, the Olympian god of fire, dropped his seed on the earth while attempting to force himself on the goddess Athena. But it wasn't until the early twentieth century that premature ejaculation began to be understood as a medical problem, and it wasn't until the 1960s that the problem expanded to encompass not just men who ejaculated before intercourse began but also those who climaxed before their female partners did. Where the famous mid-twentieth-century sex researcher Alfred Kinsey "seemed to regard the quick ejaculator as a superior male," equipped to efficiently spread his genes with minimum fuss, today the premature ejaculator is treated as a sexual failure.

These shifts reflect changes in our attitudes toward sex more generally. In a culture that is concerned with sexual pleasure, whether as a marital bonding agent or for its own sake, early ejaculation is a problem. It not only reduces the likelihood that women will orgasm during intercourse but also reduces the duration of men's pleasure, too.

Despite this concern, there is still no clear consensus on what premature ejaculation actually is. Is it reaching orgasm more quickly than the average male? Ejaculating more quickly than 70 or 80 percent of men? Coming before your partner does? Kinsey's 1948 studies found that 75 percent of American men orgasmed within two minutes of commencing intercourse. But more recent studies have reported a median time of between 5.4 and 7.5 minutes—suggesting that men may be adapting their sexual behavior to better fit the social ideal. It is no longer acceptable for the sex act to end before one party has even begun.

Our beliefs about what causes sexual problems have also changed. Nineteenth-century medical circles were deeply concerned by male impotence, but they viewed it as a moral issue rather than an anatomical one. Men who were unable to perform intercourse were viewed as weak, drained of their life force, and losing sperm in any noncoital context—be it intentional (masturbation) or otherwise (the dreaded "wet dream")—put a man at risk of "total and sometimes permanent impotence." But the problem was also considered easily resolved by a return to "normal," upstanding sexual behavior. "Marriage alone is sufficient to bring about a cure," one doctor, a medical professor at New York University, wrote in 1877. "There is nothing which will relieve the abnormal congestion of the genitals so much as moderate sexual intercourse."

Today, by comparison, our sexual norms and ideals are often cast as physiological issues: framed in terms of function and dysfunction. We blame impotence not on masturbation but on hormones or alcohol, and we treat it not with marriage but with a small blue pill. We approach premature ejaculation as a mechanical problem, enthusiastically investigating how long it takes the average man to orgasm following penetration in order to determine what time frame is acceptable.

What is "normal" is not a value judgment in and of itself. In any group of people, some beliefs, experiences, and physical traits will be more common than others—there will be an average height, for example, and an average number of friends and acquaintances. The issue arises from the moral and emotional weight that we attach to these numbers, when we start using them as a guide not just for what *is*, but for what we should be.

Rationally, most of us know that just because an experience is statistically common doesn't mean it is something we should aspire to—and that just because something is statistically rare doesn't mean it is inferior. But emotionally, it can be difficult to shake the feeling that what is typical is also better. "I always have this paranoid suspicion that everyone else is in consensus about appropriate sexual practices, and I am an awkward, immature, insecure anomaly," admits Cara, an apple-cheeked twenty-three-year-old office administrator with shiny, dark hair and a chirpy, slightly nervous energy.

Cara lives in downtown Seattle, one of the most socially liberal communities in the United States, where "you can proudly buy your BDSM accessories in the sex shop across the street, see drag shows in abundance, and stuff cash into the thongs of pole dancers at night-clubs," as she puts it. "It's a really positive expression of sexuality, which is a great thing, but it also makes me feel like a prude." Cara's best friend owns eight vibrators, has had "countless threesomes," and wants to be a sex therapist someday. As for Cara? Her dating life is "virtually nonexistent." Cara has never had a long-term boyfriend, and she has only had sex twice in her life, with three people: a one-night stand and a threesome.

Cara first reached out to me via e-mail, explaining that she had been feeling confused about her sexuality: questioning not whether she is attracted to men or women, but whether she is attracted to anyone at all. She is drawn to men on a chemical level, she says—when she sits close to one, she feels a physical buzz—but that doesn't often translate to wanting to have sex with them. Women don't appeal to her in the same way, but she sometimes makes out with them anyway. "It's almost like this mothering instinct," she explains brightly when we meet at a grungy inner-city diner two months later. "As a woman, I know what it's like to feel unworthy, so I feel bad turning [other women] down. I just want to show them that they're loved and I accept them in all their sweaty bodily fluids. And just be like, you're human and this is great."

Much of the time, though, even the thought of sex makes Cara uncomfortable. It's too messy. Too physical. Too vulnerable. "The possibility of someone seeing me naked is cringe-inducing," she says. Cara is a casual dresser; when we meet, she is wearing slim-cut jeans and a red flannelette shirt. Her makeup is minimal, as is her grooming; she doesn't color her hair or paint her nails. But Cara does carefully monitor her appearance in other ways—like contorting her body into the most flattering pose, for example, or cutting down how much she eats for a week or so if she knows she will be spending a lot of time around men. "I'm hyperaware of how other people see me," she says. "So I know how to create an image that is desirable to men. But that doesn't equate to a desire to have sex. Being sexy involves taking down this act that I've spent a lot of time creating."

Cara's nerves aren't helped by her belief that she is less sexually available than most men her age expect or desire from a relationship. "It really baffles people that I'm not more sexually active," she says. At one point, her friends were convinced that she was a lesbian and tried to help her come out. More recently, Cara's closest girlfriend—the same one who wants to be a sex therapist someday—suggested that she might be asexual, a burgeoning sexual identity used to describe people who do not experience sexual attraction to other people.

When Cara first heard the term, she didn't know what it meant, assuming her friend was calling her a prude. But then she got curious and looked it up online. She could relate to a lot of what she read and found it "pretty empowering," she recalls. "Putting a name on it and seeing that there are other people out there who don't want to have sex all the time made me realize that, okay, I'm not totally weird." It also made her feel more comfortable saying no to the sex that she didn't want. "It gave me a reason," she says. "I'm asexual. This is my special classification, and it seemed like that's something that would be more respected than just saying, 'I don't want to have sex with you.'"

Buoyed by what she had read, Cara told a guy she had been dating—a self-described feminist she had first met on OkCupid—that she had started to think she might be asexual. They had only met in person a few times, but they'd had some great conversations—about sexuality, their families, and their insecurities about the way they looked—and she trusted him. It would turn out to be their final date.

"It wasn't like some big confession or anything," she recalls. "But it was something I'd been thinking and fretting about, and I wanted to share it with him." She was hurt when she didn't hear from him again. "I'd told him quite a lot about myself, so it really felt like someone was dissolving a friendship with me. Like, I had no value to him whatsoever because I might not have sex with him anytime soon." That same night, he gave her a link to his blog. She looked it up the next day, and the most recent post—written only a day or two before their conversation—was about how he could "never date an asexual."

A week or two later, Cara stumbled upon a blog post by Seattle sex columnist Dan Savage, who was introducing the concept of asexuality to his readers. Savage argued that while asexual people "may have the same emotional needs as anyone else," most "sexuals"—that is to say, most non-asexual people, or most people who experience sexual desire—expected their romantic relationships to meet their sexual needs. "Someone who is incapable of meeting a sexual's needs has no business dating a sexual in the first place, if you ask me," he wrote. Savage's words hit Cara like a slap in the face. "It made me feel like there was something wrong with me," she recalls.

The comments on the post were even more disheartening. "At least for me, if I'm not fucking you, I'm not dating you," one read. "This is the 21st Century . . . if they're not unzipped and ready to rumble by the time I've buzzed them in, the date is OVER . . ." read another. A third comment was more damning still: "I can deal with same-sex lust, diaper fetishes, BDSM, even the whole dress-up-as-a-furry-mammal thing, but the idea of there being NOTHING inside, no juice, no drives at all . . . well, to my mind that is the ULTIMATE FREAKINESS, the one eternally unfathomable kink."

By the time we meet in person, Cara has decided that the asexual label probably doesn't fit her. But the comments on Savage's blog post still haunt her, in part because they echo the attitude she observes among her friends and neighbors: that true sexual freedom means being up for any activity, and that anything less is suspect. "It makes me feel isolated, unwanted, and dysfunctional," she says.

Norms aren't only enforced by making the people who don't live up to them feel inadequate. They're also upheld by making the people who *do* live up to them feel good about themselves. If being abnormal makes us feel isolated and unwanted, being "normal" helps us to feel accepted as part of a community. And the acts and revelations that make us feel accepted aren't always the ones you'd expect.

Ben, a cerebral, politically aware twenty-year-old American, was one of the first people who reached out to me when I started researching the Sex Myth. Perhaps due to his work as a youth advocate, Ben is particularly concerned about the quality of sex education in schools. "I had quite a religious teacher in ninth and tenth grade who skewed us away from talking about contraception and toward talking about abstinence and the importance of marriage," he explains. "You can cover those things, but they should only be one component [of sex education], not the major focus."

When we meet, Ben has been dating his high school sweetheart for two and a half years. For a long time, the stability of their relationship had earned them a reputation for being prudes. "Because we didn't talk about it, people just assumed that we weren't having sex at all," he explains. But that changed after a drunken party game in his first year of college, in which he and his girlfriend revealed they had experimented with BDSM. "[After that], we were kind of judged on the fact that we'd had a lot of sex, and we were kind of adventurous in terms of that," Ben admits.

But for Ben, that "judgment" wasn't a bad thing. "If anything, it meant my friends treated us more normally. Until that point, we were seen as horrendously innocent. But after that night, they saw our relationship as a normal, working relationship." His serious face breaks into a smile. "It actually felt really good," he reflects. "I liked that they saw me as a normal person, just like anyone else."

From Kinky to Kosher: What's Normal Now?

Handcuffs and silk scarves won't earn you back slaps and congratulatory guffaws from everyone, but they are no longer as contentious as they used to be. Nor is it only young progressives who have embraced sexual liberalism. In 2012, the New York Times reported that young Republicans were distancing themselves from the conservative social policies of their party, embracing hot-button issues such as abortion and same-sex marriage. "The students I know who are conservative are far less so on social issues than our parents," Zoey Kotzambasis, the vice president of the College Republicans at the University of Arizona, told the paper. "People are more accepting of different lifestyles. . . . Honestly, there's about zero judgment of [gay people] from the people in our club, and I think that reflects the direction my generation wants to take the party in."

In the early 1980s, the queer American anthropologist Gayle Rubin argued that there was an unspoken social hierarchy of sexual acts, in which a small number of practices (such as heterosexual marriage) were embraced, and the rest were demonized as dangerous or perverted. In an influential essay titled "Thinking Sex," Rubin made this usually implicit hierarchy visible, arguing that its invisibility served to "rationalize the well-being of the sexually privileged and the adversity of the sexual rabble." Thirty years later, her arguments still feel deeply familiar, holding up a mirror to long-held Western beliefs about the boundaries between "good" and "deviant" sex.

Rubin illustrated her theories using drawings and diagrams: one of two concentric circles marking out "the charmed circle" of normal sexuality and "the outer limits" of deviant sex, and another a series of concrete walls demarcating the lines between "good" and "bad" sexual behavior and the contested areas between. If you wanted to be let into the charmed circle, the criteria were strict. "Normal" sex was heterosexual, monogamous, and preferably married—reproductive sex conducted in private within a single loving, paired relationship.

Abnormal sex, on the other hand, was limited only by your imagination. Those condemned to the "outer limits" included people who were gay or lesbian and those who had sex outside of marriage or with too many people. "Abnormal" sex spanned masturbation, sex toys, and pornography; people who had sex in public or who found pleasure in pain; and finally, people whose desires were directed toward those much older, younger, or outside their species.

The demarcations Rubin identified were grounded in a moral framework that asserted two things above all others: that sexual gratification should be free of exploitation (thus the blanket prohibition of bestiality and pedophilia), and that sex was meant for procreation. Straight people weren't exempt from that second qualifier, either. When the word "heterosexual" was first coined in the late 1890s, it was used to describe someone who had a "pathological" attraction to the opposite sex—just as the word "homosexuality" was coined to describe people with a pathological attraction to the same sex. It wasn't the gender of the people having sex that made it problematic, but the fact that it was being pursued for pleasure rather than reproduction. It was this relationship between sex and reproduction—or lack thereof—that defined perversion in the late nineteenth century and the first half of the twentieth.

Even when Rubin was writing in the early 1980s, the moral frameworks surrounding sexuality were beginning to change, and along with them the boundaries separating normal and deviant sex. Medical advances such as the oral contraceptive pill mean that the link between intercourse and childbirth is no longer inevitable. Within the secular, Western mainstream at least, the driving sexual ethic is no longer about continuing the species but about pleasure, intimacy, and fun.

The upshot? Sex no longer has to be reproductive in order to be considered moral. Casual sex may be berated in the newspapers, but it is also expected—in numbers and frequencies much higher than it actually occurs. Sex before marriage causes consternation only in the most conservative of quarters. Purchasing a vibrator or having sex on the beach might be seen as marginally transgressive, but only in the sense that it marks the person doing it as modern and daring, rather than dull and inhibited. Certain kink practices, such as handcuffs or spanking, are no longer the exclusive purview of "perverts" and outcasts but are a mainstay of women's magazines, advertising, and bestselling erotica. In short, people and practices that were relegated to the margins thirty years ago have become part of the mainstream.

The other major transformation in sexual attitudes has been in relation to gay and lesbian people. Research by the Pew Forum on Religion and Public Life has found that 68 percent of Americans born after 1981 support same-sex marriage. In the United Kingdom, the numbers are even higher: one 2012 poll found that 76 percent of people across all age groups agree with the statement that "gay couples should have exactly the same rights as heterosexual couples."

These numbers are a reflection of changes that have had a concrete effect on the lives of young same-sex-attracted people. I meet Portia, a twenty-three-year-old gay woman, over lunch in South London. A young trainee lawyer with olive skin and a heart-shaped face, Portia tells me she has never experienced homophobia in her life. "If people are horrified or disgusted by me, it has completely passed me by," she says. Portia's experiences are partly a reflection of her privilege. She is white and conventionally feminine looking, with long, honey-colored hair and a conservative sense of dress, clothed in chic tailored pants and a collared shirt. She is also upper-middle-class, having grown up with professional parents in a well-to-do but progressive pocket of the United Kingdom, which, Portia puts it, was "more Lib Dem than Tory. It wasn't exactly a backward place."

But Portia's comments are also generational, a concrete expression of the changes wrought to mainstream values by popular TV shows like *Queer Eye for the Straight Guy, Will and Grace,* and *Glee.* For most gay and lesbian people I spoke with who were even five years older than Portia, "coming out" was a major emotional undertaking, a leap of faith and identity that risked alienating family and friends. Portia's coming out, by contrast, involved "no fanfare" at all.

That's not to say that it unfolded easily. When Portia was a child, the Barbie dolls she played with ditched Ken and dated each other instead. But when puberty hit and her classmates started their first awkward forays into dating, she "toed the line of fancying boys just like everyone else." It wasn't until Portia was fourteen that it occurred to her that she might be anything *but* straight. Even then, she didn't act on it right away, waiting instead until her final year of high school to, as she puts it, "test the waters."

"You don't want to go and declare to everyone that you're a lesbian, and then change your mind and say, *Oh no, I'm not anymore,"* Portia explains. When she was ready to tell her family, she didn't say that she was "gay" or "a lesbian," only that she was dating a girl. "I wasn't ready to fully let go of heterosexuality at that point," she recalls. Portia has well and truly discarded heterosexuality now, but she still takes the same no-fuss approach when the subject of sex or relationships comes up in social situations.

"I still do get that pause when I tell people I've got a girlfriend," she observes. "But most people gloss over it quickly and just say something like, 'Oh, fab.' You're not meant to make a big deal of [someone being gay or lesbian]; you're meant to just acknowledge it and move on." It is an attempt to experience the same "ordinariness" that heterosexual people take for granted—not because they are mistaken for something they are not, but because their sexual identity is so uncontroversial that it doesn't come up in conversation at all.

Redrawing the Borders:
Who's In and Who's Out

Not all young gay and lesbian people feel the same desire to be ordinary that Portia does. In an essay for the queer blog *In Our Words*, Chicago college student Ariana Barreto writes about her frustration at being told that she is "too pretty" to be a lesbian. "At one time, I genuinely considered 'looking gayer' and changing my appearance entirely," she writes. "I wanted it so that when I walked into a room, everyone would just know that I love women, based off society's silly stereotypes." But for the most part, to *not* have your sexuality endlessly discussed is a privilege.

And it is a privilege that not everyone has. Like Portia, Edward grew into his sexuality incrementally. A gentle, slightly goofy twenty-seven-year-old LGBT rights activist from the working-class suburbs of Massachusetts, Edward was always "into boys' things, but from a different angle than most other boys." When his classmates would play at being X-Men during lunch at school, he would want to take the part of Jean Grey or Storm, while the other boys argued over who would play Cyclops or Wolverine. "It was like I was on the precipice of having something in common with my peers, but it was always very clear to them that I was different. It was clear to me as well, and it caused me a lot of anxiety." The only place Edward felt at ease was at his family church, a suburban redbrick cathedral where he served as an altar boy.

When he got to high school, Edward fell in love: with punk rock and with a girl who looked "just like Joan Jett." He says, "She introduced me to feminism and Bikini Kill and all this progressive stuff that I'd never had any exposure to. It was shocking to me—like, you're allowed to think that way?" He told his parents he was bisexual at fifteen, and they told him he could call himself whatever he wanted, as long as he did the "right thing." That is to say, as long as he continued dating girls.

Where Portia was able to emerge from the closet when and as she chose, Edward was forcibly removed from it. The defining moment came when he was in college, at a Patti Smith concert with his "Joan Jett" girlfriend. Edward was starting to wonder if he might no longer be so bisexual after all—if he might now just be gay. Others were less tentative about his sexual status. At the concert, Edward ran into a guy his girlfriend had dated during one of the "off" periods of their on-again, off-again relationship. He approached Edward aggressively, pushing him around and calling him a "faggot."

It wasn't just the threat of physical violence that threw Edward off balance. It was the words his aggressor was using. "I was already struggling with the feeling that my relationship wasn't going anywhere—that I was gay—but to have it thrown in my face like that, I just was not prepared for it," he explains. "I don't know how anyone could be prepared, to be honest. It was like the whole world had figured me out. I felt like I didn't have an option to hide anymore."

Edward had dealt with anxiety before, but never anything of this magnitude. He found himself unable to speak or even form a sentence. "It wasn't a matter of fight or flight, it was like fight or flight or freeze," he says. So instead of fighting, he took so much Xanax that he was admitted to a psychiatric ward for a week and a half. When he returned from the hospital, he logged on to MySpace, changed his sexual orientation to "gay," and said nothing more about it.

The understatement was intentional. "Because it felt like such a big deal on the inside, I didn't want it to be a big deal outside as well. I just wanted to kind of fly under the radar and let it be what it is, and if people wanted to talk about it, we could do that at some other point—which was my kind of coded way of saying 'never,'" Edward recalls. "I spoke about it with the people I felt like it affected, like my ex—who is still a very good friend of mine—but I didn't want to be having that conversation with my roommates. It just wasn't comfortable for me. I didn't want to hear them say all that, 'Oh, we always knew!'-type stuff. It's like, 'Yeah, I know you did. Let's just move on.'"

Portia's and Edward's stories are similar in many ways. As children, they both played traditionally gendered games in nontraditional ways. They both came to terms with their sexuality slowly, taking years to try it on and think it through before eventually making a public declaration of identity. And when they did make that declaration, they both wanted to do it as quietly as possible.

But their ability to come out quietly, to blend into the social wallpaper in the same way that a young straight person would, has been very different. Portia is a femme woman with glossy hair and a discreet sense of dress; Edward is an alternatively styled man with a nose ring and pierced ears. Portia grew up in the relatively secular United Kingdom, with liberal upper-middle-class parents; Edward was a Catholic altar boy whose family was on the poorer side of the working class. Where Portia tells me that almost half of her high school friends later came out as gay or lesbian, Edward's high school Gay-Straight Alliance was told by the school administration that to hang a rainbow flag in the hallways would have the same impact on Christian students that a swastika would have on Jewish students.

In other words, it is not just the acts we partake in that call us out as normal or abnormal; it is also the bodies that engage in those acts. Our race, our class, how we dress, and how conventionally attractive we are all influence the way our sexual orientation is ultimately received.

That Edward and Portia sought to make their sexuality unremarkable at all—however successfully or unsuccessfully they were able to do so—speaks to the fact that being "unremarkable" is now an option for some young same-sex-attracted people, and to the folding of same-sex experiences into the mainstream. But not all gay and lesbian people have the option of "passing," and those who are most able to exercise that option are those whose physical appearance, sexuality, and gender expression are otherwise as expected.

In 2011, the Australian online activist organization GetUp! produced a YouTube video as part of their campaign to legalize same-sex marriage. The video follows an attractive young man of indeterminate ethnicity, with tanned skin and curly, light brown hair, through the eyes of his unseen lover. It opens with the man sailing across Sydney Harbor on a ferry, laughing as he meets his lover for the first time, and scrawling his phone number in the pages of a novel. The two ride a Ferris wheel at an amusement park, shop for groceries at a supermarket, and play cricket on the beach. They later move into the same house, scrub the dishes, and watch movies on the couch, celebrate birthdays together, and care for his mother while she is sick in the hospital. At the end of the video, the young man drops down on one knee and pulls an engagement ring out of a red box. Finally we see the person behind the camera—who is, of course, another attractive young man. "It's time," the video declares.

It is a beautiful video that effectively shows that a love story is a love story, regardless of the genders of the people involved. It was also extremely popular, attracting more than fifteen million views on YouTube at the time of this writing. But intentionally or not, it also illustrates how the acceptance of previously marginalized sexual groups like gays and lesbians hinges on their fitting the "norm" in every other way. It is relatively easy to embrace a pair of conventionally attractive, conventionally masculine men who also happen to enjoy middle-class domestic pursuits like dinner parties, barbecues, monogamy, and the beach. But what about gay men who are naturally more effete, or lesbians who eschew the markers of conventional femininity? What about the same-sex-attracted people who don't want marriage or monogamy, or who build their families around the communities they choose rather than the people who raised them? Same-sex relationships may be more accepted than they used to be, but the relationships that are embraced most are the ones that most closely mirror the old standards.

The same ambivalence can be observed in the mainstreaming of another previously marginalized activity, BDSM. Kink is cool now when it is merely a "naughty" posture tried on for novelty and variety. But it is less so when it is part of the more serious work of identity—that is to say, when it is something you need in order to get off rather than just an adventurous addendum. Would Ben's alcohol-inspired confessions of handcuffs and bondage have been so positively received if they had been seen as the raison d'être of his sexuality, rather than as an entrée to the main event of intercourse?

On the less trendy side of the nonnormative divide lie people like Nyn, a twenty-three-year-old sex-positive, polyamorous trans man living in the northwest of England. None of those qualities make him unusual within the progressive, sexually open scene he inhabits. "I live in a community which is pretty comfortable with alternative genders and sexualities," he explains. But people like Nyn are still largely invisible in most parts of the media. Gay and lesbian people may be "normal" now, but trans and genderqueer people are still treated as puzzles that need to be solved. And while no-strings-attached sex is expected among people of a certain age and class, monogamy is still assumed to be the desired endpoint of any relationship.

Even within Nyn's own group of friends, there are norms and expectations to grapple with. "Because I am honest and open about my preferences, people expect me to have far more sex, and in far more interesting and exotic ways, than I actually do," he observes. "Mentioning that I spent the evening with my partner and two other people who are part of my poly group can lead to speculations of orgies, rather than us sharing a meal and watching movies. When I sleep in a friend's bed, I now realize that I need to clarify that we didn't have sex. And while I will happily give people condoms and lube when I'm being activisty, the assumption people take from that is that I have a great deal of kinky, penetrative sex."

If being "normal" means having your sexuality removed from discussion, people like Nyn, who still exist at the margins, are seen only through the lens of their gender and sexuality. "There's this idea that because you're kinky, you're vastly experienced and up for anything," Nyn says, jokingly referring to what he calls "the Land Where People Have More/More Interesting Sex."

"People who believe in this land, and believe that they are outsiders to it, don't want to offend people who live there by saying the wrong thing," he says. "They realize that a lot of what they might have heard about could be wrong. But they assume there must be *something* interesting happening. So if you try to ask people what they expect of you, or why they jump toward thinking that sleeping over at a friend's house means some kind of kinky orgy, you end up with a weird miscommunication, where they are trying to allude to this Big Secret which they are sure you know about and demonstrate that they are accepting of your wild ways. At the same time, you actually had a Disney film marathon and don't think that there is any Big Secret, because even if there *is* a mysterious Land Where People Have More/More Interesting Sex, you certainly don't live there. After all, your experience is just normal for you."

Nyn's version of "kink" doesn't look like anything you'd find in the pages of a women's magazine. As a trans man whose gender identity is not reflected in his physical body, there are parts of Nyn's body that "don't exist for all intents and purposes" when it comes to sex—his chest, for example, and his genitals. Intercourse is off the table, and much of the sex he does have is fully clothed, concerned more with the thrill of a power differential than with penetration. It is as valid a form of sexual expression as any other, but it is one that never even crosses many people's minds. When kink is talked about in the mainstream, it is treated as a prelude, a form of foreplay used to get everyone excited before a penis enters a mouth, an anus, or a vagina. Without that reliable conclusion to the carnal narrative, many people find it difficult to imagine "sex" as they know it at all.

As much as the borders between "normal" and "deviant" have been redrawn, there are still people who are excluded from them. In order for something to be normal, there must be a counterpoint that is *abnormal*. And in order for new groups to be folded into the mainstream, there must be others that are defined as unacceptable or dangerous.

For those who are most in the outer group, the risk of being classed as "abnormal" goes far beyond an abstract sense of isolation and inadequacy. It still can—and often does—result in concrete discrimination. A 2011 report cofunded by the National Center for Transgender Equality and the National Gay and Lesbian Task Force found that transgender and other gender-nonconforming people were four times more likely than the general population to have a household income of less than $10,000 per year. Forty-one percent had attempted suicide, compared to 1.6 percent of the general population. Ninety percent had been harassed or mistreated at work, and 61 percent had been victims of physical assault. And although forty-seven US states have anti-hate-crime laws, only twenty-four of those include sexual orientation in their legislation. The lines between "good" and "bad" sex and gender identities may be more flexible than they used to be, but they are not as open as we would like to think.

Vanilla Disguise: The New Deviance

The behaviors that are embraced as normal and those that are rejected as deviant are not always imposed in obvious ways—through a law upheld in court or a pronouncement from a religious leader, for example. Just as often, they are something we learn through subtle repetition: a result of similar stories played out on television shows, in online comments, and in conversations between friends and acquaintances until they are internalized as truth. And we are not just passive consumers of these stories. We participate in their creation, consciously or otherwise, in everything we do or say when it comes to sex.

It is through repetition of ideas and assumptions that we come to believe that only social outcasts don't date in high school, that college students will sleep with anything they can get, and that sex all but dries up once you sign a marriage license. It is through the duplication of the same stories, over and over, that we come to absorb the message that men will do anything for sex or that women only have sex out of a sense of duty and obligation (but that "cool girls"—or "sluts," depending on the circles you move in—want it all the time).

Repeated often enough, these stories add up to what sociologists call "heteronormativity": the systematic elevation of heterosexuality over all other forms of sexual activity and expression. But heteronormativity isn't just an implicit pressure to be straight. It is a pressure to be a certain *type* of straight person. It is no longer only the traditional deviants of the queer, the transgendered, and the kinky who attract public censure and self-flagellation. As Gayle Rubin put it in her "Thinking Sex" essay, now even the "small[est] differences in value or behavior are often experienced as cosmic threats" to the self and the status quo.

Norms are always in the background, shaping our attitudes and expectations. But it is often only when we step out of line with them that we feel their full weight. Fortysomething Baltimore writer Pamela Haag spent little time thinking about her sex life until she stopped having sex with her husband after she gave birth to her first child at the age of thirty-five—and found her relationship suddenly at odds with perceptions of what constituted a good marriage. "Only when I fell out of step with marriage norms—when I stopped having sex—did I realize how much I'd been calibrating my marriage to other people's standards," Haag wrote in a 2011 feature for the UK's *Times Magazine*. "Before, I hadn't noticed, because I wasn't a marital misfit."

Where other people stop having sex "because they care too little about their erotic life," Haag says she stopped because she cared "too much about it—too much to fill up on 'junk food' sex." Physically and emotionally, Haag was comfortable with her temporary celibacy, but socially, she didn't feel like she had the right to be. " 'Preferring not to' [have sex] didn't feel like a legitimate, non-pathological choice," she wrote in the *Times*. "I was left thinking that we're not permitted to not want sex, or, more accurately, to be happily autoerotic."

Haag's story reminds us that norms aren't just oppressive instructions of what not to do. They also serve to tell us what we *should* be doing, urging us to modify ourselves to better reflect their scripts and standards, whether that means changing our stories or literally changing our behavior.

Courtney, twenty-two, is smart and outspoken, a bisexual, sex-positive feminist with short blond hair, a nose ring, and a maroon T-shirt with the words "Love Your Body" emblazoned across the chest. But she deeply regrets the first time she had sex. Not because, as stereotype would have it, she feels like she lost a treasured part of herself, or because she was exploited for someone else's short-term pleasure, but because she feels like she "used" the guy she lost her virginity to—all in the service of feeling normal.

It happened two years ago, when she was still at college, with an acquaintance who had "a reputation for being a giant man-slut." Courtney didn't realize he was interested in her at first. "I'm just not used to thinking of myself as attractive," she explains. "I'm getting better at it, but it seems so inconceivable to me that anybody would be interested in me that it tends to take me a really long time to pick up on signals. Like, *This person wants me to come home with them and have sex?*"

When Courtney finally realized her friend was into her, she responded by pursuing him relentlessly, showing up in places she knew he would be and making sure he knew she was interested in return. It culminated in a drunken night of brief, unenthusiastic sex. "It was not good," she recalls. "Partly because I had to be drunk in order to make the moves in order to get into the place where we were actually having physical sex. Because I was a little tipsy my brain wasn't working fast enough to realize, hey, we could change positions. And then it might have sucked less. I don't think either of our hearts were really in it."

She cried when it was over, regretting the way she had treated him and the fact that she had compromised her own desires just so that she could say she'd had sex. She had thought the experience would be fun, but instead she just felt empty. "I wanted to have sex so badly that I ended up doing it just to prove that I *could* do it," she reflects. "Just to prove that I was attractive enough and that I was brave enough to have sex."

Courtney would still like to be more sexually active than she is, but she wants to do it on her own terms. "It's not trendy to only want to have sex in a relationship that you're comfortable with," she observes. "The news anchors expect that, as a young woman living in a city, I'm having a lot of sex and it's terrible. Other twentysomethings expect that I'm having a lot of sex and it's awesome. Or [they think that] if I'm not having sex it's because I have negative views about sex and that's bad. But in actuality, I'm really not having any sex that's not with myself right now, and that's okay. You can be comfortable with your sexuality and still have valid reasons for not being sexually active."

While Courtney dealt with her feelings of difference and defect by changing her behavior, I dealt with my own by carefully moderating the way I spoke about my experiences to other people. I never outright lied about my sexual history. I just kept quiet when the conversation turned from banter to specifics. I didn't contradict the assumptions other people made about me and brushed away questions when they were asked directly. "Oh, I don't talk about that stuff," I declared blithely when a friend I was driving to the train station one night asked me how I lost my virginity. When acquaintances traded sex stories, I would laugh and joke along with everyone else. As a consequence, I passed: not as heterosexual, the way that other "deviants" before me might have, but as fun. Modern. "Normal."

But whether or not we see ourselves as normal has less to do with how typical our desires and experiences are than with how closely they align with what we believe they *should be*. In the next few chapters, we will take a deeper look at some of the attributes that comprise today's sexual ideal, starting with desire and desirability.

4

Hot, Horny, and In Control:
The Importance of Desire

Growing up in small-town Wisconsin, Alice spent much of her time feeling like a nerd. She was into art and theater rather than football and cheerleading. She made her own clothes and was a member of the math club. But there was one thing that Alice felt set her apart from her fellow geeks: she'd had sex, losing her virginity at the age of seventeen to her long-term boyfriend.

"I felt like such a vixen," Alice, now twenty, recalls. "Looking around the math club and knowing that I was probably the only person in the room who'd had sex." Even now, she feels a rush of that same "vixen vibe" when she thinks about having sex with her current boyfriend. Her back straightens. She stands a little taller. Her lips curl into a smile, like someone in possession of a delicious secret. "I'll be honest—I feel better about myself when I'm sexually active," she admits. "It's such an ego boost in a really specific way. If someone is willing to have sex with you, it means such a specific thing."

And what, specifically, does sex mean to Alice? "Just that you're generally attractive," she says. She also thinks that being sexually active makes you a little bit cooler. "People who hook up often are cool because they don't have any attachments to the experience," she reflects. "They're able to just let sex be fun." Alice has never had casual sex herself, which she thinks is "a bit weird" for someone in their second year of college. But it's something she'd like to try one day. "I feel like [a one-night stand] is a unique experience," she says. "I'd like to have one at some point."

Alice's open and optimistic take on casual sex is typical of a generation for whom an active sex life is no longer a point of fear or shame, to be swept under the carpet, but a matter of personal pride. But her comments are also emblematic of the particular modes of sexual interaction that our era celebrates. In a culture that elevates sex as the heart of human vitality, being sexually successful means two things: desiring sex, and being desirable enough to be able to get it from the people you want to have it with.

Desire is entwined with promises of pleasure, adventure, and personal fulfillment. When we are in the thick of desire for another person, the world seems richer and more vibrant. When we are desired in return, the thrill is heightened further still—not only from the gratification of having our needs fulfilled but also from the affirmation that we have been deemed worthy by another person. Who and what we desire is the foundation upon which our sexual orientations are publicly cataloged and defined: are we gay, straight, asexual, kinky, or something else entirely?

Sex has long been a vessel through which we have attempted to realize our hunger to be seen by others. But that yearning for recognition is directed at more than just our partners. We seek out sexual contact not only for its own pleasure and intimacy, but also for what it projects about our social standing more generally.

Desire has historically been considered a force that strips us of our control, as we relinquish reason in the pursuit of animalistic pleasure. But it has also become a means by which we jostle for power, not only within individual sexual relationships, but within our broader social and peer networks. Under the Sex Myth, sex is not just a raw biological urge. It is also a status symbol, with success within the bars and bedrooms of the sexual playing field serving as an affirmation of our success outside of them.

The winners on today's sexual playing field? Those who are hot, horny, and firmly in control.

Hot:
If You're Sexy and You Know It . . .

The evidence that our culture prizes physical beauty is inescapable— from Victoria's Secret billboards to the toned, partially clothed bodies that populate Hollywood sex scenes and San Fernando Valley pornography; from the magazines that make a sport out of ranking the world's "sexiest" men and "hottest" women to the portrayal on television and in the movies of anyone who is not sexually active as awkward and unattractive.

The intended equation is clear: having sex makes you hot, and hot people have more sex. "In the movies, you always have the really attractive male lead and the really attractive female lead, and they always seem to get together," observes Nicholas, a clean-cut psych and finance major at a small Midwestern liberal arts school. "That's the message I'm seeing. That if you're hot, you can have sex all the time." Chinara, an eighteen-year-old college freshman who intends to abstain from sex until she marries, agrees: "When I was younger, I always thought that the only reason people had sex was because the other person was really, really pretty."

The symbolic link between beauty, sex, and social desirability is reinforced in real life, especially during adolescence, when our bodies begin to shape the way that we are received by the world. Meet the requirements for middle-school-approved attractiveness and find yourself catapulted to preteen popularity. Hit puberty before your peers and become the target of adult attention you're not yet equipped to understand. Get a boyfriend—or a girlfriend—before the other kids in your grade, and become an object of admiring whispers and potentially poisonous gossip.

Sam, a twenty-eight-year-old computer engineer with dark hair and piercing blue eyes, cuts the figure of a classic alpha male. He is confident and charismatic, with a demeanor that alternates between East Coast enthusiasm and West Coast laid-back cool. Sam is good-looking, and he knows it. This first became clear to him when he was in the seventh grade and transferred from his small Jewish private school to a larger public school with four hundred kids enrolled in each grade. Sam had nine girlfriends that year, which was "possibly the best dating year of [his] life," he jokes.

When he got to high school, Sam's dating life slowed down. "I wasn't a jock, and I wasn't the cool new kid anymore," Sam recalls. "I was about twenty pounds overweight, didn't have great skin, and I lost my appeal." In college, though, it picked up again, and he had sex with more than fifteen women over four years. Today, his "number" is close to fifty, placing him significantly above average for his age group: according to statistics from the Centers for Disease Control and Prevention, less than a quarter of men age twenty-five through twenty-nine have had more than fifteen sexual partners in their lifetime. For Sam, sex and dating are a source of confidence, proof that he is attractive and that he has the social skills to charm whoever is the object of his affections at any given time. "When someone wants to go on a date with you or have sex with you, it's validating," he observes.

Sam's appearance and his positive sexual experiences are self-reinforcing and symbiotic. His good looks saw him embraced by his peers at a crucial point in his emotional development, which gave him the confidence to pursue dates and hookups, and meant that his early dating experiences were largely affirming. Those positive experiences in turn enhanced his attractiveness: his peers viewed him as someone worth spending time with, and this boosted his social skills.

This reciprocity is reflected by studies that look into the social and psychological benefits of being attractive. Research shows that people like Sam, who are conventionally good-looking, are beneficiaries of what is known as the "halo effect," meaning they are presumed to be smarter, nicer, and more successful than their plainer-looking counterparts. What is more interesting is that over time, those assumptions often turn out to be true: not because pretty people are innately smarter or more talented or have better personalities, but because years of positive social reception and enhanced opportunity become a self-fulfilling prophecy. Treat a person as though they are likeable and successful, and they will often become so.

The same principle applies to sex appeal: past successes increase the likelihood of success in the future. Of the hundreds of people I spoke with over the course of researching the Sex Myth, it wasn't those who were the most conventionally attractive who had the most confidence in their appeal—it was the people who'd had the most positive experiences with sex and dating. Those who had encountered early rejection or who had negative early relationships, on the other hand, were more likely to perceive themselves as unattractive, regardless of the way they looked.

If hot bodies are given a license to be sexual, less hot bodies are often denied any sexuality at all. As a teenager, Natalie, a porcelain-skinned twenty-six-year-old from the evangelical northern suburbs of Sydney, had sex on the brain. She daydreamed about anonymous men, fantasized about her crushes at school, and devoured erotic fiction online. But although she felt highly sexual on the inside, Natalie didn't feel like she had the right to be. "I didn't feel worthy of being considered sexy," she recalls.

At Natalie's school, the sexual girls were the cool girls, who were simultaneously envied for their good looks and disdained for their superficiality and perceived sexual availability. Those girls were pretty, extroverted, and outspoken. In comparison, Natalie felt short, chubby, shy, and boring. Most of the time, she tried not to draw too much attention to herself.

"There was this view that you had to know your place," Natalie explains. "You know, that if you're not attractive enough then you shouldn't go on about sex because it's out of line. There was something a bit shameful about it—about wanting sex but not being attractive enough to have it." Even now, almost a decade after she first became sexually active, she still hasn't lost the feeling that her desire for sex is in some way revolting, that she is "a disgusting freak who is lasciviously cracking onto these 'innocents.'" Natalie believes she needs to be "superhuman" in order to be attractive: someone who never smells bad, never says the wrong thing, and never has a hair out of place. "I'm a perfectionist," she explains. "And I want to be perfectly desirable, which is, of course, impossible."

It is not just women who are told that their right to feel desire depends on how much they are desired by others. But although a man's perception of his attractiveness might play a role in determining the partners he pursues—or the partners who pursue him—a woman's desirability can serve as a permission slip to be sexual at all. Whether others want to have sex with him or not, a man's desire is presumed to be bubbling under the surface, aching to be set free. Too often, though, a woman's right to desire hinges on her desirability in the eyes of other people. If they don't want to have sex with her, she is presumed to be sexless.

Henry, a trainee electrician from Bristol in the UK, is tall and broad shouldered with pale, flushed skin and closely cropped brown hair. At twenty-three years old, he has never had a girlfriend and he has never had sex, though he did come close to it once. He tells me about a girl he met online, a curvy redhead with lip piercings who lived in a neighboring town. They had met in person for a drink and were back at her house making out when she received a phone call from her ex-boyfriend. Henry lay in her bedroom for three hours while she went to see her ex, before she returned to tell him they were getting back together. "It was mortifying as hell, really," he recalls. "I was in a strange city in the middle of the night with nowhere to go."

Henry is even more ashamed of his virginity, which he attributes to a combination of shyness, insecurity, and his size. "I'll just say it—I'm overweight," he says when I ask him why he is so convinced of his undesirability. He compares himself to the men his female friends salivate over, the "A-list actors with less than three percent body fat and Type A personalities." And that's fair enough, he reasons. "If that's what they want, then they deserve to be with someone they're attracted to."

Henry's self-doubt permeates his every move. He speaks softly, so that the other patrons in the converted London church café where we meet can't hear what he is saying. His hands and voice shake whenever the conversation veers to anything that threatens to be emotionally revealing. "It's hard work to make sure that I don't wake up every day and feel like I've failed," he says. "I just feel too old to be a virgin." When he was seventeen or eighteen, it didn't feel like such a big deal. "Even at nineteen or twenty, it felt like there was still time." But Henry is now approaching his midtwenties, and his friends are starting to move in with their partners and get engaged. "I just feel like, *What am I doing?* I haven't even gotten to stage one of that conversation yet."

Henry's friends shower him with what he calls "platitudes"— *there are plenty more fish in the sea, there is somebody out there for you,* and so on. But although their words are designed to make Henry feel better about himself, he doesn't believe them. "It just feels like if that was the case, surely somebody would have come along by now." He worries that he will still be a virgin when he is eighty, that he is doomed to be alone forever. "It's a horrible thought to live with every day," he says.

A month or two after our conversation, Henry is even less sure of himself, writing to tell me that he has rethought his views on sex. "I've realized that not everyone is meant to have sex," he writes. "Sometimes it's just not in a person, and after (almost) twenty-four years on this earth without 'it,' I'm one of those people." Trying to pursue sex "like a normal" person, he says, has left him despondent and filled with rage. "People in the past told me that I 'deserved' sex. But I've come to the conclusion that no one really 'deserves' sex. It just is, and on the opposing rationale, sometimes, it just . . . isn't."

"You're Ugly Because Your Girlfriend Is"

We don't just want to be "hot" because we like the look of dewy skin and washboard abs, or even because we think it would help us get laid more often. We care about beauty for what it signifies about how we are valued, both by the people we love (and those we want to love us), and by society at large.

Beauty, whether it is our own or that of someone we are sleeping with, is a marker of status and affirmation—and Meghan, twenty-four, has been the beneficiary of more sexual affirmation than most. A smart, self-effacing young conservative with a sardonic sense of humor, Meghan knows that her appearance "very much fits the cultural archetype" of an attractive woman. She is slim but curvy, with natural-looking blond highlights and, she notes wryly, "massive boobs."

In high school, Meghan was one half of her upper-middle-class New England high school's golden couple, the trophy girlfriend of the captain of the lacrosse team and president of the National Honor Society. At college, her boyfriend was the charismatic president of his fraternity and a local celebrity in the small, Midwestern town where he grew up. Today, Meghan is rarely single—and that, she tells me, is intentional.

"I've always been the girl whose single friends have been like, you *always* have a boyfriend. How do you *do* that?" she says. "And I laugh and pretend like it's not a big deal, but secretly, I'm like, *yes*, I always have a boyfriend." For Meghan, being in a relationship is not just proof that she is desirable but an indicator of success—something that keeps her mother happy and reassures Meghan that her life is progressing as it is supposed to. "I like it to be done and sealed so that I can check that box," she admits. "Like, have a boyfriend? Mission accomplished. Now I can move on with my life."

If being in a relationship is a stamp of social approval, not being in one is considered a sign that something is amiss. Chloe, a psychology major at a women's college in North Carolina, tells me that on her campus, "people who are single are lumped into the category of being losers because they can't get a boyfriend. Like, maybe they're socially awkward or not pretty enough or whatever." Chloe is critical of many of the values that dominate at her school—the focus on remaining a virgin, for example, or the rush to secure an engagement "ring by spring." But deep down, she still believes that there is something wrong with being single. "It's not like people consciously choose not to date," she reasons. At Chloe's school, having sex outside of a relationship marks you as a slut. But not having any kind of sexual contact at all makes you a weirdo.

It is not sex itself that determines whether a person is perceived as "hot" or not. After all, no one ever really knows for sure how much sex other people are having. What matters is being recognized as having the *opportunity* to have sex—especially if that opportunity is with a person of equal or greater attractiveness. If you can't be sure how much sex someone is having, you can at least have a reasonable indication of how sexy they are.

It is no coincidence that Meghan's ex-boyfriends are mostly good-looking, or that Sam will zero in on the most attractive woman in the room when he's looking for someone to hook up with. Such choices reflect and reinforce their self-perception as desirable people, and the fact that they are chosen by those people in return is part of what makes them desirable in the first place. Indeed, Meghan attributes her high school popularity not to anything specific about her, but to the popularity of the guys she went out with. "It was the halo effect of dating them," she observes. "It had nothing to do with my own awesomeness."

The link between sex appeal and social status is not a recent development. In 1937, the American sociologist Willard Waller published a paper on "the rating and dating complex," his term for the process by which young people meet and form relationships.

Today dating is seen as a time-honored, even slightly old-fashioned practice, but back then it was a relatively new phenomenon. Dating only emerged in the 1920s with the popularization of the automobile, which gave young people the means and freedom to socialize—and court—outside the home. And like the baby boomers who complain about "hookup culture" today, Waller was less than impressed with it. He described dating as a "dalliance relationship," more concerned with cheap emotional and sexual thrills than with the serious business of getting people married. (Less than two decades later, adults would be encouraging teenagers to date around more, fearing that "going steady" would lead them to commit—and have sex—before they were ready.) Drawing upon interviews with students and alumni at a large state university, Waller argued that dating operated on a market-based system, in which an individual's dating success reflected his or her status according to the broader scheme of campus values.

Students at the top of the social ladder, whom Waller labeled "Class A," dated other Class A students almost exclusively, while students at the bottom were often excluded from dating altogether. Women in particular would choose not to date at all rather than be seen dating a man their friends thought was undesirable.

But what made an individual rate highly as a dating prospect differed depending on the gender of the person being rated. For Waller's men, like Meghan's ex-boyfriends, desirability was tied to status elsewhere on campus. The men who were considered most datable were those who were members of the most prestigious fraternities, who were involved in high-profile campus activities, who were well dressed and good-looking, and who had access to a car. For Waller's women, as for Meghan, the relationship worked in reverse. Rather than a girl's popularity determining her datability, it was her desirability as a date that determined her popularity, more so than her personality, how much money her parents had, or even how pretty she was. "[In dating] as nowhere else, nothing succeeds like success," Waller wrote.

Especially in the earliest years of our sex and dating lives, what we consider desirable is shaped not only by what we personally find attractive but also by what we think other people are attracted to. If the person you hook up with reflects your status and position, your peers' approval of your partner is a proxy for their approval of you. As we discussed in chapter 2, the people you have sex with can become a kind of commodity, like the car you drive or the clothing you wear.

Caleb, a soft-spoken twenty-four-year-old from Melbourne, Australia, takes the analogy a step further. "My friends and I came up with this theory that you are only as attractive as the girl you're going out with," he explains. "So therefore if you had an ugly girlfriend it would make you ugly, and if you had a really hot girlfriend it made you attractive. And that was the guideline." He laughs. "One of our mates, pretty much all of his girlfriends were ugly."

So, it was like you're ugly and your girlfriend is, too? I ask. "No," Caleb corrects me. "It was like you're ugly *because* your girlfriend is."

Horny:
Want to Have It, Got to Have It

Being "hot" is more than just genetic luck. It is a measure of effort: of the hours you spend working out; the precision of your grooming habits; and how completely you have internalized and executed the symbols of sex appeal as dictated by your gender, age, and subculture. Jezebel blogger Emily Armstrong put it simply when she said, "Pretty is a set of skills." Desire tends to be slippery and specific to the individual: one person might have a thing for curly hair, while another might prefer a strong nose or an acerbic sense of humor. But mass-approved hotness is not about what individuals find attractive. It is a form of peacocking, a visual calling card declaring that we are a particular type of sexual person.

A waxed pubic area, for example, is sexy to many not just because it allows the genitals to be more easily seen or tasted, but because it suggests that sex is a priority in your life, that you expect to have it regularly and are willing to sacrifice time, physical comfort, and money to prepare for it aesthetically. Tight dresses and T-shirts show the labors of a gym-toned body. Fake tans, colored hair, and breast implants beckon to be looked at not only because they mimic traits we associate with youth and health, but because of the exertion they convey. At its core, what we consider to be hot is about making an effort, attractive not only for its aesthetics but because it suggests one might be open to sex.

This matters, because desirability in the early twenty-first century hinges on more than just other people wanting to have sex with you. It also means wanting to have sex with them in return— or at least looking like you might. And part of that means enacting a particular set of behaviors—being confident, outgoing, and open to a good time.

It is a set of behaviors that Stephanie, a seventeen-year-old high school senior from New England, has pursued with enthusiasm. Vivacious and analytical, with short dark hair, Stephanie has never felt like she fits the beauty standard laid out for girls her age. The exceptions to this insecurity, she tells me, are her breasts, which she describes as her "master status." When she was younger, she used to like to lift her shirt and flash them at people. "I thought it was hilarious, and it was, to be honest. It was pretty funny," she recalls. But, she concedes philosophically, she lacks "a certain bangability," that "special trait" that would elevate her from a girl people like to look at to a girl they want to have sex with.

When Stephanie was in her freshman year of high school, she and her friends entered into a race to see who would lose their virginity first. "It was an official competition," she explains enthusiastically. "I would get a boyfriend and they would be like, 'Ticktock, ticktock. When is it going to happen?'" Stephanie was the first of the group to start dating, but a year into their two-year relationship her first boyfriend came out as a transgendered woman. As such, he wasn't interested in penetrative sex. "Feeling like he had the wrong parts sort of put a damper on it," she says matter-of-factly. Her second boyfriend was an abstinence advocate who wanted to wait until marriage to have sex. "I was like, *Come on!*" she laughs, recalling her frustration. "So, that did not work out for me."

As she nears the end of high school, Stephanie is now the only virgin left in her close group of friends. She's okay with that, sort of. "If I wanted to have sex, I could," she reasons. "I'd just show up at a party with a lot of drunk people around." But her friends are more impatient for her to get it over with. "It's not like I have to have sex before prom," she jokes, "but it's kind of like a 'get a boyfriend and do it this summer' kind of deal. So that we can all be at the same stage again. So we can all have a similar level of experience."

Still, Stephanie admits, on some level she is as invested in the "race" as they are. "I don't want to still be a virgin when I'm twenty-five or even twenty," she says. She also doesn't want to be a virgin when she gets to college. At college, it's assumed that you'll be sexually active, she explains, and it's important to her to know what she's doing before she gets there.

No one in Stephanie's life right now expects her to be sleeping around. Her guy friends, in particular, are very clear that they think casual sex is a bad idea, telling her she shouldn't have sex unless it has "meaning" to her. But people do expect Stephanie to be having sex—preferably with one person, and in an ongoing relationship. Maybe it's because she'll be eighteen soon, she muses, and "you can't be an adult without having some kind of sexual experience. Sex is a rite of passage in our culture, I think." Losing her virginity would be proof that, as Stephanie puts it, "there are traits in [her] that people want, right over here."

Like flashing her breasts at strangers and entering into a teen-movie-style virginity-loss contest, being sexually active would also mark Stephanie as someone who is doing young adulthood in a particular, socially desirable way. As we learned in chapter 1, sex plays a key role in our popular imagination of what it means to be young, free, and fun. Like people who are attractive, people who are "fun" are perceived to have more opportunities to have sex—and people who are perceived to have a lot of sex are in turn considered to be more fun. Modern media and popular culture tell us that young single people are dining at a buffet of almost unlimited sexual options—and doing sex "right" means taking advantage of those opportunities.

Behind this ideal of fun and freedom lies a view of desire as a near-unstoppable force, one that shouldn't be interfered with. Left to our own devices, it says, we would fuck without fear or consequence, and anyone who does not do this must be repressed or otherwise eccentric.

But desire is also less straightforward than it is often portrayed. On-screen and in magazines, desire is powerful and immediate. But in practice, it often manifests itself more tentatively, sometimes emerging so quietly that we don't notice its presence until it achieves full bloom. Other times, especially when they do not conform to the expectations we have set out for them, we might not register our desires at all.

Courtney, the twenty-two-year-old bisexual woman we met in chapter 3, illustrates this ambiguous relationship well. Growing up in suburban America in the late 1990s and early 2000s, Courtney and her family would often visit her great-aunt Jean, who lived with a woman—known as "Aunt Susan"—in Philadelphia. It wasn't until she was in seventh grade, working on a family history project for school, that Courtney thought to ask her mother how exactly Aunt Susan fit into their family tree. "Well, Court, do you know what it means to be gay?" her mother replied.

During the same period, Courtney was starting to have her own feelings for girls, spending her evenings glued to the TV screen, drinking in images of Emily VanCamp on *Everwood* and Alexis Bledel on *Gilmore Girls*. She didn't recognize those feelings as sexual, though; all she knew was that she was drawn to the young actresses. "At that point, the only thing I knew about same-sex relationships was that it was this thing that old women did," she explains. "So even though I was having crushes on girls on TV, I really didn't have the language to say that it was a crush. There was no link in my head between what was going on between Aunt Jean and Aunt Susan and the way I felt about Emily VanCamp."

Courtney started to think that she might be bisexual in her early teens, but it wasn't until her third year of college that she fully came to terms with the fact that she was interested in girls. Even now, Courtney sometimes struggles to differentiate her desire to be sexual with other women from her desire to be intimate with them in a more platonic way. "Like, I'll see a girl and think she's pretty, and I'll have to stop to ask myself, 'Do I want to *be* her or do I want to have sex with her?'" It might just be that she has more practice being attracted to men, she concedes. "In a lot of ways, with girls, it's like being fourteen again. And realizing for the first time that, oh, maybe kissing isn't so gross after all."

Nor does every public expression of desire indicate an underlying longing for sexual release. Andrew, a twenty-three-year-old from London, is quirky and confident, with curly blond hair and an impish smile. He is in a committed relationship now, with a girl he plans to marry someday. But in his younger years, he and his friends treated hooking up as a game, picking up women and taking them home every chance they could. "It was insane," he recalls.

But on the nights when Andrew "won" the game, by meeting a girl, charming her, and bringing her back to his house, a funny thing would sometimes happen. He would find that he didn't want to have sex after all. "I couldn't get it up," he says incredulously. It wasn't nerves, he insists; it was that there hadn't yet been time to build up the chemistry between them. "I know it's a massive immaturity, but I didn't realize you had to have lust in order to enjoy sex," he says. "I thought it was all about the pickup." For Andrew, it was the *appearance* of desiring sex that mattered most, not the desire itself.

Control:
The Battle of Who Could Care Less

Part of the reason we pursue hotness and horniness is because we hope they will make us more desirable, and therefore more lovable. But we also pursue them because they promise another kind of security: the ability to control our romantic and sexual futures.

We are taught that if we transform ourselves into sufficiently enticing people, then we will be the ones deciding whether a hookup or flirtation turns into a fully fledged relationship. If we are the person who is most sought after at a party or on a dating website, we can have the power to choose who we date, rather than wait to see who chooses us. And if we need the person whom we are with less than they need us, we won't have to fear getting hurt.

Desire and desirability are more than just stamps of social approval. They are a form of emotional armor, an illusory promise that if we shape our appearance and demeanor in all the right ways, we will be safe from pain or rejection. But the bid to be "hot, horny, and in control" also turns sex and relationships into a game—sometimes literally, as in the case of bestselling self-help books such as *The Game* and *The Rules*—in which the victors are those who attract the greatest number of desirable partners without risking any vulnerability. As Nate, a confident twenty-one-year-old, puts it: "It's like Monopoly. Whoever has the most money at the end wins."

Occidental College researchers Lisa Wade and Caroline Heldman call this bid for control "compulsory carelessness"—the idea that sexual success depends on not being too emotionally invested in the person or people you have sex with. Under this model, sex is both spontaneous and disinterested, an outcome of neither emotional connection nor physical attraction, but rather a detached execution of a social script and biological urge. To care too much, either for your partner or for the act itself, would be to cede control.

"You don't ever want to drop the mask of being cool, calm, collected, and powerful," explains Ashley, a twenty-seven-year-old massage therapist from Portland. "You want to appear like you are choosing to sleep with the other person, not like they are choosing to sleep with you. You want to appear like you have the number one say."

Barefaced and bubbly, with wavy ash-blond hair, Ashley has been in a monogamous relationship with her girlfriend for three years. But she is animated when she describes the hookup scene at her university and the women she dated in the years after she graduated.

Ashley didn't sleep around when she was an undergraduate. Like most college students, she only had one or two sexual partners each year. But she kept her relationships deliberately casual, things that happened as if by chance at parties or on weekends but were never discussed directly. "You would have sex with the same person consistently for a season, but it was still very casual sex," she recalls. "It wasn't like you were doing it because you were in love and wanted to get married. You definitely would never describe them as your girlfriend or boyfriend."

After college, the arrangements evolved into something more closely resembling a formal dating relationship. "We'd go out to dinner or an activity, and then we would come home and either say good night or stay." But the importance of appearing uncommitted remained as it was before. "I would meet up with Jo on one night, and Lesley on another," Ashley says. "But I couldn't be somebody's *girlfriend*. You had to be dating multiple people. And even if you weren't, you would lie and say that you were. You didn't want the other people to think that you were falling head over heels for them. There was this mutual fear that the other person was going to go crazy on you, and you didn't want to appear like you were the crazy one in any way."

Ashley acknowledges that pretending to be dating multiple people when you're really only dating one is pretty "crazy" behavior, but the aim was to communicate that you had other alternatives, she says. "You want to show that you are independent and grounded and strong, that when you're not with the person you're seeing, you've got other stuff going on," she explains. Still, why not just say you're hanging out with friends or going to a concert? I ask her. "It's not as exciting or interesting," she replies. "Maybe in reality, I choose to be at home reading a book. But being able to say that one of the things I'm doing is another woman is very powerful."

Visibly dating multiple people doesn't just show that you are attractive and in demand. It also suggests that you have an appropriately high sex drive. "I do think that the 'wanting sex' thing plays a really big role," says Ashley. "Because if I had sex with Renee on Tuesday and Thursday, and I don't have sex Monday, Wednesday, or Friday, is that a concern? Does it look like I'm not interested in having enough sex?"

The idea is to avoid being vulnerable by limiting your emotional investment. "Needy isn't sexy," as Jasmine, a twenty-four-year-old woman from Toronto, puts it. Historically, this kind of feigned indifference might have been achieved by delaying or withholding sex. But today sex is a given, and delaying it too long can feel like a risk unto itself. Instead, indifference is communicated by withholding feeling, by refusing to show your emotional cards before you are sure of what the other person's cards might say in return.

This isn't to say that people don't fall in love. The hookup may have replaced formal dating as the mechanism by which young people in particular form relationships, but for most people, casual sex—if it happens at all—is one piece of a bigger puzzle that also incorporates love, short-term relationships, and periods of sexlessness and celibacy. Nor is it to suggest that, for all our attempts at projecting detachment, we are no longer vulnerable when it comes to sex. Sex is still a highly emotional matter, whether the emotions in question relate to how we feel about our partners or how we feel about ourselves.

The feminist psychologist Wendy Hollway has observed the way that heterosexual men will often describe their female partners as the more "emotional" figures in their relationships, arguing that it serves as a means of deflecting from their own emotional needs. By attributing any negative or overpowering emotions they might be feeling to the women they are dating, they are protected from having to deal with their own difficult emotions. But men are not the only ones who turn from their vulnerability in this way, or who recoil from people who express their emotions too readily. Women aren't lining up to date needy men either, says Pete, a smart, sensitive twenty-two-year-old from Seattle. "I've got friends who will spend an hour writing a single text message so as to appear interested but not too interested."

This desire to seem "interested but not too interested" is one reason that alcohol is so prominent in campus sexual encounters, argue Lisa Wade and Caroline Heldman. They quote Charlotte, a college freshman who writes: "A sober hookup indicates [you are] serious, which either no one is interested in or no one is brave enough to admit they want." A drunken hookup is careless, an aftereffect of inebriation rather than attraction. It is only the sober advances that are considered "real," and that pose the biggest risk to our reputations and emotional security.

The Opposite of Sex

Ironically, it is often when we feel *least* in control of our sex lives that we are most inclined to want to prove our mastery over them. The behaviors I have described in this chapter—the jostling to gain status through the manipulation of appearance, the pursuit of socially desirable sexual partners, the exaggerated performance of what passes for fun and freedom—are not usually those of people who are comfortable with themselves or their relationships with other people. Nor are they the behaviors of people who are reveling in the physical pleasure of sex for its own sake. They are postures, an attempt to turn the complex, vulnerable people that we are into the uncomplicated, emotionally impenetrable people we would like to be. As Tom, twenty, observes, "The people I know who have the most playboy-ish attitude are actually the people who are most emotionally needy."

Reflecting on my own sex and relationships history, it is when I have been most insecure in my attractiveness that I have retreated into beauty culture, obsessively monitoring and manipulating my appearance in order to more closely fit a cultural ideal. Reeling from romantic or sexual disappointment, I would color my hair, paint on a smile, and embark on a mission to become as thin as I could. When I feel more secure in my desirability, I am more content to let things be, including my appearance. It is when I have been least sexually active that I have talked the most about sex. And it is when I have been least certain that my interest will be reciprocated that I have felt the greatest need to play it cool—"to try," as I put it in a song I hummed to myself while getting ready for a college party one winter evening, "to look like I'm not trying."

Being hot and horny may have become our cultural shorthand for desire, but these traits are often less about our hunger for other people than they are about our hunger to be recognized by others. Arguably, hotness and horniness are the opposite of desire: based on thinking rather than feeling, a performance of identity rather than the realization of a sensual yearning. Ashley recalls the conversations she and her friends would have about sex in high school. "Instead of talking about how it makes your skin feel, the focus was on what you did, who you did it with, and what you produced," she says. "It was more like a scientific-method kind of thing than how you communicated on a physical level."

Just as important, chasing the hot and horny ideal doesn't work. Learning how to pattern your physical appearance to the socially sanctioned mold of "hot" might provide a short-term confidence boost, but it probably won't make you feel deeply desirable. Or at least it never made me feel that way. Nor does performing "horniness" teach us how to desire other people.

In fact, the pursuit of surface-level hotness and horniness might prevent us from fully experiencing desire, enforcing artificial limits on who and what we find attractive. For all that we are told that physical attractiveness is a formula, what each of us actually finds attractive is both broader and more idiosyncratic than what Hollywood sells us as hot. "I used to think there was one specific type of girl that was my 'type,'" says Marie, a dark-eyed seventeen-year-old from Kentucky. "Blond, or really skinny and conventionally attractive. As I've gotten older, though, I've noticed that I'm not just attracted to people who are really thin." What she really likes, she tells me, "is when people are bright." She blushes. "I feel a bit giggly just talking about it."

Nor does going through the motions of being a "fun," sexually liberated person always translate to actually having fun. As Andrew's tales of aborted one-night stands demonstrate, it is possible to have a lot of sex and not really enjoy any of it, or even to feel much desire for it.

For women, this divide between "being" fun and having fun can be even starker. Research by American sociologists Elizabeth Armstrong, Paula England, and Alison Fogarty shows that women only orgasm 32 percent as often as men do in first-time heterosexual hookups. By comparison, they orgasm 49 percent as often as men do in repeat or ongoing hookups, and 79 percent as often in relationships. This "orgasm gap" isn't just a question of emotional connection but of pragmatics: women are less likely to receive oral sex in a casual hookup than they are in a relationship, and less likely to receive the clitoral stimulation many women need to climax. "Sex in relationships tends to be better in part because . . . one has a greater incentive to treat one's partner well if a repeat is likely," the researchers observe. "Also, good sex takes practice, as, over time, partners learn what turns each other on."

A year and a half after we first met, I phone Meghan to check the details of her story and to see how she is doing. As usual, she has a boyfriend, but this one is different, she tells me. She met him online, after her relationship with her latest alpha asshole went spectacularly bust. "I was blindsided," she recalls. "I was like, *Why did this happen to me again? This always happens and it's not fun anymore.*" As she reflected, she realized there was a pattern to the guys she usually dated: she met them in bars or other social situations where it was difficult to talk and impressions were formed rapidly, on little more than the way she or they looked. "If I'd had to filter them for intellect or personality first, I never would have dated most of them," she reflects.

So she decided to change her method and find a mate in a forum where the content of what she had to say would matter as much as the color of her highlights: she'd look online. She met her new beau within two weeks of signing up for a dating service. They've now been dating for six months.

"He's very laid-back," Meghan tells me. "Funny, quirky, calm. Very successful. He has the confidence that I always got from the alpha-male guys, but none of the stupid swagger." And the most important part, she says, is that she feels like a three-dimensional human being, rather than a two-dimensional trophy girlfriend. "I've told him my weirdest, nerdiest thoughts that I wouldn't normally tell people, and he thinks that they're hilarious. All the reasons that he likes me are based on who I actually am as a person. My physical appearance is a bonus, but it's not the focus. Other guys would try to tell me how to dress and not to talk to other guys."

It's not that the usual physical attraction isn't there, Meghan stresses. "He's really cute. He's tall, he's handsome, he has broad shoulders, but he doesn't dress like he's trying to impress people. If he'd seen me at a bar, I don't know that he would have even wanted to talk to me."

Why not? "Because I didn't look like a person of depth," she jokes. "I looked like someone who had the intellectual maturity of a sloth." It was only when Meghan let go of her compulsion to treat relationships as a "game" that she finally experienced holistic desire.

5

Masculinity:
Inside the Boys' Club

It is 11:00 a.m. on a Sunday, and the men of Alpha Epsilon Eta*
are sound asleep. I am on campus in small-town Ohio to meet
with some of their members, and my first interviewee for the morning, Max, has just phoned to let me know he is running late, still on
his way back into town following his girlfriend's sorority formal the
night before. He tells me to let myself in through the back door—it's
unlocked—and to wait for him in the kitchen. I do as he instructs,
laughing as I inform him that where I'm from, no one leaves their
door unlocked, and they certainly don't invite people they don't
know to hang out in their homes when they're not there. Least of
all journalists.

I've never been inside a frat house before; we don't have them
in Australia, where I grew up and went to school. The closest thing
I've encountered is one of the all-male residential colleges at the
university where I studied as an undergraduate, notorious for their
wealthy inhabitants and for their occasional media scandals. Frater-

_____

* Not their fraternity's real name.

nity houses are the stuff of pop-cultural legend, an undiluted window into Planet Guy. I'm not sure what to expect.

Wedged on the edge of campus between a fellow fraternity and a women's soccer club, the Alpha Epsilon Eta house is smaller and less imposing than the Greek houses I've seen in the movies. Its initials are not carved in stone above stately doors but drilled into a small metal plaque, like a midlevel executive office door at a downtown law firm. It looks just as you'd imagine a house full of college guys to look on a Sunday morning. The kitchen table is scattered with red Solo cups and almost-empty beer cans. There are dirty plates and a couple of discarded bags of chips on the floor. A young woman lies on the couch in the open lounge area, sleeping off the party from the night before. On the front porch sits a table with the words "place scrotum here" scrawled on the top, and written on the kitchen wall is a rhyming manifesto espousing the virtues of brotherhood, friendship, and booze.

But Alpha Epsilon Eta is not your stereotypical fraternity. It is one of what sociologists have identified as a new breed of frat, born out of a more inclusive brand of masculinity that began to emerge in the early 1990s. Fraternity life has historically been criticized by feminists and other progressives for the negative attitudes it fosters toward women and gay men (and for good reason—research shows that fraternity men are three times more likely to commit sexual assault than other men on college campuses), but Alpha Epsilon Eta counts openly gay students among its members. They don't haze in the conventional sense, instead asking new members to study the chapter's history and recite chants from Stanley Kubrick films. As for their attitudes toward women, I was introduced to the Alpha Epsilon Eta men because a young woman I had interviewed had slept in a spare bed at the fraternity for a couple of months when she was in between houses. The manifesto on their wall urges "respect for all womankind."

And Max—a tall, analytical twenty-year-old with glasses and a buzz cut—is not your stereotypical frat guy. Like many of the fraternity men I met in my travels, Max didn't come to college planning to join a frat. A cross-country runner, he chose his school based on its athletics program. But when he neared the end of his freshman year and realized that most of the nonathlete guys he knew were members of the same fraternity, joining seemed like the natural thing to do.

Not all of the fraternities on Max's campus are like Alpha Epsilon Eta. He tells me about the "douchebag fraternity," as he and his friends describe them, "who think that they're the best thing that has ever walked the earth." Those guys, he says, are proud that they don't have any gay members and only hang out with women when they're looking to hook up.

But Max believes that the emotionally detached and macho brand of guyhood is on the decline. "I mean, you do see it," he admits. "Those guys who are all, like, *I'm the big, strong sports guy who likes to drink and party, I wear my hat backwards,* et cetera. And you will continue to see guys like that as long as there are people who think that stuff looks cool. But most men aren't like that. At least, most men I talk to aren't," he clarifies. Max doesn't think that most Greek guys are like that, either. "The stereotypes usually lag behind the people," he observes.

Masculinity scholars such as Michael Kimmel and Raewyn Connell argue that manhood has traditionally been defined by what it is not, as much as it is defined by what it is. In the conventional, orthodox view of manhood, "real men" prove their masculinity by being strong, confident, self-reliant, adept with women, and good at sports. They also assert it by distancing themselves from that which is defined as not masculine—which historically has meant anything feminine and anything that might hint at being something other than heterosexual.

These rules are starting to change, exemplified by young men like Max, who have grown up in a time in which homophobia is on a rapid decline and in which gender equality is not just a political movement but an accepted fact of life. But the conventional view of what it means to be a man hasn't disappeared entirely, either—especially when it comes to sex.

Max and his friends may be on what he describes as the "progressive track" of masculinity, but he is aware that there is a gap between his experiences and the masculine ideal that is presented in popular culture. "There is definitely an idea that men should be trying to have sex with as many women as possible," says Max, who has only slept with his current girlfriend. "I know guys who say they've slept with twenty people. It's a little intimidating."

In the same way that straight people's sex lives have historically been treated as apolitical, a state so neutral and ingrained that it does not warrant serious discussion, so too are men's experiences often left out of the ongoing public dialogue around sexuality. Female sexuality is contentious and politically fraught, bound up in questions of empowerment and oppression. But men's sexuality is framed as something that just "is"—an uncomplicated biological urge.

In some ways, this ordinariness is a reflection of men's continued institutional power: male sexuality does not need to be discussed because it is not considered a problem. But the absence of straight men from public conversations about sexuality also means that expectations of what men should do, be, and desire when it comes to sex too often go unchallenged. It renders the cornucopia of ways that men experience sexuality invisible and dissolves them into one single, streamlined march, making young men arguably even more vulnerable to the Sex Myth than young women. In this chapter, we will look at how the Sex Myth is shaping men's experiences of sex and relationships, and how young men are challenging the constraints of conventional masculinity in their own lives.

"No Memory and No Conscience": The Sexually Insatiable Man

Men, we are told, want sex in a way that women just don't. It is the impulse that puts a twinkle in their eye when they're sitting in class listening to a boring lecture and plagues them whenever they pass an attractive person on the street. Where women's desires are depicted as passive and malleable, easily influenced by the vagaries of popular culture, emotion, and how much housework they've done that day, men's sexuality is portrayed as fixed and unchanging, an unrelenting biological need. Men thirst for sex like dogs thirst for water, whereas women can take it or leave it. Men will fuck anyone who will let them, whether they find them attractive or not, but women seek to bond with a single partner who will stick around to provide for their babies.

These binaries are not just embedded in our culture; they are seemingly inscribed in the very physicality of our bodies. The alternately exterior and interior design of human genitalia means that men's sexual arousal is literally more visible than women's. If a teenage boy gets an erection at the swimming pool, everyone can see. If he has a sex dream, his semen stains the sheets. If a girl dreams about sex or fantasizes about one of her classmates as she glances at them from across the room, no one will know but her.

As most men will tell you, an erection does not always signal sexual desire—it can as easily be a response to warm air or water, a full bladder, or even the vibrations of a bus. But the erection's seemingly spontaneous nature serves as a visual reinforcement of the idea that men's desire is both an essential expression of their masculinity and something that occurs independently of their brains.

Josh, a thirty-year-old mobile phone app developer from Johannesburg, South Africa, recalls his embarrassment as a teenager when he was asked to come up to the front of the class to solve a math equation in the midst of an unwanted erection. "At first I said I didn't want to, but the teacher thought I was just being shy, so pretty much forced me to do it. I had to make some sort of nifty shirt/trousers/belt rearrangement, and walk with my arm by my side in order not to be seen," he remembers. "It can be very frustrating to realize that you don't have full control of how your penis behaves in certain situations."

A man's penis is not just another part of his body, like his torso or his knees. It is treated as a force unto itself that, as the actor Robin Williams once put it, "has no memory and no conscience." It is a view that simultaneously abases men while privileging their sexual needs over the needs of their (presumably female) partners. If men are unable to control their own desires, it falls to women to manage them instead, whether that means having sex they don't want in order to maintain a relationship, being more sexually inventive to preserve their partners' interest, or changing their clothes or behavior to avoid unwanted sexual advances.

But men's desire for sex is not as uncontrollable as we think. At twenty-three, Christopher, a slightly built, charming Texan with dark hair and eyes, has had a lot of sex: with women and with men, in long-term relationships, threesomes, and one-night stands. But at no point in any of those encounters has there been a time when he "couldn't stop and say no," he says. "There might be a slight twitch, but even if the other person wants to stop halfway through, that's that. The idea that guys 'can't help themselves' is completely ridiculous."

But if Christopher has always been physically able to slow down, he hasn't always felt like that was something he is permitted to do—even when it has been exactly what he wanted. "In every sexual relationship I have had with a woman, I have felt pressured to do more than I am comfortable with," Christopher says. Sometimes that pressure has come directly from the women he's dating, other times from some internalized ideal of how guys "should" approach sex. He recalls a night he spent watching movies on the couch with his first girlfriend when he was fifteen. "I was quite happy to just kiss, but I remember feeling this pressure to initiate something more. *You're alone and she turned off the lights, so I guess that means you're supposed to take it further.*"

He felt the same pressure when he started dating the girl he lost his virginity to a few years later. He'd had a crush on her for two years, and the first time they hooked up, they gave each other oral sex. "It was really wonderful," he says. "But I still remember feeling like I hadn't gone far enough. Like maybe we should have had [vaginal intercourse], because that was 'real sex.'"

Christopher's comments echo qualitative research into young men's sexual attitudes and experiences. A 2004 study funded by the Ford Foundation found that many teenage boys and young men felt they were expected to be sexually active, even before they wanted to be. One thirteen-year-old boy interviewed for the study, "RZA," described feeling like he had to "be a man" and "get some" with a girl his friend had described as an "easy target." The two had been left alone together with the expectation that they would have sex, and were kissing when RZA realized he didn't want to have sex with her—or with anyone at that moment. "I don't know what it was, I just didn't want to, like, do anything," he told the researchers.

Another boy who participated in the Ford study, the self-described "Nervous Guy," described feeling pressured to kiss a girl in a game of truth-or-dare. "You gotta do something, so I did. And, like, it was terrible." He recalled the kiss as "disgusting," and told the researchers that he later went home and washed his mouth out. "It was kind of a rip-off, man . . . Like, 'cause it really didn't mean anything, it was just really dumb. In a way, that's just, like, rude to myself [to kiss a girl he wasn't attracted to]." It was his first kiss.

A 2010 survey commissioned by the National Campaign to Prevent Teen and Unplanned Pregnancy and *Seventeen* magazine found that 21 percent of fifteen-to-twenty-two-year-old guys had been pressured by a female peer to go further sexually than they wanted to, with more than three-quarters (78 percent) agreeing that there was "way too much pressure" to have sex. Fifty-six percent said they were "relieved" when a female partner wanted to wait to have sex.

Expectations that young men be sexually active don't just apply to intercourse. A 2013 Australian study on sexting, the practice of exchanging sexually explicit photographs, videos, and text messages via cell phone, found that teenage boys sext in part because of pressure from other boys to have girls' photos on their phones and computers. They are also more likely than girls to share explicit messages that they receive with their friends.

This isn't to say that men *aren't* interested in sex. Most of them are—at least some of the time, with some people. But the reality of male desire is more complex than is portrayed in the media, popular culture, or everyday conversation. Stereotypes about male sexuality aren't designed to reflect actual men you might meet and know in your everyday life. They are an imagined ideal of how men *should* be, and it's selling many men short.

"Find, Fuck, and Forget": Love Is a Battlefield

You don't need to like a stereotype to fold it into your understanding of how the world works or how you ought to behave. Like Christopher, Ben, whom we met in chapter 3, is not fond of the way that media and popular culture pigeonhole male sexuality. He finds it "demeaning" and hates that it is "just kind of an accepted fact." But he acknowledges the ways in which those stereotypes have shaped his attitudes and experiences when it comes to sex, especially when he was a teenager.

Ben attended an all-boys private school that had a regular Monday-morning ritual: the guys would meet in the leafy schoolyard before the first bell rang and exchange stories of the girls they had met and hooked up with over the weekend. "The idea was to get as much as you could from girls," he recalls. "One of my friends described it as the 'three-Fs' culture. Find, fuck, and forget." Most of Ben's friends didn't make it past the first step—"finding"—but the point of the ritual wasn't what had actually transpired. Its appeal was embedded in the bravado itself: it gave the boys an opportunity to play the role of the stud, even if the reality of their weekend escapades didn't live up to the stories they told at school on Monday morning.

Guys aren't the only ones who internalize these expectations of how men should behave when it comes to sex. A University of California, Santa Cruz study into young people's first dating relationships found that young women so much expected their male partners to pressure them for sex that they were startled if their boyfriends wanted to take things more slowly. "I was really surprised, because I didn't know that guys felt like that and stuff," said one young woman whose boyfriend wanted to wait until he was married. "He didn't want to force anything," said another. "It wasn't his goal to sleep with as many people [as possible] or anything, he was just very, very sensitive." The young women expected coercion— whether it came in the form of begging, wandering hands, or threats to end the relationship and take up with someone else. As a third woman put it, "[Guys] think that they have to ask [for sex] in every relationship . . . just in case, like, there [is] a glimmer of hope that it [will] happen." Trying to get your girlfriend to have sex with you, however you went about it, was just part of being a "regular guy."

One reason young women expect their boyfriends to push for sex is because, statistically speaking, sexual pressure is the norm in adolescent relationships. Just over half the female college students interviewed for the University of California study reported some form of pressure from their partners to advance their sexual activity beyond the point that they were comfortable with. One in twelve described experiences that fit the legal definition of rape. But they may have also anticipated pressure because the dynamic of male initiator and female gatekeeper is one that each of us is taught to play out and expect, years before we ever have sex.

For boys and men, these messages are found in knowing remarks from friends and family about how "boys will be boys." They are in all the films and TV shows in which the male hero pursues an

initially unwilling female lead. And they are in the deeply embedded but dangerous notion that women need to be persuaded to have
sex—because it is not something they could ever possibly want to
do of their own accord.

For girls and women, the same messages are found in teen magazines, television dramas, and well-intentioned warnings from authority figures to hold on to your virginity because boys are "only
after one thing." The sealed sex-education supplements in the magazines I read as a teenager set up sex as a battlefield, on which boys
would always push for more ground and girls needed to be armed
with the weaponry to hold their own—not just physically, but mentally and emotionally. It wasn't bad advice per se, but it put girls on
the defensive, poised to fight off predators even when there were
none, while simultaneously positioning coercion as unavoidable,
one of those things that guys "just did."

The expectations change a little as we grow older, but not as
much as they should. In their 2006 study examining women's magazine representations of male and female sexuality, New Zealand
psychologists Panteá Farvid and Virginia Braun found that men
were depicted as naturally more sexual than women, their desires
needing to be managed by any women wishing to build and maintain a long-term heterosexual relationship. In one of the articles
they cite, a male informant declares, "Most of us guys are raring
to go anytime, anyplace, anywhere." In another article, a man confesses: "[B]eing male, I find that sometimes your groin can take
over, and it's only after the deed is actually done that you regret
sleeping with a particular girl." Men's magazines talk about male
sexuality in the same way, depicting their readers as insatiable when
it comes to sex, forever on the hunt for a new partner or source of
sexual novelty.

One effect is that men like Christopher feel pressured to pursue and initiate sex, even when they don't want it. Others, meanwhile, pursue the conventionally masculine role with gusto, transforming themselves into players and pickup artists.

"The MVP of Getting Laid": Sex as Sport

In a culture that equates manhood with sexual insatiability, it is no surprise that some men seek out sex with the fervor of a professional athlete approaching a major game. At twenty-one, Nate is a self-described "bro," defined on the website UrbanDictionary.com as "an alpha male idiot" who is "obsessed with women, beer, and sports."

A final-year science student at UC Berkeley, Nate is passionate about environmental issues and wants to work in renewable energy after he graduates. He is also passionate about women. Self-assured and smoothly charming, Nate has been an athlete and a partier his whole life, playing competitive basketball and cruising with college kids when he was still in high school. "It was an interesting juxtaposition," he says. "I didn't like the popular people, but I still hung out with them, even though I thought lots of them were douchebags."

Nate spent his first two years of college "sleeping around and juggling girls," racking up more than twenty-five partners in that time—a rate that puts him in the top 2 percent of men in his age group. It was a period of adventure that boosted his confidence and gave him a sense of social accomplishment. "Like being a really good basketball player or being the MVP of getting laid," he jokes. He still relishes the thrill of the pickup now: last weekend, he tells me, he collected two women's phone numbers and made out with another two women for the first time. But that was an unusually active few days, he explains. He isn't as into the hunt as he used to be.

Last year, Nate fell in love with an American girl he met when he was studying abroad in Brazil. They hit it off the moment they met, exchanging stories about where they were from and what had taken them to South America. But it was only after Nate was injured playing basketball that their casual hookup turned into something more serious, and they continued to date for nearly a year after they returned to the United States.

Now that Nate has been in a relationship with someone whose company he enjoyed as much as her body, hooking up with other women isn't as much fun. "It's hard to find a girlfriend, because a lot of the people you find attractive won't have the right personality for you," he says.

Then there is his growing ambivalence toward bro culture. "The idea is that you get drunk a lot, you have your bros, and you all go out together and have the confidence that you are going to get laid," Nate explains when I ask him about his attraction to the subculture. "You're smart, you're charming, you're business oriented—I'm pretty sure [bro blogger] Tucker Max went to Duke for law school, so he's real smart. He gets lots of girls, and he parties a lot. So he is kind of the ideal bro, you know.

"It all sounds pretty fucking good," he admits. "But at the same time, the ideal bro—he treats women like shit. He's the guy who sleeps with a woman and then automatically says, 'All right, are you ready to leave now?' When it comes to sex, the 'bro culture' often comes down to 'be the biggest asshole in the room and get laid.'" It is a strategy Nate used himself, hitting on girls with boyfriends to try to get them to cheat, bailing on plans when a better option came along, and brushing off girls after he had sex with them. "But at the end of the day, is that who I want to be? Is that who I want to tell other girls I am? Or tell my parents I am? There is a fine line between being an asshole as a hookup strategy and having it become who you are."

When I ask Nate why he engages in this kind of behavior if he doesn't like it, he says the answer is simple: it works. He points to the "hot girls" he went to high school with, who dated guys who were "mean to their teachers, mean to their parents, and mean to the people who weren't their friends." And playing the role of the confident, emotionally unavailable bro has helped him to succeed with women time and time again. In his early college years, he explains, the end justified the means. "I was having sex with attractive girls and I felt good about that. The good feeling definitely outweighed the bad feeling. Nowadays my goal is not to have intermittent sex with hot girls that I don't really enjoy being around. I'd rather have consistent sex with girls that I actually enjoy spending time with."

Playing the "asshole" is more than just an effective route to getting laid. It is also a distancing mechanism, demonstrating that although you may have sexual *relations* with women, your relationships with them are not as important as your friendships with other guys—or as important as fulfilling the promise of the type of guy that you aspire to be.

University of Pennsylvania sociologist David Grazian believes that the enthusiastic pursuit of sex practiced by men like Nate is often less about physical pleasure than it is about the pleasure of bonding with their male friends. In a 2007 study drawing on the testimony of 243 young men aged between eighteen and twenty-four, Grazian observed the ways in which what he called the "girl hunt" serves as a collective social ritual: from the music the men listen to before they embark on a night out to the confidence-boosting banter they engage in about their prospects to the stories they exchange in the days, weeks, and months after.

Indeed, Nate admits that one of the things he enjoyed most about his years as a "bro" was the bank of stories he built up to share with his friends. "The story is definitely the part that is best about it, the pickup story," he says. He tells me he'd love to have sex with a woman who models for Victoria's Secret—not for her body, but so that he could tell his friends about it after.

But while Nate enjoys "the satisfaction of knowing that other people are attracted to what [he is] attracted to," he tries to shy away from boasting. "Personally, my favorite stories to tell are the funny ones," he tells me. "When something happens with a girl you never thought you'd hook up with, or the girl you thought hated you finally gives in, or you hook up with a girl you and your friends make fun of. When there is an element of humor to the story, that's definitely the best type of story to tell."

Andrew, twenty-four, also employs humor when talking about sex with his friends in pubs around trendy East London and Leeds, the city in the north of England where he attended university. Sex is "a massive social icebreaker," he says. "You go into a room and sit down with your mates, and immediately within five minutes you're talking about sex." A lot of the guys he hangs out with talk up their conquests, comparing them to popular celebrities like Megan Fox and British glamour model Kelly Brook. Andrew, however, is more "brutally honest"—especially when there's the possibility of getting a few laughs. "I'll say things like, *Yeah, she was ugly as sin, like Lindsay Lohan on coke.*"

If Nate is a "bro," Andrew is his British equivalent—a lad. Like Nate, Andrew devoted his late teens and early twenties to, as he puts it, "getting [his] tally up"—whether he was attracted to the women he was sleeping with or not. Cheeky and self-deprecating, with messy, curly blond hair, Andrew had sex with thirteen women before meeting his first serious girlfriend three years ago. Eight of those encounters happened within one four-month period. The rest of the time, he admits with a smile, he didn't have much success at all. "It was mostly getting nowhere. You know, going to house parties, going to bars; not just not having a shag, but not getting any kind of action at all. No pulling [British slang for 'picking up'], no nothing."

But although Andrew and his friends suffered more failures than successes in their quests for action, the ritual was nonetheless central to their bonding as a group. Back then, Andrew lived in a house with eight other guys: a three-story Edwardian building with large, elegant windows and sticky floors. In the kitchen, they kept a cork bulletin board hanging over the refrigerator, covered with photos of the housemates drinking and having a laugh. On the other side, hidden from the view of visitors, was a piece of white butcher's paper on which they kept a chart rating the women each of them had slept with. It was a complex grading system that Andrew likens to the popular UK automotive show *Top Gear*, which ranks cars according to their lap times, "sex appeal," and popularity. "We took it to an advanced level," he laughs. The first column listed the woman's name and Facebook URL, followed by an overall performance grade out of ten, a rating for her breasts, and one for her ass. The succeeding columns were given over to other housemates, who would add their own ratings based on pictures they found online, resulting in a "final score" for each woman, on which the housemates were ranked against each other.

Where David Grazian's guys ranked each other according to how many women they had sex with, Andrew and his friends evaluated each other according to the "quality" of the women they slept with— with quality determined by how attractive the women were deemed by the group. One of Andrew's friends became an object of ridicule when he slept with a string of women the rest of the group rated poorly, while another "won for, like, two months running" when he hooked up with "an absolute stonker [British slang for 'stunner']." Andrew was usually in the bottom half of the league. "No one really took it that seriously," he tells me. It was mostly an opportunity for them to have a laugh with each other. But with a few years' distance from those events, he admits that the fridge "was more important to [their] house of male bonding than [they] realized."

Pigs on a Spit: Masculinity and Sexual Violence

Taken to extremes, this kind of masculine bravado can have violent consequences, particularly in environments like sports clubs, fraternities, and the military, which bind men who fit the mold together at the expense of everyone else.

In a 2008 paper looking at how men's relationships with other men shape their sexual interactions with women, masculinities researcher Michael Flood spoke with Tim, a twenty-one-year-old naval officer cadet at the Australian Defence Force Academy and alpha male of the most conventional variety, whose social life revolved around drinking, fighting, bedding women, and impressing his "boys." At the time he was interviewed by Flood, Tim had a steady girlfriend who was a bartender at a local pub popular with

Defence Force cadets. "I don't like socializing with females very much, unless I'm out to pick them up or have sex with them," he said.

Like all of the men interviewed for Flood's study, Tim said that he would stop any sexual activity if his partner asked him to. But the stories he shared with Flood suggested that wasn't always the case. On two occasions he described participating in a game he called "Rodeo," in which one member of a group was assigned the task of finding the fattest woman he could and persuading her to come back with him to his hotel room, where his friends lay in wait. They would start having sex, and he would tie her to the bed with her stockings, positioning her on her hands and knees. Then, when a certain amount of time had passed, he would shout the word "rodeo." The lights would be switched on, and his friends would emerge from their hiding places as he jumped on the woman's back, trying to hold on for as long as possible while she struggled in humiliation. On another occasion, Tim recalled a friend bringing home a woman who was so drunk she fell asleep, after which his friend removed the woman's underwear, retrieved some golf balls from elsewhere in the house, and the group "tried to play a hole in one."

Tim's stories echo similar incidents of gendered violence and humiliation in hypermasculine environments that have been reported in the news media in recent years. In 2013, a cadet at the same Australian military academy Tim attended was accused and later found guilty of using Skype to stream video of him having consensual sex with a female student to his friends. In the United States, high-profile high school rape cases in Steubenville, Ohio, and Maryville, Missouri, have raised questions about how male athletic culture enables sexual assault and allows it to go unpunished. "The jock culture/rape culture dynamic should be obvious to anyone with any connection to organized sports," wrote sports journalist Dave Zirin at the *Nation.* "The fact is that too many young male athletes are taught to see women as the spoils of being a jock." The UK National Union of Students has now produced two reports on "lad culture," a term used to describe the daily sexual harassment experienced by female university students at the hands of their male classmates.

These incidents do not reflect the behavior of most men. While one in five American women reports having experienced sexual assault at some point in her life, research shows that the vast majority of offenses are committed by a very small proportion of men—approximately 4 to 8 percent of the population, many of whom are repeat offenders.

Nor do the values that facilitate them reflect the majority of young men's attitudes and aspirations for their lives. In his book *Challenging Casanova: Beyond the Stereotype of the Promiscuous Young Male,* psychology professor Andrew Smiler reports that only a quarter of guys say they'd prefer to hook up than be in a relationship, and most rate their partner's physical attractiveness a lower priority than "being funny, nice, outgoing, understanding of others, able to make decisions, and reasonably self-confident." Similarly, only one-fifth of the students that University of Pennsylvania sociologist David Grazian surveyed talked about "girl-hunting" as a key component of their social lives. The rest, presumably, went out to drink, dance, and spend time with friends—or avoided nightclubs altogether.

But incidents like the ones Tim describes do represent the worst excesses of a culture that teaches men that their power and success are directly linked to their ability to conquer women and impress their male friends. And while the majority of young men might not be trying to be "the MVP of getting laid," the idea that assuming the role of the player is the route to masculine triumph is hard to escape entirely.

Caleb, whom we met in chapter 4, is one jock who pursues the "progressive track" of masculinity that Max described at the beginning of this chapter. Tall and classically handsome with broad shoulders, Caleb could hook up on a regular basis if he wanted to. And he does from time to time, making out with girls he meets at parties and out at bars. But at twenty-four, Caleb is still a virgin—partly by choice, and partly because the right woman hasn't come along yet.

Until recently, Caleb played cricket on a semiprofessional level, for a competitive team in his hometown of Melbourne, Australia. But Caleb's attitudes toward women set him apart from his teammates and meant that no matter how well he played the game, he was always on the outside of the group. "It was a high-grade team, so you got a lot of egos," he says. Not to mention a lot of bragging. In warm-ups, the team would play a game they called "roots and pulls," in which they'd go around the circle and discuss who had had sex, who had jerked off, and who had done nothing sexual at all the previous week.

One of Caleb's teammates kept a topless photo of every woman he'd had sex with on his phone, while another claimed to have bedded forty-five people when he traveled through Canada for three months. "You're in an environment that encourages high performance," Caleb explains. "Who can run the fastest? Who can do the most sit-ups or the most push-ups? It's a very competitive kind of masculinity, and that competition is applied to sex as well." And like Nate's and Andrew's sexual banter, those competitive exchanges serve as a bonding agent. Caleb recalls an incident in the UK when a couple of his teammates "got a girl on a 'spit roast,'" a slang term used to describe group sex in which a woman is orally and vaginally penetrated by two men at the same time. "That story was being talked about for three or four weeks. You get this extraordinary amount of detail about it," he says. "But why do I need to know how much hair she had down there? It turns sex into this club bonding experience."

Caleb never bought into that culture of one-upmanship, preferring to stay silent when the subject of sex was raised, which made him "pretty much the resident gay bloke" in his teammates' eyes. "You could be the biggest player going around, but if you don't talk about it, they immediately assume that nothing happened. It's a bizarre environment." Eventually, he decided to switch to a lower grade of cricket. "You play a sport because you love it, but in a team sport, so much of your enjoyment comes down to getting along with your teammates." In Caleb's new club, the players are of a wider range of ages and skill sets, which he thinks fosters a more respectful environment. "The younger guys still talk a lot about women, sex, and relationships, but once the older guys show up, it comes back to the actual sport you're playing. You know, instead of the number of people you bedded over the weekend."

I ask Caleb why he thinks he is more able to resist that culture than some of his guy friends. He puts it down to his emotional reserve. A lot of young men are very concerned with what other guys think of them, he says, but he is more concerned with what he thinks of himself. "A lot of people use that pickup environment as a form of self-validation," he explains. "Even if they're not attracted to the girl, it's going to make a good story, and they can put her underwear in their cricket bag and bring it with them on the weekend. Whereas for me, I'm a very insular person. My first instinct is to withdraw until I'm sure of where I stand."

But even the men he knows who draw most on their sex lives for validation turn that side of themselves off when you remove them from the group. "If you get the jocks alone you can have a good conversation with them. And then one of the other jocks walks around the corner and they start talking about how their cock is ten inches long. I try to engage with the individual," Caleb says. "It might only be a two-second question, but there's got to be something more interesting to talk about than *Did you sleep with that girl over the weekend?* Because ultimately, who gives a fuck?"

"Dirty Little Bottoms" and "Very Straight Gays"

Being vocal about your attraction to and success with women serves another purpose in the pursuit of masculinity as well. It "proves" that you are not gay, a quality that has historically been considered antithetical to true manhood. If "real men" are strong, dominant, and powerful, gay men have often been portrayed as the opposite: weak, submissive, and powerless. As a result, as much as men have sought to prove that they are "not women," they have also sought to prove that they are "not gay."

This has not been the case in all times and all places. For the ancient Greeks, what separated the "real men" from the fakes was not the gender of the people they had sex with, but *how* they had sex with them—that is to say, whether they were the penetrator or the penetrated. In the Middle East, South Asia, and parts of Africa, men walk down the streets holding hands without anyone batting an eyelid, not because of an absence of homophobia so much as because affection between people of the same sex has no sexual connotation.

But for most of the last century in the English-speaking West, male homosexuality and femininity have been considered one and the same. The stereotypical gay man is a fashion-conscious, clean Lady Gaga fan who is more femme than most women—think the "flamboyantly feminine" Jack in the popular '00s sitcom *Will and Grace*, or fashion stylist Carson Kressley on the Bravo reality show *Queer Eye for the Straight Guy*. These stereotypes emerged hand in hand with what American sociologist Eric Anderson calls "homohysteria"—a state of panic about homosexuality that casts gay men as deviants and predators, and all men as potentially gay.

In his book *Inclusive Masculinity: The Changing Nature of Masculinities*, Anderson uses photographs of men's sports teams to show how perceptions of masculinity and appropriate male intimacy have evolved over time, from the 1890s to the present day. Prior to the 1920s, he writes, teams were photographed smiling, hugging, and draping their arms around each other, this kind of physical contact perfectly compatible with their status as men. But soon after, the men in the photographs began to keep more distance from one another: first arranged in rows with their hands by their sides and later, in the hypermasculine 1980s, not touching or emoting at all, posed sitting with their arms crossed and blank looks on their faces.

Homohysteria requires two things to thrive, argues Anderson: an awareness of homosexuality as a sexual orientation, and a fear and disapproval of its existence. In the photographs from before the 1920s, the men were permitted to touch each other because it was assumed that they were straight. Hugging another man was a sign of friendship, not desire. By the 1980s, at the height of the HIV/AIDS crisis, even being remotely affectionate with someone of the same sex was considered suspect. To be a "man" meant distancing oneself from even the slightest hint of homosexuality.

The belief that masculinity and homosexuality are incompatible is starting to erode, though. Along with looking at photographs of men's sports teams in the past, Anderson watched male athletes posing for portraits in the present as well—among them a group of (gay and straight) male cheerleaders. Anderson observed how the men's first instinct was to pose with their arms by their sides, and how the photographer—a man in his forties—encouraged them to fold their arms across their chests instead. "They have worked hard for those muscles," he told Anderson. "They should show off their masculinity." When the team's captain learned what the photographer had said, the young men rebelled, throwing their arms around each other instead. Such changes, Anderson argues, reflect broader changes in masculinity as homophobia has declined.

For the past decade, Anderson has been interviewing and observing men in conventionally masculine environments, like sports teams and fraternity houses, across the United States and United Kingdom. Some of his results have been surprising—and controversial. In a 2008 study published in *Sex Roles*, Anderson argued that the "one-time rule of homosexuality" (which dictates that even a single same-sex experience is indicative of a hidden homosexual orientation) was on the way out, with 40 percent of the sixty-eight straight-identifying men surveyed confirming some kind of same-sex experience. In another study, published in 2012, Anderson and his co-researchers Adi Adams and Ian Rivers reported that 89 percent of young British men have kissed another man on the lips—not as an expression of sexual attraction but of friendship.

The straight-identifying men I spoke with did not report anything close to the same levels of same-sex experience that Anderson's men did. But much of what they told me did support his assertion that the relationship between masculinity and homosexuality is changing. As Tom, twenty, put it: "It's a lot more acceptable to be attracted to a guy than it was before. I think it's become a little more okay to try it out." Michael, the thirty-two-year-old London call center worker we met in chapter 3, was blasé on the subject. "I have kissed guys before," he said. "It doesn't really matter to me."

Most of the time, when the straight guys I interviewed reported kissing other men, they did it for the same reason they told stories about the women they had sex with—to get a laugh. Max tells me that where he lives, in small-town Ohio, only a very small percentage of guys "will engage in any kind of homosexual behavior." Max's friends, though, are more relaxed on the subject. "We joke about it a lot more," he says.

One of the ways in which Max's fraternity brothers "joke about it" is through a game called gay chicken, in which men compete with each other to see who can withstand the highest threshold of man-on-man sexual behavior. Young men in other countries do this, too. Will, a twenty-five-year-old living in the north of England, told me: "It's like, 'I bet I can run fastest' or 'I bet I can get highest up this tree,' except it is a test of how 'gay' you can get without squirming." By demonstrating that he is willing to be more "gay" than other men—by holding hands, touching thighs, and even kissing—a man shows that he is not concerned with proving his heterosexuality (and therefore, ironically, shows that he is less gay than other men).

Max says that the game "feeds into the whole new masculinity thing, where it's more masculine to be okay with homosexuality"— and he's not wrong. But the humor at the heart of gay chicken isn't as progressive as it might seem. "The only way you can kiss another guy [without people questioning your sexuality] is if you can prove yourself to be otherwise hetero," Australian masculinity researcher Clifton Evers tells me. "It has to be a particular context. There is a very fine-tuned awareness of when you're allowed to kiss and when you're not allowed to kiss; when you are allowed to hug and when you're not allowed to hug."

In other words, it is easier to embrace new standards of masculinity in one arena if your identity as a man is already being affirmed in another. Men whose masculinity is not so readily affirmed—men who are poorer, less educated, or indeed, even gay men—might be more inclined to keep their behavior within the bounds of conventional gender roles.

Yusuf, whom we met in chapter 2, grew up in the working-class western suburbs of Sydney, in a devout Muslim family where liking boys was not an option. When he came out at the age of nineteen, his best friend didn't speak to him for months, afraid that Yusuf might hit on him. Yusuf buoyed himself with fantasies of his future life, in which he "was going to be beautiful and extremely masculine and hot"—and have regular, exciting sex with a rotation of equally hot guys.

Yusuf's teenage self would be pleased with the way his life has unfolded since then. Now twenty-six, Yusuf lives with a friend in Bondi, a beachside Sydney suburb famous for its body-beautiful residents. With his tall, muscular build and striking features, Yusuf fits right in. Yusuf is what is known in gay online dating circles as a "straight-acting gay man"—a man who has sex with men but who otherwise embodies conventionally hetero-masculine traits. He speaks in a low, broad Australian accent and drinks beer. His car is a mess, filled with empty drink cartons, books, and random pieces of paper. He moisturizes and exfoliates, but he couldn't care less about fashion or pop music. Combined with his dark skin and masculine physique, these traits have made him a sought-after commodity in Sydney's same-sex dating market.

"A lot of gay guys don't like 'gay guys' very much," Yusuf observes. "They're trying to set themselves apart from a way of behaving that they see as very trashy, very low, very effeminate, very something . . . [They're] trying to redefine being gay as something that is also very masculine and identifying more with straight men than with gay men."

He's not proud of himself, but Yusuf admits that sometimes, when he and his friends are walking down Sydney's famously campy Oxford Street, they will make fun of the more feminine guys they see. He describes men who receive rather than give anal sex as "dirty little bottoms." Yusuf's physique means he is usually assumed to be a "top": the guy who does the fucking, rather than the guy who gets fucked. It is internalized homophobia, and he knows it. But "masculinity and femininity are portrayed as these two opposites, and you kind of feel you have to pick a side," he explains. And in that particular binary, Yusuf has chosen masculinity.

Yusuf's comments are reflected in findings by University of Oregon researcher C. J. Pascoe, who argues that the epithet "faggot"—popularly thrown around by high school boys across America—is now employed less as a comment on a boy's sexuality than on his masculinity. "While it is not necessarily acceptable to be gay, at least a man who is gay can do other things that render him acceptably masculine," Pascoe wrote. "A fag, by the very definition of the word . . . cannot be masculine."

It is a message that Yusuf has taken to heart. "If you're not completely polarized," he says—if, for example, your identity as a man's man is compromised by the fact that you like to have sex with other men—"then you're going to feel insecure."

Yusuf wasn't the only gay man I spoke to who felt this way. "In the media, you're either a flaming queer or a raging straight person," says Scott, a twenty-three-year-old music writer with a slim build and fine facial features. But Scott feels he sits somewhere in between: a man who has sex with men, but who is no more defined by his sexual preferences than he is by his love of indie music and hip-hop.

Scott runs with a liberal crowd of punks, artists, and writers—the kind of people "who think ambiguity is cool," he says. But although his friends are happy to experiment with same-sex encounters, most of them identify as straight. "Half the reason I've had so much trouble in my life is because to me the ideal guy is a straight guy," he says. "And that's fucked up, but it's what is in my head. I'm, like, searching for the guy who is as un-gay as possible."

A preference for "straight-acting" gay men is not necessarily an indication of homophobia, internalized or otherwise. Nor is it a recent phenomenon. In a 1992 paper on gay masculinities, the acclaimed sociologist Raewyn Connell noted the tendency for gay men to identify as "very straight" when it came to their gender identity and performance. And this should come as no surprise. As Connell observed: "The choice of a man as a sexual object is not just a choice of body-with-penis; it is a choice of embodied masculinity. The cultural meanings of masculinity are (generally) part of the package. In this sense, most gays are 'very straight.'"

But Yusuf's and Scott's comments demonstrate that while having sex with men is no longer antithetical to "being a man," men who have sex with men—whether they identify as straight, gay, or bi—are still expected to compensate by meeting the masculine ideal in other ways. A gay man can now be a "real man," but a "fag" still cannot.

Removing the Masculine Straitjacket

The conventional parameters of manhood don't just lock out the men who flagrantly defy them—men who are gay or bisexual, men who do not have high sex drives, men who are emotionally sensitive or otherwise effeminate. They also limit the choices and behavior of men who, on the surface, appear to meet the conventional standards pretty damn well. Orthodox masculinity teaches men that they can't say no to sex, be physically or emotionally close to other men, or display any kind of vulnerability without putting their status as "men" at risk.

The stoicism and deliberate self-assurance required by conventional masculinity also make it difficult for men to speak about their experiences with sex and relationships without the cushion of protective humor that underlies Nate's hookup stories, Andrew's refrigerator rating system, and Max's accounts of "gay chicken." Christopher recalls the sex-education classes at his Catholic high school in Texas. "You never wanted to ask questions, because you always assumed that everyone knew more about sex than you did," he says. "I was fifteen and curious about what my girlfriend's parts looked like and how they worked, but I would never ask that question for fear of social rebuke."

A 2008 study published in the *Canadian Journal of Human Sexuality* found that men actually have a narrower spectrum of acceptable sex and gender behavior than women do. Men were more likely than women to be considered "abnormal" if they fantasized about being intimate with a member of the same sex, if they dressed in clothing associated with the opposite sex, if they were celibate, if they didn't masturbate, if they enjoyed receiving pain during sex, or if they were aroused by being urinated on. The only behavior that was considered more unusual in women than in men was voyeurism.

There is evidence that young men are beginning to challenge these standards, throwing off the orthodox masculine straitjacket in favor of a masculinity that is more inclusive and accepting of difference. In a 2012 opinion piece published in the *New York Times*, University of Massachusetts researcher Amy T. Schalet wrote that American boys were becoming "more like girls" when it came to sex, citing data from the Centers for Disease Control that shows that to-day's teenage boys are having sex later than their counterparts in the late 1980s were, as well as her own interviews with teenagers in the United States and the Netherlands. And it's not just men's experiences of gender that are evolving, either. As we will see in the next chapter, women's sexual ideals are changing, too.

But it will take more than a shift in gender roles to combat the idea that a guy's manhood is a product of what he does with his penis. Our belief in the physically dominant, sexually insatiable man reflects more than just our investment in "men being men" and "women being women." It is a reflection of our desire to believe in sex as a transformative force—one with the power to overcome our old selves and make us new.

6

Femininity:
The Madonna/Gaga Complex

As a high school freshman in rural Illinois, one of Brit's favorite ways to spend a Sunday afternoon was curled up in her friend Jessa's bedroom, eating Girl Scout cookies and reading *Cosmopolitan*. The two would sit together on Jessa's twin bed, surrounded by stuffed animals and Backstreet Boys posters, and flip through the pages of the magazine, exchanging notes on how the content therein stacked up to their own nascent sexual knowledge, and laughing over the illicit and sometimes outlandish nature of their reading material.

As teenage girls go, Brit was not particularly "girly," and nor did she want to be. Introverted and bookish, with dark hair pulled back into a loose ponytail, she found the traditional femininity that was celebrated in her tiny Midwestern community left her cold. In a school where there were only fifteen girls in her grade, she felt like the odd woman out, a lone wolf in an ark full of platonic pairs.

But those evenings she spent sitting in Jessa's bedroom, talking about sex, gave Brit a window into a world that was as intimate as it was rebellious, and as transgressive as it was conformist—what Brit describes as "that space between girlhood and womanhood that seems to be designated by sexual acts."

Simone de Beauvoir famously wrote that "one is not born, but rather becomes, a woman," and one of the chief ways in which girls learn womanhood is through their engagement with sexuality. As Brit puts it, "When you had sex, you were a 'woman,' whether you were ready for it or not."

"A lot of it was just reading magazines and giggling," Brit, now twenty-three and living in New York, recalls. "But it was also about having a space to speak openly about sex—to say, *Oh, I'd do that*, or *That's totally nuts*."

Conversations like the ones Brit describes above are more than just a clumsy adolescent attempt at playing grown-up. They are an exercise in the learning and creation of gender, a drawing of the boundaries not only of what it means to be an adult, but of what it means to be *female*.

And just as men are taught that their masculinity is contingent on their sexual prowess, so too are women taught that being "feminine" means being sexual in particular ways. It is a process that begins long before puberty, manifest in everything from the plastic baby dolls and pink beauty kits that dominate the designated "girls' aisles" at most toy stores to the inevitably heterosexual happily-ever-afters that conclude fairy tales and Disney movies. Years before we ever have sex, sexuality is as much a part of the toolbox through which we are taught to communicate and decipher gender as the clothes we wear, the amount of space we take up when we sit on the train, or the length to which the hairdresser intuitively goes to cut our hair.

The symbolic and symbiotic relationship between sex and gender was apparent in the conversations I had with young women every place I traveled. Heather, a shy twenty-four-year-old from Geelong, Australia, told me how her boyfriend's lower sex drive and reluctance to experiment sexually had left her feeling like she wasn't "a good enough woman." Brooke, a college student from Montreal, talked about the responsibility she felt to "pleasure" her partner, saying, "[If] I don't live up to certain standards of attractiveness or sexiness or availability, he'll leave me for someone who does." Stephanie, the high school senior we met in chapter 4, referred to Margaret Atwood's reproductive dystopia *The Handmaid's Tale*, using its term "unwoman" to articulate the link between "doing" femininity right and doing sexuality correctly. "If you are labeled a whore, you're 'unwoman.' If you're not fertile, you're 'unwoman.' If you refuse to have sex, you're 'unwoman,'" she explained.

Like boys and men, the ways in which girls and women are taught to be sexual are changing. Once being a "good woman" meant being passive and "pure"—refraining from sex until you were married or in a serious relationship, for example, or engaging in it as an act of service while ignoring your own sexual needs. But today's "good woman" takes as much pleasure from sex as any man does. For the modern young woman, sex is no longer something done to assuage others but an expression of identity and empowered self-determination. Being sexually active has become a means through which women demonstrate and exert control over their sex lives.

But this shift has done more than just multiply the ways in which women are permitted to be sexual. It has also expanded the ways in which a woman can be designated "unwoman." This chapter looks at sexuality as an arena in which womanhood is created and reinforced, and examines how the female sexual ideal has changed over time.

How to Be a Woman:
Sex and Femininity

If having sex for the first time made her a woman, Brit crossed the threshold into adulthood the spring before her sixteenth birthday: the same year her parents divorced and she was diagnosed with an autoimmune disorder. She and her then boyfriend had been dating for a few months, and although he was happy to linger on kissing, touching, and oral sex, Brit was keen to move things along to intercourse. "Oral sex did nothing for me," she recalls—and that was true whether she was giving or receiving.

When they finally did have sex, Brit didn't enjoy it as much as she had expected to, although she pretended she did, putting on a show of fake-but-dramatic orgasms for the next two and a half years of the relationship. But sex did make her feel more grown-up, even though at that point in her life she had yet to learn to cook, drive, or even properly insert a tampon. Still, at fifteen, Brit felt mature and self-composed, more like an adult than she did a child. And being sexually active affirmed her sense of having arrived in the world.

"I feel like a guy can go through high school and be a virgin and still be cool," she muses, sitting on a bench in Manhattan's Union Square. "I went to a really small school, and if a guy wasn't having sex, people figured it was because he chose not to. Whereas if a girl wasn't having sex, the only explanations were that she was religious or because she was undesirable." Later, she tells me, "The marker of girlhood to womanhood is virginity, and I think it's something we wrestle with for the rest of our lives, because so often we're *not* adults when we first have sex."

Even the act of becoming a *girl* is bound up in the symbolism of sex and romance. In 2008, two Illinois sociologists, Kristen Myers and Laura Raymond, brought together small groups of elementary-school-aged girls to talk about their experiences of girlhood, anticipating conversations about school, friendships, and common extracurricular activities such as dance class and soccer. But once they were in the room with their subjects, the study took an unexpected turn. Whether the girls were in kindergarten or about to graduate to middle school, they all wanted to talk about one thing: boys.

"Are we going to talk about boys?" one girl asked anxiously at the beginning of the third-grade group's first get-together. "Because if we do, I'm going to freak out. No talking about crushes!" Fifteen minutes later, she had changed her mind. "I want to talk about crushes," she announced. "I just want to talk about that now." She decided that the group should go around the circle, declaring in turn which boys they "liked" and which boys they "like-liked." She would go first. "I like-like Toby," she said. "I have a big crush on him."

Other groups of girls Myers and Raymond spoke to engaged in similar banter. The kindergarteners and first graders spoke about what it meant to have a crush ("If a boy really likes you, they have a crush on you. If they like-like you, then they love you"), while the older, fourth- and fifth-grade girls talked about their infatuations with Disney stars such as Zac Efron and the Jonas Brothers. Conversations about boys were high energy and full of excitement, punctuated by shrieks and laughter as each girl revealed to the others who she liked.

Like Brit and Jessa leafing through *Cosmopolitan* on a Sunday afternoon, for the girls in the Illinois study, boy talk was a means of cementing female friendship. Girls bonded over exchanging secrets, the thrill of liking the same boy, and how hilarious it was to have a crush on a boy in the first place. But the degree to which boy talk dominated their conversations—and conversations that had been framed at the outset as being about *girls*, at that—suggests that boys hold another, deeper significance in female interaction. That almost by definition, to be a girl is to be vocally interested in boys.

The notion that there is something "special" about the relationship between boys and girls is pervasive in media targeted at children. A 2009 study published in *Gender & Society* found that although G-rated films were not allowed to show sex, violence, or nudity, many popular children's movies contained a suite of *implicit* messages about sexuality. In particular, the researchers observed the way that heterosexual romance was portrayed as "magical," "exceptional," and "transformative," with relationships between opposite-sex characters accompanied by soaring music, soulful eye contact, and sweeping natural vistas in a way that other types of relationships—such as those between friends, or between children and parents—were not.

In Disney's *Aladdin*, Jasmine and Aladdin fall in love as they glide through the sky on a magic carpet; in *The Lion King*, childhood friends Simba and Nala discover their feelings for each other as they run through the jungle to a chorus of heartfelt music. By comparison, Simba's friendship with Timon (a meerkat) and Pumbaa (a boar) is treated as comic relief. In these movies, love is literally transformative: in *The Little Mermaid*, Ariel must secure a kiss from the prince to keep her voice and legs, while in *Beauty and the Beast*, a kiss from Belle turns the prince into a man again. "The primary account of heterosexuality in these films is one of heteroromantic love and its exceptional, magical, transformative power," the researchers wrote.

It is little wonder, then, that the girls in the Illinois study were so eager to talk about boys, or that doing so was such a source of excitement for them. They were responding to a culture that teaches us that romantic relationships are the most interesting types of relationships there are, and that these exciting connections properly unfold between girls and boys—not between girls and other girls, or between boys and other boys.

Talking about boys as a bonding mechanism isn't solely a childhood thing; it is a social theater that continues into adulthood. Sarah, whom we met in chapter 1, recalls a woman she encountered when she was backpacking through South America. They didn't hit it off at first, until one evening when they were walking through town with a mixed-gender group of friends, and the guys split off to walk ahead. The girl started telling Sarah about her ex-boyfriend, and Sarah began to feel like she knew her better, that she could understand and relate to her more. "I've always felt like talking about boys and love and sex is a really good tool for connecting with women," she observes.

Good Girls Go to Heaven

Learning heterosexuality—and learning femininity—entails more than just being attracted to men. It means learning to perceive yourself as the *opposite* of men, and learning to perform and express your sexuality in all the opposite ways to those that men are taught.

Where men are taught that their sexual power derives from their ability to chase and win the people they desire, for most of the past two hundred years, being a "good woman" has meant playing the role of the sexual sentry, of saying no however much you might want to say yes.

But although it might seem timeless, the belief that women are naturally less sexual than men is a relatively modern invention. In ancient Greece, women were considered the weaker and more passive sex, because they had no penis with which to penetrate their partners. But their weakness was also believed to make them more licentious, not less. In the Old Testament, it was Eve, not Adam, who was vulnerable to the temptation presented by the serpent. Indeed, some scientists believe that early human females behaved much like other female primates during periods of peak fertility, having sex up to fifty times per day with numerous male partners.

It wasn't until the 1800s that women—or more specifically, white, middle-class women—were repositioned as enforcers of virtue, the angels of their respective houses, as the famous nineteenth-century English poem put it. And it was only in this era that excess female desire began to be conceived not just as a potential social problem but as a matter of spoiled identity, exemplified in the emergence of the "nymphomaniac"—ambiguously defined as anything from a woman who masturbated in public to one who desired more sex than her husband.

Echoes of this idea that too much sex "spoils" a woman can be found today in what feminist author and activist Jessica Valenti refers to as "the virginity movement": the religious lobby that urges young people to abstain from sex until marriage but puts most of the onus of maintaining said abstinence on young women. Within the virginity movement, women also stand to lose more—socially and morally—if they do have sex.

But if purity is a source of esteem for some women, the idea that sex corrupts it can have calamitous effects. I meet Annabelle, a college freshman at the University of North Carolina, at a Starbucks a few hundred yards off campus. Small and blond, with a bohemian sense of style, Annabelle grew up in a small Baptist town where virginity mattered a lot. It mattered to her parents. It mattered to her church. It mattered to her school. And it mattered to Annabelle as well. "Growing up, I was always, always, always taught that your purity is part of who you are as a woman," she explains. "Not even a part of who you are. Your purity *is* who you are as a woman."

Virginity mattered to Annabelle's high school boyfriend, too, enough that he didn't want to have sex, at least in the penis-in-vagina sense of the word, until he was married. "He thought it was immoral," she explains. He did not think it was so immoral, though, to force Annabelle to have sex with him in other ways, raping her orally and anally on a regular basis for a period of almost two years.

It was a cycle of abuse that destroyed Annabelle's confidence and drove her to depression, to the point that in her final year of high school, she attempted to take her own life. She couldn't talk to her friends about what her boyfriend was doing to her, because they believed that sex before marriage was a sin. "And even though I wasn't initiating it," she says, "that's what was happening to me." She couldn't bring herself to tell her parents, either, until after the relationship had ended. The shame was too grave. "I wasn't a virgin anymore, and that meant I wasn't whole or pure," Annabelle explains. "And if I wasn't whole and pure, I wasn't, like, a *woman*."

This idea that being a "good woman" means refraining from sex is more pronounced among some groups than others: women from more conservative, religious, or rural backgrounds, for example. But you don't need to be religious to internalize the idea that "good girls" don't have sex.

I grew up an atheist in Sydney, in Australia, a relatively secular country. But although my high school friends and I talked about sex constantly, we were also wary that it was dangerous. We were afraid that if we had sex too soon, we might get pregnant while we were still teenagers—something that would jeopardize the futures we were beginning to plan for ourselves. As children of the eighties and early nineties, the specter of HIV loomed large in the backs of our minds, too. But pregnancy and disease weren't the only things we were afraid of. We were also scared of being hurt or used, of being declared a slut.

I still recall a conversation I had in eighth or ninth grade with one of my closest friends, the gregarious daughter of Turkish Muslim immigrants. She was bolder and more confident than I was, and also more religiously devout. Chewing on sandwiches in the schoolyard one lunchtime, we were speculating together over what point in a relationship you could trust a guy enough to be sure he wasn't using you for sex—and accordingly, at what point you could safely have sex with him. I suggested that engagement might be a reasonable marker, if you wanted to be *really* safe. My friend countered that you couldn't be sure even then. It was best to wait until you married. I told her that I felt the same way, more because I didn't want her to think I was slutty than because I actually agreed with her statement.

As we grew older, waiting until marriage was no longer a desirable option, either personally or socially. But my friends and I were still wary of the havoc that sex had the potential to wreak on our reputations and emotions. When we watched *Grease*, it was naïve Sandy, not rebellious Rizzo, whom we identified with, whose songs we sang theatrically as we walked down the school corridors. Our favorite film was *Clueless*, and we would toss the line "You are a virgin who can't drive" at one another flippantly—not because we saw it as an insult, as it was delivered in the film, but because we took it as a given that *everyone* we knew was a virgin who didn't yet know how to drive. And we did all these things as girls who didn't take the idea that our value lay in our virginity particularly seriously.

Like me, Katie, a soft-spoken twenty-three-year-old from Detroit, didn't grow up in a household that advocated abstinence. If anything, her parents were more liberal than she was. Katie's father encouraged her to go on the Pill when she was in high school, "just in case," and when she went away to college, he sent her off with a pack of condoms. "My parents definitely stressed that there was no shame in expressing my sexuality," she says. "They didn't push it or anything, but they were definitely more comfortable with it than I was."

But Katie's mother and father weren't the only influence on her early beliefs about sexuality. When she was in middle school, Katie spent her afternoons in after-school care with her classmates, and like Brit and Jessa, the girls would pass the time by talking about boys. Then only eleven, Katie was still nearly a decade away from having sex for the first time, but she already had strong beliefs about when and how she would do it when the time came. She planned to wait until she finished high school, or until she met someone she fell in love with.

Katie's friends had thought about their future sex lives, too. They intended to stay virgins until they married and were vocal about their opinions on the subject. "They made it sound really romantic," Katie recalls. "They talked a lot about how special it would be to only have one partner, and I was like, *Yeah, that does sound kind of cool.*" During the same period, Katie was starting to spend more time at church and began to internalize "some of those messages, for better or for worse, about being abstinent." When she was twelve she made a private commitment to herself not to have sex until she married, and in the summer after she finished high school, she made that commitment public in the local newspaper.

Katie didn't judge other people for being sexually active, she stresses. "It wasn't like I thought they were dirty or anything." But she did place a lot of value on her own virginity. She spoke about her decision often with friends and acquaintances, in the same way that her sexually active peers would talk to her about their hookups. She even made mention of it in her Facebook biography: "I'm proud to say I'm a virgin," she wrote. "I felt good about the fact that I was waiting," she explains.

Sitting across from Katie in a burger chain perched along the banks of the Detroit River, I am struck by how beautiful she is: tall and slim, with dark skin and high cheekbones. She is smart, too. When we met, she had recently been accepted to graduate school at Harvard. But she also suffers from cripplingly low self-esteem, and being a virgin was one thing that made her feel special, she tells me. That's one of the reasons she was so determined to hold on to it. "I felt like my virginity set me apart, and I liked that because there was so much other stuff about myself that I didn't like. I feel like I'm too skinny—I don't have big boobs or a big butt, and I wish I was curvier. Being a virgin was the one thing I was proud of."

But Katie didn't stay a virgin for as long as she intended. She had sex for the first time in her junior year of college, with the man who is now her fiancé. Although he didn't put pressure on her to have sex, she worried that if she didn't, he would end the relationship. When she did have sex, she cried about it almost every day for a year. "I thought: *I can't believe I gave in. Now I'm just like everybody else. I fucked up.*"

Katie concedes now that she probably "put too much emphasis" on the fact that she wasn't having sex. She also believes she had too much confidence in her ability to halt the physical aspects of her relationship before they went further than she was comfortable with. "I would go over to his place and spend the night. We wouldn't do anything, but I was sleeping in the same bed. Then we started messing around, but I still thought I could handle it. And then the bar kept being raised. We were doing more and more, but I was still convinced that we weren't going to go all the way. I was sure that I wasn't going to mess up." If she was able to rewind the clock and start over again, she believes she would do things differently. "I think that if you want to stay abstinent you need to not put yourself in certain situations," she says carefully. "You need to just keep it at kissing or holding hands or whatever your limit is. I far exceeded my limit."

Katie is now caught in what she describes as a "limbo space," where she is no longer a virgin but she does not feel able to be freely sexual, either. Sometimes she and her fiancé will go through periods in which they will have a lot of sex; other times, they will go weeks or months having none at all. For Katie, the only sex that it is okay to have is accidental. In her mind, each encounter is the last—a momentary slip-up born alternately of passion and resignation.

That Katie's sex is deliberately unintentional means that, like many lapsed abstinence pledgers, she is also reluctant to use contraception. "That would be like admitting I have a sex life," she says. "Every time we have sex, I'm like, *Please, God, let my period come.*"

Sitting Pretty: The Submissive Sex

Like stereotypes of men's sexual insatiability, the belief that women are sexually passive is bound in the symbolism of the female body. As Simone de Beauvoir wrote in *The Second Sex*: "The sex organ of a man is simple and neat as a finger; it is readily visible and often exhibited to comrades with proud rivalry; but the feminine sex organ is mysterious even to the woman herself."

Even today, some people assume that when a woman has sex, she is doing it in exchange for something else: emotional intimacy, commitment, or family and children. Women who have sex outside the bounds of a monogamous relationship are depicted as doing sex and relationships on men's terms, even if they believe they are pursuing their own desires. Within committed relationships, we are told that women's libidos are "fragile" and "easily distracted," prone to fizzle under the pressures of everyday life.

Where young men are taught that desire will burst forth from their bodies whether they like it or not, young women are taught that their sexual urges need to be awakened by someone else, like Snow White waiting for a kiss from Prince Charming. In her book *The Power of Beauty*, author Nancy Friday recalls how powerless she felt in the matter of her own sexual initiation. "Was there anyone more starved than I in adolescence, more vulnerable to 'that feeling' boys aroused when I was held and kissed?" She wishes that she had known she was able to produce the same sensations in her own body, instead of depending on a boy or man to arouse them. "Until [a girl] discovers that her own hand touching herself unleashes some of this same feeling," she writes, "it will be the boy-prince who holds the key; she will sit by the telephone and wait and wait in expectation of the next magical moment when he holds her in his arms and 'makes' her sexual."

The same male-as-teacher and female-as-student dynamic can be found in the bestselling *Fifty Shades of Grey* series, in which the virginal Anastasia Steele learns about sex in the arms of the wealthy and charismatic Christian Grey. "We can start your training tonight," he tells her before they have sex for the first time. Later, she describes her libido as "woken and tamed by him."

But being sexually passive doesn't just make it harder to take ownership of your sexual desires. It also makes it more difficult to say no to sex that you *don't* want. If women are taught that their sex drives are naturally weak, not wanting sex is not sufficient reason not to have it. If sex is supposed to hurt the first (and second, and third) time you do it, it is okay to have sex that doesn't bring you pleasure. If sex is framed as a duty, something that "must" be done in order to keep your partner happy, is it any wonder than many women in long-term relationships start to view it as a chore? If you are taught that your value lies in being "chosen" by someone else—for a date, a hookup, or even a marriage proposal—it matters less than it might otherwise if you would choose to be with that person in return.

In a 2013 article for the *New York Times Magazine*, author Daniel Bergman suggested that over time, the message that women want sex less than men do might become a self-fulfilling neurological prophecy. "If boys and men tend to take in messages that manhood is defined by sex and power, and those messages encourage them to think about sex often, then those neural networks associated with desire will be regularly activated and will become stronger over time," he wrote. "If women, generally speaking, learn other lessons, that sexual desire and expression are not necessarily positive, and if therefore they don't think as much about sex, then those same neural networks will be less stimulated and comparatively weak."

Jennifer, twenty-four, reached out to me via e-mail after reading a story I'd written for a women's magazine about what I'd called "the new sexual double standard"—the misconception that women were so indifferent to sex and men were so insatiable that male consent was assumed, rather than needing to be negotiated or asked for. It had made Jennifer think about her own relationships, she told me—not only the way she had treated her male partners, but also the way she had been habituated to the role of sexual sentry, able to say yes or no to men's advances but unable to initiate sex or set the terms of her own engagement. "I would let people have sex with me, rather than sex being something that we did together," she wrote.

Jennifer grew up in the peaceful northern suburbs of Adelaide, on the southern rim of Australia, the daughter of Vietnamese immigrants who raised her to be independent and strong willed, but who also held very conservative views about sex. She didn't meet her first serious boyfriend until she was twenty-three, when she moved out of her family home and bought her own apartment, living alone for the first time. Until then, her only engagement with sex was through flings and one-night stands, conducted clandestinely at the houses of the guys she slept with, with Jennifer sneaking back home to her parents before the night was over.

But although she was sexually active, Jennifer didn't feel in control of her sex life. She tells me about Oliver, a guy she hooked up with on and off for a year and a half before she started dating her current boyfriend. They met shortly after she finished college, as her friends were dispersing in different directions and beginning their adult lives. Jennifer felt isolated and lonely, and "it was nice to think somebody wanted me and loved me and enjoyed being in my company," she says.

Maintaining that sense of approval meant saying yes to sex, whether she wanted it or not. She describes her role in that relationship as that of a titular gatekeeper. Oliver set the terms—Would she come over to his house? Would they have sex tonight? Would she have a threesome with him and another girl he was seeing?—and in theory, Jennifer had the option of accepting or declining his requests. But in practice, she felt her only real choice was to say yes. "In a superficial sense I was completely in control of the situation, but in another sense I wasn't at all," she says. "I didn't feel like I could ask for what I wanted; I could only respond to what *he* wanted, and in a way that was agreeable to him."

That Jennifer never had an orgasm in these encounters only exacerbated her feelings of powerlessness. "It's not like I just lay there, but I felt like sex was my duty," she recalls. She likens herself to Kristen Wiig's character in the opening scenes of the film *Bridesmaids*, thrashing about in a succession of porn-inspired positions with a bored glaze over her eyes. "You're not just saying yes to sex in that situation, you're also saying yes to not pleasing yourself," says Jennifer. "And the longer you spend pleasing other people at your own expense, the harder it is to do anything else."

Jennifer's passivity didn't just impede the pleasure she took in sex. It also impacted the way she felt about herself. Meeting the obligation she felt to be constantly sexually available meant ceding her desire to fulfill another contemporary feminine ideal: that of the "strong, independent woman." She explains: "I just felt like being with him meant that I was lacking self-respect." In other ways, Jennifer's relationship with Oliver strengthened her affinity to that archetype. "I guess having this secret sex friend made me feel like I was living the *Sex and the City*–type life, being all in charge of my sex life by actually having sex," she says with a note of irony. "But it didn't really seem glamorous, fun, or fulfilling." On reflection, she thinks, "choosing not to have sex seems like it would have been the more independent decision."

Fun, Fearless, and . . . Feminist?
The New "Good Woman"

The passive and pure feminine ideal hasn't disappeared entirely. She still looms large in the hearts and minds of many women. But she was not what most of the women I spoke with aspired to, especially once they moved out of adolescence and into adulthood. The modern feminine ideal is confident, independent, and empowered, built more in the mold of the fearless Lady Gaga or 1980s Madonna than Madonna, the mother of Christ.

It is an ideal that is epitomized by *Cosmopolitan*'s "Fun, Fearless Female," who, according to the magazine's South African edition, "embodies ambition, passion, and a confidence that breaks all barriers." Today's "good woman" is attractive, self-assured, and pursues sex with the same enthusiasm with which she goes after everything else in life. She may not explicitly refer to herself as a feminist, but her modus operandi is shaped by an ideal of female empowerment.

Priya, twenty-three, is a proud feminist and has identified as such since she was a teenager. Her feminism is shaped as much by the freewheeling thirtysomethings on *Sex and the City* as by the well-worn copy of Germaine Greer's *The Female Eunuch* she used to read during her high school lunch breaks—and sexual freedom is an important component of it. "A lot of people assume that casual sex hurts your self-esteem, but I don't see it like that," she tells me.

Like the women whose sexual adventures she enjoys watching unfold on television, most of Priya's relationships to date have been casual. Not one-night stands, necessarily, but short-term liaisons predicated more on physical chemistry than on any ongoing emotional commitment. Nor does she really date—at least, not in the dinner-and-a-movie sense. "I meet someone, I sleep with them, and we go from there," she explains. Sometimes the sex turns into something longer-term, other times the relationship stays informal, but either way, she is content with the outcome.

For Priya, the freedom to have sex when she wants it and with whom she wants is a feminist act in and of itself. It's not that she avoids committed relationships; she has been in one before, and she expects that she will have another at some point. But she also believes that having sex outside of a relationship shows confidence and strength of character. "It's pretty gutsy to decide that you don't care about the stereotypes that might be applied to you if you have casual sex," she argues. "Women should be able to have sex without being judged for it." And when Priya and her friends have casual sex it is because they want it, "not because [they're] looking for validation," she says.

Priya's thoughts on casual sex echo those of many women of her generation. They also reflect the broader transformations that have taken place in how we expect women to behave when it comes to sex and relationships. Just as sexual freedom is a symbol of political liberalism, so too are our perceptions of women's power and agency intertwined with what they do with their sex lives.

In many respects, this shift has been a positive one. Jennifer hated casual sex when she was cast in the role of the sentry, saying yes or no to other people's requests. But when *she* was the person choosing her partners and setting the terms of their interaction, she felt bold and powerful. Hooking up with Oliver made her feel manipulated and demeaned, but one-night stands were an act of liberation. "Because I wasn't going to see them again, the sex was spontaneous," she explains. "There was no obligation to do it again and again, whether I wanted it or not." It wasn't casual sex that made Jennifer feel bad about herself, but the circumstances under which she was having it.

Similarly, Annabelle still lives in a community where purity is highly prized. Some of the girls she is friends with at college date, but most of them are still virgins. But Annabelle doesn't feel "broken" the way that she used to. She recalls one of the first dates she went on after she ended her relationship with her abusive ex-boyfriend, how she phoned her mother after to tell her, with bittersweet relief and delight, "Mom, I was with a guy and he didn't rape me."

Annabelle is dating another guy now, a fellow student at her university. They are sleeping together. When Annabelle told her roommate that she was sexually active, her roommate replied that she would pray for her to stop. Annabelle says she responded by telling her: "I know you might be feeling disappointed in me, but you have to realize that this is really important to me. To be able to take back something that was taken from me and make it something beautiful."

Annabelle's current relationship is a markedly different experience from her first one. "After I lost my virginity in a consensual relationship, I was like, wait, I don't feel like I'm not a woman," she says. "I don't feel like I'm lesser or like he took anything from me. I feel happy and fine." It surprised her at first. "I'd been taught that sex is like this horrible, bad, impure thing. But I don't feel like that's the case at all now." That is to say, sex can be good for a woman's soul.

According to some experts, casual sex might also be good for a woman's bank balance. In a 2012 essay for the *Atlantic*, journalist Hanna Rosin argued that hookup culture was "an engine of female progress," the unspoken secret of young middle-class women's educational and career successes. "For college girls these days, an overly serious suitor fills the same role an accidental pregnancy did in the nineteenth century," she wrote, "a danger to be avoided at all costs, lest it get in the way of a promising future."

Rosin pointed to research by academics Elizabeth Armstrong and Laura Hamilton, which found that some high-achieving young women were consciously delaying committed relationships for fear that they would compromise their future career prospects. Casual relationships were a way to bridge that gap, to enjoy the physical intimacy and companionship of a conventional relationship without the associated outlay of time and emotion.

"To put it crudely, feminist progress right now largely depends on the existence of a hook-up culture," Rosin asserted. Her arguments were echoed in a 2013 feature by *New York Times* journalist Kate Taylor, which contended that young women at elite colleges were eschewing serious dating relationships in favor of committing to a demanding schedule of schoolwork, volunteering, and extracurricular activities. "There's this hypothetical, 'I would like to be in a relationship, because it's, like, comforting and stable and supportive,'" Pallavi, a senior at the University of Pennsylvania, told Taylor. "But then, the conversations that I've had, it's always like, 'Well, then what do I do when we get to May, because we're graduating, and so where do we go from there?'" Pallavi was planning to stay in Philadelphia to pursue a master's degree after she graduated, and later move elsewhere to do a law degree and PhD. But that, she was aware, was a ten-year undertaking, which was too much to ask anyone to commit to.

For the young women Taylor and Rosin interviewed, casual sex wasn't just a way of staying focused on their studies. It was an expression of female empowerment. "I definitely wouldn't say I've regretted any of my one-night stands," a Penn junior, who went only by "A," told Taylor. "I'm a true feminist. I'm a strong woman. I know what I want." Another young woman, a Yale sorority girl, told Rosin that she found hookup culture empowering and that she liked the control it gave her. "Guys were texting and calling me all the time, and I was turning them down. I really enjoyed it! I had these options to hook up if I wanted them, and no one would judge me for it."

Where the old feminine ideal turned women into sexual objects, today women are viewed as sexual *subjects*. In the English language, the "object" refers to a person or thing to which something happens. An object may be many things—beautiful, cherished, even revered—but it is also necessarily passive. By definition, it cannot act; it can only be acted upon by others. "Subjects," on the other hand, are dynamic. They are the creators of their own stories, sentient beings with their own desires and motivations.

But subjects are not entirely self-governing, either. The feminist term "objectification" refers to the process by which a three-dimensional human being is reduced to a two-dimensional "thing." But philosophers also use another term, "subjectification," to refer to the process by which our sense of self is shaped—not independently, according to our own free will, but by drawing upon the stories, norms, and archetypes that permeate the culture around us. This new brand of femininity, though less destructive than the compliant one, comes with its own set of issues. Sexual objects might be policed by other people, but sexual *subjects* police themselves, watching and regulating their own behavior in order to create a self-identity that fits the cultural ideal.

In a 2012 article for *Psychology and Sexuality*, UK academic Kaye Mitchell examines the emergence of the confessional sex blog and erotic memoir, dissecting in detail French art critic Catherine Millet's *The Sexual Life of Catherine M*, Brooke Magnanti's *The Intimate Adventures of a London Call Girl*, and Zoe Margolis's *Girl with a One-Track Mind*. These stories are sold as bold, real-life examples of female sexual freedom and power, and on the face of it they seem to be just that. But the power exercised in these books isn't one of self-directed sexual pleasure, Mitchell argues. Rather, she writes, it is "the secondary empowerment that comes with being able to sell yourself successfully." As Brooke Magnanti observes dryly in *Belle du Jour*, "Let's be honest—this is a customer-service position, not a self-fulfillment odyssey."

The commercial success of these stories, and their resonance with the public—*Belle du Jour* was later adapted into a television series, while Zoe Margolis now writes for the British newspaper the *Guardian*—also reinforces the idea that the most interesting stories that women have to share are their sexual ones—that the truth of women's status in the modern world can be derived from the contents of their sex lives. Mitchell wonders why the memoir, a genre concerned with the creation and articulation of the self, "has for women increasingly become the *erotic memoir*, and the blog . . . has increasingly become the sex blog."

Why the stories women are encouraged to tell are so often sexual is a question that Hannah Horvath, the twentysomething memoirist at the heart of the cult HBO series *Girls*, might ask as well. In the penultimate episode of the show's second season, Hannah has a meeting with her book editor, who tells her he didn't finish reading her drafts—not because he didn't have the time to read them, but because he didn't want to. "Where's the pudgy-faced liquid semen and sadness?" he asks, vocally disappointed by her decision to focus her work on friendship rather than sex. "We were talking about Anaïs Nin, you know, your life on your back. Right? That's actually a great title. *My Life on My Back*." If she's not having sex right now, he suggests, she can "make it up." "Can you make it a novel?" he proposes eagerly.

Women's sexual memoirs appeal for the same reason that news stories about spring break, hookup culture, and online pornography do: they play into familiar narratives about the depths and dangers of sexuality, while maintaining an appearance of being transgressive. We hear them as often as we do because they are stories we *want* to hear. But we only want to hear them from certain types of women.

One of the most common criticisms of the new, sexually fearless feminine ideal is that it doesn't apply equally to all women. The women who are celebrated as empowered sexual subjects are usually young, thin, white, and heterosexual. Women who deviate from this model—who are older, fat, or have a disability, for example—still find their sexuality marginalized, whether it is framed as a problem, dismissed as revolting, or ignored entirely.

One reason Priya derives such a sense of power from casual sex is because it defies the expectations people have of her as a young woman of South Asian heritage. "The first guy I slept with asked me if he had ruined my arranged marriage," she reveals with a mix of horror and amusement. Priya's ethnicity shapes her sense of what it means to be a sexually powerful woman in other ways, too. When I ask her what sexual liberation means to her, she laughs and tells me, "Just being able to go out and stuff without people judging." Many of the taxi drivers in the city in which Priya lives are Indian, she explains, "and when they see that I'm Indian, too, they ask questions, like: *What are your parents doing letting you out this late?*" For Priya, being sexually active is a way to take control of her social life and live on her own terms.

The question of which women are cast as independent sexual agents and which are pitied is also tied to class. For upper-middle-class women, to be visibly and actively sexual is viewed as an expression of empowerment and self-determination. In magazines like *Cosmopolitan*, *Marie Claire*, and *Glamour*, sex forms part of a bigger aspirational "lifestyle" package, perched alongside a high-status career path, close-knit friendships, and access to designer clothes and shoes as symbols of female power.

When an upper-middle-class woman takes pole-dancing classes, wears a short skirt, or experiments with swinging or BDSM, she is read as being modern and edgy. When a poorer woman does the same things, she is seen as tacky, distasteful, or worse, dangerous. As part of their Christmas 2011 campaign, the UK luxury retailer

Harvey Nichols released a commercial showing a succession of young women, mostly aged in their late teens and early twenties, making their way home in the early hours of the morning after a night out. Stockings torn and high heels in hand, they tug at their skirts—suddenly too short now that the sun has come up—to keep themselves from showing too much flesh. "Avoid the walk of shame this season . . ." the advertisement urges, before cutting to a slim, slightly older woman making the same journey in a designer dress and immaculate hair and makeup. She smiles and says hello to the mailman before entering her riverside apartment.

The wealthier woman in the Harvey Nichols ad presumably stayed out just as late as the younger, poorer ones; the sun is rising and the postman is already at work when she arrives home. And she may well have drunk just as much, or had just as much or as little sex as they did. But because her dress is more expensive and her body is model thin, her night out is positioned as aspirational, where the other women are objects of ridicule—sending the message that it is not the act itself that is trashy, but the dress and demeanor of the person doing it.

These contradictions filter through from popular culture into real life. A 2014 study by Elizabeth Armstrong and Laura Hamilton found that "slut-shaming"—the practice of attacking a woman for being or appearing sexual—is less a reflection of how many people a woman has had sex with than of her economic class and social status. Although the more affluent women Armstrong and Hamilton spoke with had a higher number of sexual partners on average than their middle- and working-class counterparts (and were far more likely to engage in casual sex), it was the poorer women who were labeled sluts.

Slut-shaming, they argued, was not a punishment for engaging in stigmatized sexual behavior, but for "failure to successfully perform an affluent femininity"—to wear the right clothes, date the right guys, and socialize in the right circles. One young woman was even labeled a "slut" for the crime of eating ketchup for dinner. "She has some issues," her classmates said, laughing.

The fun, fearless, and sexually liberated feminist might be the prevailing ideal of our times, but she remains an ideal that only a small subset of women—chiefly those who are young, white, and middle-class—are permitted to lay claim to.

Rewriting "Girl Power"

Of course, even if a woman does have permission to approach sex in this way—if her mind is assessed as sufficiently self-determining, if her body is deemed desirable—that doesn't necessarily mean she will want to. A model of sexual freedom that requires having as much sex as you can, minimizing your emotional attachments, and looking as conventionally "hot" as possible while you're doing it might not be the one that feels most free to her.

She might prefer to be monogamous, or to only have sex when she meets someone she really, really likes—or even loves. She might find it more "empowering" to be judged on her heart or mind instead of on her sexual appeal or appetite. She might find her freedom in dressing in a manner that pleases *her* when she looks in the mirror, whether it makes her attractive to other people or not. She might prefer not to have sex at all.

More so than men, the ways that women are expected to be sexual closely track our hopes and ideals about the role of sex in our society at any given time. So it is little surprise, then, that as we have moved from a culture that idealizes sexual restraint to one that celebrates sexual freedom and autonomy, so too have our female ideals become more "free" and autonomous. On the whole this has been a positive shift that has allowed many women to seek out and enjoy sex with less shame or fear of censure. But it has also created new sources of shame and anxiety, and like the old feminine ideal, the new one still places sexuality at the core of a woman's femininity.

Nor is the new fun and fearless feminist as self-governing as she might at first seem. She may be a subject rather than an object, the author of her own sexual stories, but she does not write those stories or make her choices in a vacuum. The ways in which she can choose to exercise her "freedom" are determined by the options available to her—set out not only by her class, her race, and the shape of her body, but by her knowledge of how each sexual choice she makes will be responded to and how she wishes to be perceived.

True female sexual autonomy doesn't just necessitate the right for women to have sex without stigma or judgment, although this is of course important. It also needs to entail the right to confidently *not* have sex when it is unwanted or unavailable on the terms she might prefer. And ultimately, it means rejecting the idea that there are only two options for explaining women's engagement with sex—that any of us are either wholly "pure" or "empowered," innocent Madonna or self-assured Gaga.

7

Use It or Lose It:
The Performance Premium

To succeed under the Sex Myth, it is not enough to be sexually active. The sex you are having must be of a particular type. Good sex is exciting and spontaneous, a product of passion rather than duty or routine. It is novel and inventive (never boring), taking everyone involved to sublime heights of pleasure. Glossy magazines, sex advice columns, and pornography teach us that "good sex" is a skill that is essential not only to attracting a partner and maintaining a relationship, but to our competence as human beings.

In the summer of 2013, Los Angeles–based tech company Ardenturous LABS launched a mobile phone application to help us assess just how good the sex we are having really is. Cheekily titled Spreadsheets, the sound-and-motion-sensitive tool measures how often you have sex, how long each session lasts, and the average number of "thrusts per minute," allowing users to keep a record of their average, peak, and aggregate performances—and improve their sexual prowess in the process. Users can earn points for "achievements" like morning sex, sex that lasts longer than forty minutes, or having sex more than five times in one day.

Ardenturous wasn't the first company to use technology to monitor and improve our sex lives, and it won't be the last. Kindu, a phone app released in 2009, helps couples talk about which positions, fetishes, and other activities they might like to explore by surveying their responses to more than eight hundred sex acts. Another app, Kahnoodle, sends users push notifications to their phones to remind them when it is time to initiate sex. In 2014, one enterprising design student announced his intention to use Google Glass to create a program that would give people the ability to watch themselves having sex through the eyes of their lover. Think of it as a high-tech, twenty-first-century version of the mirror on the ceiling.

When Spreadsheets launched in 2013, the media response to it was less than enthused. The *Huffington Post* called it "possibly the least sexy app we've ever heard of," while tech blog *Betabeat* declared that "if you need an app to figure this out, you're probably not [good in bed]." But although the particular criteria Spreadsheets tracks might not be to everyone's tastes, the model of "good sex" it depicts is decidedly more common. The sex Spreadsheets rewards its users for having is long lasting, frequent, penetrative, and lightly transgressive—the same traits that are prized elsewhere in our culture. The app is not a humorous oddity but a reflection of an existing drive for more and better sex.

In part, these standards have developed because of the sheer amount of sexual information we now have at our fingertips. We know more about our bodies and how they work than we used to, and we are also more aware of the sheer breadth of sexual possibilities than we were previously. We don't take bad sex lying down. "It's no longer normal to accept sexual dissatisfaction," observes Pete, the smart, sensitive Seattleite we met briefly in chapter 4.

Just as the Sex Myth's elevation of sex as an act unlike any other can inflame anxieties about how "normal" or attractive we are, so too can it foster a sense of inadequacy when it comes to our pursuit and experience of pleasure. As UK sociologists Stevi Jackson and Sue Scott put it in a 2004 article for the academic journal *Sexualities*, "[T]o be bad at sex is almost to fail as a human being." This pressure can manifest in performance anxiety—for example, in the reports of young men who pop a Viagra before casual sex to make sure they rise to the occasion—but they also shape our expectations of how our bodies should *respond* to pleasure. A 2011 study found that women made the most noise during sex not when *they* were about to orgasm, but when they believed their partners were. And it's not just women who perform pleasure in this way, either. A 2010 study by researchers at the University of Kansas found that 28 percent of sexually active men had faked an orgasm at some point.

There is nothing wrong with wanting sex that is pleasurable, challenging, and fulfilling. But the sex we have been sold under the Sex Myth is not just a pleasure but an imperative, something we *must* do—two to three times a week, in a variety of different places, styles, and positions—in order to be a good lover and an adequate human being. This chapter examines some of the key traits we are told are necessary for a good sex life, from the continual quest for new knowledge and adventure to the invention of new sexual dysfunctions and diseases.

Harder, Better, Faster, Stronger

A good lover knows how to please their partner and what makes their own body tick. They keep up to date with the latest sexual trends and techniques, and take joy in applying them to their own encounters. Their knowledge reflects not just their skill and experience in the bedroom but the effort they invest into their sex lives. They are informed about sex because they know that sex matters. And if you don't have the same familiarity with anatomy and technique that they do, there is an entire industry of media, celebrity therapists, and other lifestyle experts lining up to relieve you of your inexperience.

Follow their advice, and you will "reap the blissful benefits." Ignore it, and you risk becoming a sexual failure, doomed to dreary relationship sex, unfulfilling one-night stands, or involuntary celibacy. As one 2013 article in *Maxim* put it, if you want sex with the same person more than once, you'd best get it right the first time.

That there is an industry around sex advice at all reflects a simple fact: our bodies may be designed for sex, but few people are equipped to have *good* sex without at least a few initial pointers on anatomy and technique. At a time when most formal sex education is focused on preventing pregnancy and STDs, informal sex education of the kind proffered in popular sex books or magazines like *Cosmopolitan, Men's Health,* or *Glamour* fills an important gap, covering information on pleasure and technique that you won't find in most textbooks.

But popular sex advice is not solely about enhancing pleasure. It is also a form of labor, a series of tasks that *must* be completed, not for money or some other concrete reward, but for the emotional reward of being a good partner or successful individual. Sex is not just a form of recreation but a project for developing a desirable self-identity, not unlike the self-improvement work involved in the other arenas these publications cover, like fitness, beauty, or building a professional career that is also glamorous and fun.

In a 2012 article published in *Glamour*, sex bloggers Em & Lo present a tongue-in-cheek adaptation of the traditional women's magazine summer diet plan, describing sex as "the easiest—and most fun—way to get a bikini body." Just like weight loss, they explain, an active sex life can have a host of health benefits, including "less stress, more intimacy, improved mood, better body image, heightened relationship bliss, a recharged libido, and one *very* grateful man."

The parallels between sex and food continue throughout the article. Like a diet, *Glamour's* "summer sex plan" runs over four weeks, with six sex-related activities to complete each week. Activities are categorized using food metaphors. "Appetizers" are small tasks designed to get you in the mood for sex. "Lie-down meals" are for when you have the time to "properly indulge." "Decadent desserts" help readers to be "adventurous with everything from toys to kink." Activities are recommended for their fat-burning properties, with readers advised to "go long" because "an hour of sex burns 170 calories" or to reach for their partner instead of reaching for sweets during TV commercial breaks.

These parallels are clearly intended to be humorous, and it works—the article is clever and funny. But like a weight-loss plan, it also treats sex as a series of assignments to "accomplish" and "complete." Only instead of dining on carrot sticks or going for a run after work, the tasks are to send a dirty text message, pin your partner against the wall, and go outside to kiss the next time it rains, just like in the movies. And just like a diet, these activities are designed to create results. "Using a plan is great, because it takes on a life of its own," reader Michelle, thirty, tells the magazine. "Even on days when I didn't really want sex, I did want to tick the box and say I'd completed the task."

It is not just women's magazines that blur the lines between work and play when it comes to sex. *Men's Health* offers workout tips to improve sexual "power, endurance, and control," advising: "Like many a sport, sex is a legs game, and this position [having sex while standing up] is a case in point. 'It requires a mixture of isometric strength in your legs to hold her weight, and enough power in the tank to create the thrusting motion,' says [personal trainer] Cathy Brown ... 'What's more, you'll need to hold her up with your arms for quite some time, so strength in your forearms and biceps is key.'" Incorporating the right moves into your exercise routine, it promises, will make you better at sex.

Both men's and women's magazines assume that their readers are sexually active and experienced. *Cosmopolitan* presents its readers with a "summer sex bucket list," reasoning that "if you're going to be having lots of sex"—as *Cosmopolitan* readers presumably will be over the summer—"how do you stop it from becoming same-same?" *FHM* advises readers on "how to close the deal with beautiful women," with a cast of female characters drawn straight from a porn film: the new intern at work, the "hot friend," and the best friend's younger sister among them.

In publications targeted at both men and women, sex forms part of a broader "taste culture," as Finnish communications researcher Kaarina Nikunen describes it, that binds readers together as part of the same tribe. Doing sex in the "right" way is just as important—if not more—to being a *Cosmo* girl or a *Maxim* man as wearing the right clothes, having the right kind of job, or going to the right parties. It is an ideal that means not only being sexually active and experienced but also constantly seeking to improve your sexual abilities. Like the old adage "you can never be too rich or too thin," you can never be too good at sex, either. There is always room for improvement, no matter how much you know or how well you perform.

Being Boring:
The Rise of Lifestyle Kink

Being literate in anatomy and technique will score you a passing grade in the school of sexual adequacy. But to truly excel requires an additional layer of commitment: to novelty, innovation, and avoiding being seen as "boring" at all costs. It means not just being, as the celebrated sex columnist Dan Savage puts it, "good, giving, and game," but actively seeking to expand the ground on which sex is played. An interest in trying new things is considered a skill in and of itself, a sign that you are worth the time and effort to have sex with.

As we have become increasingly well educated in the basics of human sexual response, standing out as a sexual partner means upping your game. And being exceptionally good in bed doesn't just mean knowing how to produce a mind-blowing orgasm—it means being creative with positions, locations, and your own fantasies. The same media outlets that push the need to be sexually skilled also promote a diluted, mass-market brand of "kink," advocating once-transgressive acts such as BDSM, threesomes, sex in public places, and more as ways to enliven both long-term relationships and casual hookups.

"Instead of playing it safe and boring, why not kick it up a notch?" suggests *Maxim* in a 2013 article on how to turn a first-time hookup into second-round sex. "Being bold with your position choice can make the first time more significant . . . and more fun." Nikki, a model featured in Australian men's magazine *Zoo Weekly*, tells readers to "mix it up a bit and be adventurous. Nothing's worse than having sex in the same way and in the same place all the time." Especially, presumably, during a one-night stand. When it comes to longer-term relationships, *Glamour* sex adviser Dr. Pam Spurr advises against routine. "Tender sex can be intense and produce amazing orgasms," she counsels. "But it still requires variation to stay fresh. Try different positions, such as face-to-face while lying on your side, or sitting up in bed."

There is evidence that sexual variety is good for relationships. A 2012 study published in the *Journal of Sex Research* found that couples who are more willing to adapt their sexual behavior to meet their partner's needs and desires have higher levels of relationship satisfaction. And in a culture in which penetrative, heterosexual intercourse is still considered the most legitimate of all the forms of sex, lifestyle kink can expand our sense of what is possible.

But these acts aren't just presented as an exciting expansion of sexual options. They are framed as an expectation: something that you *must* do, or else risk being thought inhibited, ungenerous, or old-fashioned. A low-level kink is now near compulsory, a way to prove that you are sexually at ease, modern, and "with it." To be "vanilla," on the other hand, is an insult or a source of embarrassment—as journalist Catherine Scott put it in an article for the feminist blog *Bitch*: "a byword for 'sexually pedestrian.'"

This dichotomy between intrepid sexual adventure and lackluster vanilla sex can be seen in an early episode of the sitcom *Friends*. Trapped in Monica and Rachel's apartment during a blackout, the group exchanges stories of the strangest places they've ever had sex. Monica says she once did it on a pool table in her senior year of college. Joey had sex in the women's bathroom on the second floor of the New York Public Library. Ross boasts that he and his ex-wife once did the deed on a Disneyland ride. Finally, Rachel admits with a sigh that the most exciting place she and her ex-fiancé Barry ever had sex was at "the foot of the bed."

Later in the episode, Rachel worries what her confession says about her former relationship—and about her. "I just never had a relationship with that kind of passion, you know, where you have to have somebody right there, in the middle of a theme park . . . Barry wouldn't even kiss me on a miniature golf course." The lack of sexual novelty in Rachel's former relationship is a metaphor for the lack of desire between Rachel and Barry, as well as of his unsuitability as a partner. As Ross asks sarcastically, "And you didn't marry him *because . . . ?*"

Rachel's comparatively cautious sexual history is a motif that continues later in the series. In the show's seventh season, Rachel runs into one of her old sorority sisters, Melissa. When she tells Phoebe that the two of them kissed in college, Phoebe laughs in disbelief. "It just seems a little wild and you're so . . . vanilla," she says. "Vanilla? I am not vanilla," Rachel protests. "I've done lots of crazy things!" In the eyes of her friends, Rachel's perceived lack of sexual adventurousness is almost as great a perversion as if she weren't having sex at all.

By contrast, engaging in small acts of lifestyle kink is seen as a sign of sexual potency. Small with rosy cheeks and curly blond hair, Lacey grew up in a small town in the South. Sex was commonplace at her rural high school, and many of the people in her grade were married by the time they graduated, if they made it to graduation at all. Of her class of one hundred and twenty students, Lacey was one of only seven who went on to college.

In some respects, Lacey is more conservative than her fellow students at the small public university where she now studies. At twenty-one, she has been dating her boyfriend for four years—and where for many of her classmates dating doesn't mean much more than meeting up for sex, Lacey and her boyfriend schedule time together and hang out with each other's family. She doesn't like Rihanna and her "half-naked, vagina-thrusting" music videos, and she's not a fan of the MTV reality series *Teen Mom*, either. "All it does is show how easy it is to have a teen pregnancy," she says. "I think that's why there are so many high school girls who want to have kids."

But in other respects, Lacey prides herself on being a little more "out there" than her peers. She has slept with only two people, but she and her boyfriend are "the most sexually active people" she knows, she tells me—and the most sexually experimental as well. They've role-played and dressed up in costumes, made love in an open field, and engaged in *Fifty Shades of Grey*–style BDSM power plays—although she clarifies, "Nothing too extreme, I don't like paddles or chains." The BDSM stuff makes her feel a bit "abnormal," she admits, but it's what she likes—and mostly, she is cool with that. And anyway, she says, "I can't imagine sitting there and doing the same thing over and over. It might 'work,' technically speaking, but it's going to get boring after five, ten, or fifteen times of doing the same thing."

Like being skilled and sexually active, lifestyle kink isn't promoted only for its potential to "spice up" a relationship. It is also celebrated for its capacity to transform the self, for the way that it identifies an individual as modern, sexy, and open-minded. But the kink that is advocated in magazines like *Cosmopolitan*, *Maxim*, and *Glamour* is different in essence from the kind favored by people for whom kink is a way of life. Lifestyle kink is like a fashion accessory— something you try on to impress your partner or experiment with a new way of being. You might lock your partner to the bed with a pair of fluffy pink handcuffs, but the power play is understood to be a prelude to the main act of intercourse. Perhaps you try out a threesome or head to a swingers' party, but integrating multiple partners into your everyday life would be a step too far. Fetish is often specific and idiosyncratic—one person might be turned on by dressing up like a nurse, while another will get off on being whipped with a riding crop. But in lifestyle kink, all fetishes are interchangeable. The turn-on is in the sense of transgression, not in the act itself.

Although lifestyle kink is presented as a fun, even essential, addition to one's sex life, articles about less conventional sexual practices are often infused with an air of ambivalence—that is to say, kink may be exciting, but it is also a little bit weird. For a 2013 story published in *Glamour*, sex writer Anna Davies embarked on a "personal pleasure hunt," vowing to live out—and document—all her hottest sexual fantasies before her thirtieth birthday. Over a period of five months, Davies tries sex with another woman, books an erotic massage, has a fling with an older man, goes to "orgasm school," and experiments with BDSM. But in each case, the fantasy falls flat. Hooking up with a woman only confirms that she is more attracted to men, and she leaves the orgasm workshop early, coming to the conclusion that she needs "connection to climax." Her short-lived relationship with a sugar daddy turns her on, but she is turned off by how grateful he is that she is willing to have sex with him in the first place.

The only experience Davies enjoys is the spanking, but even that leaves her conflicted. "When I thought about what had gone on . . . I found I couldn't put it into words without people seeming concerned about my sanity," she writes. As her experiment comes to an end, Davies concludes that although it has led to "some sexy moments," it also made her feel lonely. At the end of the article, she reveals that she is now dating again, and this time she is looking for a more serious partner. But monogamy doesn't have to mean monotony: chief among her requirements is "a partner in crime to help [her] come up with a new list" of acts to experiment with.

The same ambivalence toward non-vanilla sexual acts can be seen in other women's magazine articles about sex. In a *Cosmopolitan* article about the risks of living out your sexual fantasies, a woman who takes off her clothes at an amateur strip club breaks up with her boyfriend the next day. "I realized I'd never have wanted to do it if I truly loved him," she explains, warning that "it's easier to live out fantasies with casual boyfriends" than with people you're emotionally invested in. Another woman in the same article purchases an erotic massage while on vacation in Thailand and worries that it means she is secretly gay. Sex therapist Tracey Cox offers words of warning for anyone considering following in their footsteps. "Fantasies about you and your partner doing relatively 'vanilla' things are relatively safe," she advises, but anything too edgy—like non-monogamy or BDSM—is risky to reveal. "Even if you have no desire to act out the fantasy . . . he may still find it disturbing."

Which leaves it unclear exactly *how* sexually adventurous the reader is supposed to be. If you are not experimental enough, you risk losing your partner's interest—and outing yourself as someone who is uninteresting in return. But if nontraditional sexual acts are more than just an experiment for you, you risk being seen as a pervert. There is no "right" way to engage in lifestyle kink—only endless ways to get it wrong.

"You Can't Make an Appointment for Sex"

Sexual skill and lifestyle kink aren't just designed to make sex more interesting. They are also designed to keep us *interested*—to make us more likely to continue having sex, after the honeymoon is over and the initial rush of hormones runs dry. It is this desire to maintain sexual passion against all odds that underlies so many of our collective anxieties about sexual performance.

You don't need to be having sex to understand the importance of a good sex life. At twenty-three, Mariam is saving herself for marriage, a decision she made when she was sixteen and the Christian abstinence organization True Love Waits visited her Catholic high school. "I think people admire me for [waiting], but at the same time they think I'm an idiot," she says matter-of-factly. But just because Mariam isn't sexually active doesn't mean she doesn't have some very detailed ideas about what she would like her future sex life to look like. When Mariam gets married, she and her husband are going to have sex at least once a day, she tells me. "Morning and night sounds good," she says. They will be adventurous, continually incorporating new positions, activities, and sexual techniques into their relationship. Most important, their sex will be spontaneous, resisting the dreaded malaise of marital "routine" for as long as possible.

Mariam's plans are based on more than just theory. She has been with her boyfriend for four years when we meet, and a few days after our interview, she e-mails to tell me they are engaged to be married. Mariam is a virgin, but her boyfriend isn't—by the time they got together in their late teens, he had already slept with eight women. "He says he's not going to let me rest when we get married, because he has to make up for four years [of no sex]!" she jokes. She has also learned plenty about what a good sex life should look like from friends who are sexually active. One friend, for example, had sex three times a day for months when she met her last boyfriend. "And it wasn't even the first time she had sex. It was just some new guy she'd been dating."

Mariam is as clear on what she *doesn't* want from her married sex life as she is on what she would like it to entail. "Anything less than two times a week is bad," she says. "Or less than three times a week, even." She is dismissive of the notion of scheduling sex. "My partner has one rule," she explains. "We can't book in our sex time. That is something that is not allowed. Like, you can't make an appointment for sex."

Mariam is not alone in her hunger for a sexually exciting relationship. The passion she desires is the unspoken imperative that resides behind everything we speak of when we talk about good sex. We value spontaneity because it suggests that our libidos are still strong; we promote sexual variety because we hope it will stop our urges from waning. In movies, new couples tear off their clothes before they make it through the door and stay up all night talking and touching, their enthusiasm for each other a mark of their compatibility. When their relationship begins to atrophy, their sex life does as well. In a 2012 interview with *New York* magazine's *Vulture* blog, actress Olivia Wilde advised women to listen to their vaginas if they wanted to know if a relationship was right. "Sometimes your vagina dies," she explained. "Then you know it's time to go." Under the Sex Myth, after all, sex isn't "just sex." It is a barometer of the quality and status of your relationship.

"Sex is a very easy thing to measure your relationship by," admits Tom, a tall twenty-year-old with wire-frame black glasses and sandy blond hair. "It's like a yardstick. Are we doing well right now? Are we having a good time?" As indicators of relationship success go, sex is clearly defined and simple to tally. Although Tom would feel strange counting the number of restaurants he's visited in the last month, or how many bunches of flowers he bought for his long-term girlfriend, keeping an eye on the number of times they have had sex feels natural. "If you happen to be in a good spell, sex is a very easy way to notice that." Likewise, if they haven't had sex in a while, "you know that it's not going so well."

Psychologists used to define a "sexless relationship" as one in which a couple had had no sexual intimacy in more than a year. More recently, that definition has expanded to include couples who have had sex less than ten times in the past twelve months. But for many people, the point at which not having had sex becomes a problem kicks in much sooner: not at less than a certain number of times per year, but at a certain number of times per *week*. For some, this is a matter of libido. But for others, it is also a matter of living up to the standards that have been set out for them. Most sex therapists stress that being in a sexless relationship isn't a problem in and of itself, that relationships can be full of love and satisfaction without being sexually active so long as everyone involved is happy with the situation. But when sex is considered shorthand for vitality—whether our own or that of our relationships—the idea of a loving-but-sexless union can be a difficult concept to swallow.

"I get scared if I don't have sex at least a couple of times a week," admits Holly, a New York artist who grew up in the Deep South. "Like I'm not showing the right amount of affection, or like there is something wrong with me. It's not even about whether I'm enjoying it. It's about whether I've hit that number." She's not sure why it matters so much to her. "I mean, when I say it out loud it sounds totally ridiculous. Like, why that number? What's so special about two or three times a week? But in my head, it makes so much sense."

Ashley, whom we met in chapter 4, also keeps close tabs on how often she has sex with her girlfriends. "There is this thing called lesbian bed death," she explains, referring to a term coined by American sociologists Philip Blumstein and Pepper Schwartz to describe

the typical decrease in sexual activity among long-term lesbian couples. "It is a huge, big deal in the lesbian community. People talk
about it all the time."

When she was younger, Ashley and her friends used to swap
notes on how often they had sex, checking in with each other to find
out what was normal and find out how their own relationships were
faring. "If you haven't had sex however many times that week, people talk like you're doomed," she says. "It shows that it is the end
of your relationship, that you may as well just be friends." Ashley
would talk about how often she had sex with the women she was
dating, too, trying to fix any emergent issues before they grew too
serious. "It's like this *disease*," she pronounces. "If you haven't had
sex in a couple of weeks, then you have to deal with it right away.
There is always crying. And you just feel like shit about yourself."

Ashley is more relaxed in her current relationship, which she has
been in for three years now. "It is the most beautiful, balanced relationship I have ever had," she says, and it has given her the security
to let her libido ebb and flow. "We'll have loads of sex for a month or
two, and then two weeks will go by when we won't have sex at all. I
used to think that meant I was failing."

When sex therapists talk about sexless relationships, they are referring to partnerships that are absent of sexual contact of any kind.
But when most people worry about the frequency of sex in their
relationships, they are concerned with a more specific type of contact: how often they are having penetrative, usually heterosexual,
sex. Even Ashley, who only dates women, defines whether or not
"sex" has happened by whether or not there has been penetration.

But although pleasure and physical touch are an important part
of nurturing intimacy for most people, penetration is not the only
way that sexual intimacy can be achieved. It is not even the only way

we can achieve orgasm—or, for many people, women especially, the easiest or most pleasurable way to do so. Making penetration the standard-bearer for "real sex" diminishes other activities that can bring just as much pleasure: kissing, stroking, flirting, oral sex, spanking, role play, sex toys, and more. If it is the sensual bond between lovers that matters, why do we put so much emphasis on one particular form of sensuality?

For one, not everyone prefers penetrative sex. Edward, the gay rights activist from Boston whom we met in chapter 3, has been sexually active since he was fifteen, but he didn't have anal sex until he was twenty-five. He liked it, but it's not a major part of his sex life even now. "I have a healthy sexual relationship, but it doesn't look like what most people expect gay men's sex lives to look like," he says. The idea that "real sex" means a penis entering a vagina marginalizes gay, lesbian, and non-gender-normative people. But it also alienates anyone who doesn't want to make penetrative sex the center of their sex life, whether due to personal preference or medical reasons.

I meet Jasmine, twenty-four, on a humid spring day in Toronto. A grad student with short dark hair, Jasmine first had penetrative sex when she was nineteen; a little later than most of her peers, but not *so* late that it marked her as different or caused her concern. Nor was Jasmine worried when, once she did lose her virginity, it hurt—a lot. First-time sex was supposed to be painful, after all. "I just figured it was because I hadn't done it before," she says. But sex didn't stop hurting, and after a few weeks Jasmine began to wonder if something was wrong. "I had friends who would tell me about their sex lives, and none of them had mentioned this kind of pain. I realized this should not be happening."

Jasmine suffers from vulvodynia, a neural condition that causes burning and irritation in the genital region. For some women, the condition is so severe that it is difficult to sit down, but Jasmine's vulvodynia is concentrated in the ring of muscle that surrounds her vagina, meaning she experiences pain only when she has penetrative sex.

At first Jasmine tried to think her way through the problem, hoping that if she practiced "mind over matter," the pain would disappear. She thought she might be allergic to latex, so she tried using polyurethane condoms. She visited the campus doctor, who responded by giving her antibiotics for yeast infections. But the pain continued, and it began to take a toll on her relationship. "My partner found it difficult to relate to me," she recalls. "And I found it hard to talk about because I felt like there was something wrong with me."

Jasmine and her boyfriend found that they were ill equipped to carve out an erotic life that didn't look like the straightforward scenarios they'd seen on TV or learned about in sex-ed classes at school. "I think especially when you're young, you kind of feel like you have something to prove," she explains. "You feel like in order to be a real man or a real woman, you need to have real, heterosexual sex. And when that doesn't happen—if for whatever reason you're thrown out of that paradigm—it's hard to know who you are or what to do. It can be really scary."

At first, Jasmine was determined to have a "normal" sex life, but she found it difficult to sustain enthusiasm for sex that felt like sandpaper burning against her skin. "There were times when I wondered if I even had a libido," she recalls. "I didn't know what turned me on anymore. If I couldn't have sex within the narrow definition that society had given me, could I have sex at all? And how could I have a relationship without sex? That's, like, not even a relationship, right?" she asks dryly.

Jasmine and her boyfriend eventually broke up, and for a long time she felt like her sexuality had gone dormant. It was only a year later, when she briefly dated another guy she had met at college, that she felt like she had gotten her sex drive back. They didn't attempt intercourse, but the attraction Jasmine felt for him was enough to reassure her that she was still capable of feeling desire, even if her body found it difficult to have penetrative sex.

Now Jasmine's sex life is dormant once more, and she's okay with that. Sex isn't a priority for her right now, and she'd rather put her energies into her studies. And when she does date people occasionally, she focuses her attention on building intimacy through open dialogue and alternate forms of physical intimacy. She is seeing another doctor, though, and trying to get her condition addressed slowly. "I'm unattached right now, so it's not something I have to deal with on a daily basis," she explains. "But I would like to get it cleared up before I'm thirty."

Fake It Til You Make It: Orgasm Inc.

There is a final characteristic of "good sex," one that hinges not on your ability to provide pleasure but on your capacity to feel it. Leonore Tiefer, the author of *Sex Is Not a Natural Act*, is also the founder of the New View Campaign, which challenges the medicalization of sex. Over the past three decades, she has noted an increase in what she terms "response anxiety": a condition experienced by people who "fear they don't *feel* enough, that their inner experience isn't properly passionate."

In a culture that places so much emphasis on sexual vitality, such concerns are not surprising. Behind our fixation on sexual performance lies a belief in the transformative properties of sexual pleasure. Scientists say an active sex life can boost your immune system, relieve pain, and improve bladder control in women. Psychologists believe it reduces stress, boosts self-esteem, and serves as a natural antidepressant by releasing endorphins into the brain. The free-love evangelist Wilhelm Reich believed that a satisfactory orgasm was a cure for all problems, from individual neurosis to the political fascism that forced him to leave Europe for the United States. But response anxiety isn't solely a reflection of a culture that places a high value on sexual pleasure. It is also a reflection of a culture that demands the *performance* of pleasure, irrespective of what is happening to our bodies.

For women especially, part of being seen as good in bed is knowing how to play the role of what sex writer Clarisse Thorn labels "the Sex-Crazy Nympho Dream Girl," who squirms and moans whenever her partner touches her and is "Super Excited" by whatever her partner wants her to do. The Sex-Crazy Nympho Dream Girl is a character that Thorn learned to play early. "Before I had any actual sexual partners, I knew how to give a good blowjob," she wrote in a 2011 article for the Good Men Project. "I also knew how to tilt my head back and moan . . . and I knew what my reactions and expressions were supposed to look and sound like—I knew all those things much better than I knew what would make me react."

Thorn's critique isn't about the expression of sexual enthusiasm but the extent to which that enthusiasm can be faked. She is wary of how easily the performance of pleasure can become an acceptable substitute for pleasure itself. "I just got rewarded for it so much," she tells me when we speak on the phone. "And it's really hard not to play that role when afterward the person you're sleeping with tells you you're amazing." Even now, she says, it is much more difficult for her to ask for what she wants out of a relationship than it is for her to create "that sexy dream girl shell."

Thorn is not the only woman to have bought into the idea that her ability to dramatize sexual desire matters as much as, if not more than, her ability to experience it. Lucy, twenty-five, tells me that when she was at college, her sex life was more performative than it was pleasurable. "You make the right noises, you give the right looks, but you're experiencing it all in the third person. It doesn't belong to you," she says. But Lucy's sexual performances weren't just a matter of pleasing her partners. They were an expression of hope: that if she faked her pleasure for long enough, eventually she would find someone with whom she wouldn't have to "act" like she enjoyed sex. She would be able to slip out of the role she was playing and actually enjoy it.

Like being skilled, adventurous, or sexually voracious, performing pleasure helps to construct a socially desirable identity—to become the sort of sexual person you believe you ought to be. As we saw in chapter 4, the current sexual ideal means not just being attractive to others, but demonstrating your desire for and interest in sex. And part of demonstrating that desire means performing great heights of pleasure.

At the heart of this performance lies the orgasm: the objective measure of sexual pleasure and the logical end point to any sexual encounter. In our culture, orgasm is positioned as the "ultimate meeting with our true (sexual) selves," argues psychologist Annie Potts in her book *The Science/Fiction of Sex: Feminist Deconstruction and the Vocabularies of Heterosex*—and the ultimate way to gain understanding of another person. Not to orgasm, on the other hand, is to be alienated from an essential aspect of yourself. But not all orgasms are created equally. Orgasms that occur during partnered sex are superior to ones that are a by-product of masturbation. Sex that culminates in mutual orgasm is better than sex in which only one partner orgasms. Orgasms that are man- (or woman-) made are more valid than those that are generated by sex toys. And in a contemporary holdover of the theories of Sigmund Freud, who believed that they were a mark of greater maturity than "infantile" clitoral ones, the vaginal orgasm is still positioned as the crème de la crème of female pleasure. This is despite the fact that 75 percent of women will never reach orgasm from penetration alone.

When Brit, whom we met in chapter 6, started having sex in her midteens, her orgasms ticked all of these boxes. They were loud and enthusiastic, they required no clitoral stimulation, and they always happened at the exact same moment her partner came. There was just one problem: they weren't real.

Brit faked her orgasms in part because she didn't want to disappoint her boyfriend. He wanted her to climax, so she did—in exactly the way they had both been socialized to expect her to. But she also faked them to take the pressure off herself. "I would lie about the orgasm, and then I had the freedom to just let the 'second' one happen or not, even if for me it was my first," she recalls. There was no shame in not achieving a second orgasm, but there were great expectations attached to the first.

It was only when she was flicking through a magazine one evening, reading about how some women's toes clenched when they came and contemplating how she could use this information to improve her performance, that she realized things had gone too far. She told her boyfriend she'd been faking it, and he flipped out. At the time, she found his reaction understandable. "I had lied about it," she reasons. But, she notes, "There was no move to have a conversation following that about what we could do to make sex more enjoyable. And at least in my experience, sex can be enjoyable without ending in an orgasm."

Others are less content to go without. The 2011 documentary *Orgasm Inc.* tracks the race among pharmaceutical companies in the early 2000s to create "a female Viagra." One of the most fascinating stories in the film is that of Charletta, a sixtysomething woman living in Winston-Salem, North Carolina, who reveals she has had difficulty achieving orgasm her entire life. Diagnosed with female sexual dysfunction (FSD), a catchall term used to describe the struggles with pleasure, arousal, and desire that are experienced by up to 43 percent of American women, Charletta is a regular participant in clinical trials for anything that might aid her condition. The latest of these is a device named the Orgasmatron, a small box, surgically wired to the spine, that is said to stimulate orgasms with the push of a button. Charletta is dismayed by her diagnosis, telling filmmaker Liz Canner, "Not only am I not normal, I am diseased. That sounds real bad." But she is hopeful that the Orgasmatron will help her achieve the pleasure she desires.

The Orgasmatron doesn't give Charletta an orgasm, although it does make her left leg twitch. But after having it removed, Charletta reveals something else to Canner: she does in fact have orgasms, and she has been having them all along. Her "dysfunction" is that she has never been able to orgasm in what she describes as "the normal situation"—during penetrative intercourse with her husband. When Canner tells her that most women are unable to orgasm without clitoral stimulation, she is delighted. "That's wonderful," she laughs. "To heck with all that disease stuff."

The last two decades have seen the emergence of a suite of new products and procedures designed to help people achieve greater sexual pleasure and perform better between the sheets. The most famous of these is Viagra, the small blue pill credited with solving male impotence and allowing men to enjoy active sex lives into old age. But there is also the O-Shot, an injection of blood platelets into vaginal tissue to "generate healthier and more functional tissue in the areas of sexual response"; the G-Shot, which injects collagen into the vaginal wall to enhance sensation; and Femprox, a cream designed to enhance the female libido. New York gay lifestyle magazine *Next* reports that some male porn stars use Caverject, an injectable drug that creates a "superhuman erection."

These technologies have been marketed as great liberators, which advocates argue will free men and women to enjoy sex without physical limitation. And certainly, treating deficits of desire or pleasure as physiological issues rather than psychological ones has the potential to make them less personal. If you don't feel like having sex, it doesn't mean there's something wrong with your relationship, or worse, with you. It's an easily solvable medical issue that can be fixed by going to the doctor. But the use of medical rhetoric to discuss sexual issues also serves to entrench ideas of what a "normal" sex life ought to look like. Not experiencing orgasm, not being able to produce an erection on command, and waning interest in sex in a long-term relationship are not just less-than-ideal situations. They are, as Charletta put it, a *disease*.

And sexual dysfunction is a disease that has the potential to be very profitable indeed. In a 2003 article published in the *British Medical Journal*, health journalist Ray Moynihan argues that female sexual dysfunction—the condition Charletta was diagnosed with— is a "corporate sponsored" disease, created by pharmaceutical companies to "build markets for new medications" in the wake of the financial success of Viagra. FSD is ill defined, he argues, encompassing everything from waning desire to anxieties regarding sexual performance to difficulty achieving lubrication. What's more, the claim that 43 percent of American women suffer from it is questionable; the number was achieved by including any woman who has experienced any sort of sexual difficulty for two months or more during the previous year. Even Edward Laumann, the researcher who administered the study, has conceded that many of the women among his 43 percent were "perfectly normal."

The category of female sexual dysfunction, Moynihan argues, takes what are potentially temporary sexual difficulties and turns them into "diseases" that need to be treated with medical intervention. In addition, it promotes the idea that if you do not desire sex all the time, there must be something wrong with you.

Then there is the matter of what is labeled a sexual dysfunction in the first place. Why is it our bodies that we so readily question, rather than our assumptions of what a "good sex life" is supposed to look like?

More Pleasure, Less Angst

If there is anything "dysfunctional" about our current approach to sex, it does not reside in our bodies, but in the way that we perceive sex and sensuality.

We treat sex as something that can be mechanized and perfected, through the acquisition of skills and techniques, the development of "signature moves," and a focus on the performance of pleasure rather than the sensation of it. But the problem is not that we are "doing it wrong." It is that we have been told that there are only a handful of very specific ways to do it *right*. That "good sex" is whatever looks sexy through a camera or sounds exciting written down on the page, rather than what feels good in our bodies in the moment.

Orgasms aren't the only route to sexual satisfaction, as many women and men who struggle to climax during sex will happily tell you. Fluffy handcuffs, costumes, and a Kama Sutra's worth of sexual positions aren't the only ways to keep your sex life interesting. And checking off three rounds of "spontaneous" sex each week isn't the only way to measure the vitality of your relationship—or of your life.

Rather than engaging in acts that don't interest you in order to avoid seeming boring and old-fashioned, the truly "radical" act might be to turn your focus to the sex you actually want to have—however "kinky" or "vanilla" it might be. Rather than assessing the state of your sexual relationships by how often you penetrate or are penetrated by your partner, it might take the pressure off to stop focusing your sex life around intercourse—to make kissing and touching and holding as valid a form of sexual intimacy as what we usually call "sex."

And finally, as we will soon see, you might shift the focus away from what sex says about who you are and bring it back to how it makes you feel.

8

You Aren't What You Do:
Why We've Got It Wrong

I f the Sex Myth makes us feel anxious and inadequate, why is its grip on us so powerful? Most of the people I spoke with in the course of writing this book knew on a gut level that there was something wrong with the way that sex is spoken about in our society. They understood that the glossy, stylized images that dominate our media and popular culture were exaggerations that bore little resemblance to the lives of the people they knew. And they believed, deeply and viscerally, that their value and identity lay in something more than how often they had sex, how many people they had slept with, or how adventurous (or not) they were between the sheets. It was why they volunteered to meet and speak with me, in floods of e-mails that numbered almost one thousand.

But being able to identify a false ideal is one thing. To reject it, even in the most vulnerable, uncertain parts of your being, is another. And although the young women and men I interviewed were adept at dissecting social norms and deconstructing their least favorite TV shows, their hearts too often remained open to emotional subterfuge.

Yusuf, the "straight-acting gay man" we met in chapters 2 and 5, knew that he wouldn't really be shielded from sexual rejection if only he were sufficiently good-looking, but he still felt insecure when he measured his experiences against the gay male ideal. "I often feel like I'm rejected," he told me, "and I don't know what to take from that." Jasmine, the Canadian graduate student for whom intercourse felt like sandpaper, was armed with a catalog of feminist theory, but she was still uncertain of how to carve out an erotic identity when she was unable to have what most people thought of as "sex." Katie, the lapsed abstinence pledger we met in chapter 6, understood intellectually that her value wasn't bound up in her virginity, but on an emotional level, she believed it was the only thing that made her special.

I still feel those same contradictions between intellect and emotion myself, albeit not as much as I once did. I can tell you the cultural and historical origins of every negative or limiting belief about sex that I have. I can throw studies and statistics at you designed to prove that you, and I, and everyone reading this are just fine the way we are. I can tell you that there are other people experiencing the same fears and challenges you are, whatever your challenges might look like. And indeed, you could argue that I have done just that over the course of this book.

And yet, I still can't entirely shake the fear that I have crossed some kind of line if I make a dirty joke, or when I speak about pornography with an almost scientific detachment. I still feel like a bad lover—and a subpar human being—if I am too busy or distracted or disinterested to have sex one week. I still evade and obfuscate when it comes to the exact details of my sexual past, posturing as someone who more closely resembles the fun, free, sexy woman I would like to be seen as—to the point that I often don't notice I'm doing it until the words slip out of my mouth.

One night at the end of 2013, I was hanging out with my friend Penny, discussing potential cover designs for this book and contemplating how the Sex Myth might be distilled into a single image. She suggested a twist on the "walk of shame": the young women you see traveling home in the clothes they wore the previous night who, as she put it, "really just fell asleep at a friend's place after staying up too late watching DVDs." I instinctively escalated the conversation. "And why do they call it 'the walk of shame' anyway?" I quipped. "Whenever I've done the walk of shame, it has been a *stride of pride*."

Never mind that the one sex-related "walk of shame" I've done in my life to date has been after sleeping with the man who ended up becoming my husband. Or that, as someone I have known since I was seventeen, Penny knew perfectly well that I didn't have a past scattered with one-night stands. I called myself out on it immediately. "Look at me," I said. "I'm being totally Sex Myth–y right now!"

The Sex Myth wouldn't be so insidious if it were solely a negative force, a cultural killjoy bent on telling us what not to do. The truth is, believing in the Sex Myth can be a lot of fun. Elevating sex as the ultimate pleasure inflames our imaginations, which in turn makes sex more pleasurable. Believing that it reveals the barbaric truth of human nature makes it feel more titillating and transgressive. Setting it apart from other acts transforms it into something more potent and dramatic. The Sex Myth may fuel our anxieties about our sex lives, but it is also a source of physical and emotional pleasure. We believe in the Sex Myth in part because we want to.

But the pleasures of the Sex Myth are ultimately outweighed by the damage it causes. The Sex Myth doesn't just make sex more exciting; it also renders it more dangerous, weighing down our sexual desires and histories with an excess of significance. And by inflating the importance of sex in this way, we have unwittingly bonded ourselves in chains of our own creation.

You Are Not Your Sex Life

The Sex Myth teaches us that sex is a subject of almost otherworldly importance that matters not just for the pleasure and intimacy it can contribute to our lives but also for its status as a harbinger of "truth," a window into who each of us "really" is. The Sex Myth transforms acts into identities, defining us on the basis of our sexual histories and desires in ways that are often negative or otherwise compromised. Under the Sex Myth, you haven't just had sex with a lot of people; you *are* a slut, a player, or a potential sex addict. You are not just sexually inactive but a virgin or a loser, someone who is alternately "pure" or ridden with unspecified emotional issues. You don't just happen to be attracted to people of the same gender; you *are* gay, lesbian, or bisexual.

The British sociologist Anthony Giddens has argued that humans derive our sense of self not from the raw details of our experiences but from our capacity to weave those details into a consistent story. If we are liberal in our attitudes, we expect our sex lives to be similarly liberal. If, on the other hand, we value tradition and conservative values, we expect that, too, to be reflected in our sex lives.

In real life, many people hold identities that might seem to be at odds with one another at first glance. Nyn, the polyamorous trans guy we met in chapter 3, told me that he struggled with the expectation that because he had multiple partners, he was "vastly experienced" and up for anything. "I'm quite young, still," he said. "People tend to ascribe a lot of experience to me that I don't actually have." Greta, the twenty-five-year-old fashion blogger from chapter 2, considered herself politically radical but had a sexual history most people would associate with someone more conservative, having had only one partner since she was eighteen.

Meghan, the sardonic blond Republican we met in chapter 4, told me about one of her best friends from high school—"a bleeding-heart liberal" who was studying to become a public defender and didn't have sex until she was twenty-three. Meghan's experiences, on the other hand, have been the opposite of her friend's. "People tell me all the time that I look really sweet," she observes. "Good girl, conservative, take her home to Mom . . . And it's like holy shit, I have had sex with a *lot* of people!" Where Meghan's friend spent her college years thinking she wasn't "normal" because she was still a virgin, Meghan felt like being sexually active had put "a black mark next to [her] name." Meghan, after all, had been brought up to believe that nice girls didn't have sex until they were married. And yet Meghan had sex well before that, in her first semester of college.

But while Meghan's and her friend's trajectories might outwardly appear to be opposites of each other, they share an emotional experience in common. When the stories we tell about who we are don't seem to correspond with our experiences—when we lack "integrity of the self," as Giddens puts it—shame and anxiety are the all-too-common results. To resolve this discord, we will often try to make our experiences and the stories we tell about them consistent.

When it comes to sex, this consistency can be achieved in a number of ways: By omitting details of our histories that don't fit with our desired self-image, or by hinting at events that never happened in order to better project an image that fits the ideal. Maybe we avoid sexual activities that don't fit with our beliefs about who we are, or pursue experiences and relationships we are ambivalent about in order to maintain a particular self-image. A 1997 study of the relationship between young people's self-image and their sexual practices found that the more important a belief or ideal was to a person's self-perception, the more likely it was to be enacted in their behavior.

In practice, achieving this alignment between sex and self might mean responding as Meghan did and staying in a relationship you're not happy with in order to validate a decision you now regret. But it could just as easily mean having sex with someone you're indifferent about—like Courtney, whom we met in chapter 3—just to prove that you're worth having sex with. It might mean not trying an act that intrigues you, because you're afraid people will think you're a freak. Or it could mean engaging in activities you have no interest in, because you don't want to seem boring or inhibited.

The belief that our sex lives define us in a unique and profound way doesn't just shape the acts we partake in. It also influences the experiences we believe we are *capable* of partaking in. When Henry, the twenty-three-year-old virgin from chapter 4, e-mailed me a few months after I interviewed him, he expressed his embarrassment about the things he had told me. When we had first spoken, he said, he had thought that he would eventually meet someone he cared about and who cared about him. "I seem to remember having a bit of an 'it'll happen when it happens' rhetoric," he wrote. But now he was more somber in his assessment of his sexual prospects. If he hadn't had sex by now, he argued, who was to say he would have better luck in the future? For Henry, the belief that his sex life defined him had become a shackle that limited his capacity to change his situation.

The stories that are told in media, popular culture, and in everyday conversation set out the parameters of what we *should* do when it comes to sex. But it is through our efforts to match our sex lives to our self-image that these standards are enforced, as we regulate our behavior and self-presentation not only to conform to the ideal but also to manage the way that we are perceived by ourselves and others.

The French philosopher Michel Foucault coined a term to describe this process: subjectification, which referred to the mechanisms through which individuals became objects not of other people's authority but through which they learned to exert control over themselves. For Foucault, this process of self-discipline was exemplified by the panopticon, a type of eighteenth-century jail that allowed the guards to observe any prisoner at any time, without the prisoners' knowing whether they were being watched. The effect was that prisoners behaved as though they were being monitored at all times, and thus learned to regulate their conduct to fit the prison's rules and norms whether someone was observing them or not.

The same dynamic can be seen in the relationship between sex and the self. For the most part, sexuality is not regulated by a tyrannical external force. It is something we manage internally, as we continually monitor our behavior to befit the type of person we think we ought to be.

Foucault believed that the significance Western culture ascribed to sex was ultimately destructive—a tool not of liberation but of regulation and control. He was wary, too, of the degree to which sexuality was intertwined with the self, arguing that it would not lead to people being freer in their sexual practices, but that it would compel them to behave more conservatively and experiment less. "If the perennial question [people] ask is 'Does this thing conform to my identity?' then, I think, they will turn back to a kind of ethics very close to the old heterosexual virility," he predicted.

Foucault's words have not come true in the manner he expected. In today's sexual climate, the dominant ideals are liberal—at least insofar as the values and aesthetics they promote, if not in the diversity of practices they preach. And as the stories I have shared throughout this book show, not everyone marches to the same sexual drum. Different people are drawn to different behaviors, identities, and desires, influenced by their life history, the people they surround themselves with, and their own tastes.

But the peculiar "specialness" that we attribute to sex limits our inclination to explore it as freely as we otherwise might. If sex reveals who we really are, to step outside the bounds of the identity and practices we are already comfortable with poses a profound emotional risk.

Still, just as our sense of self can evolve over time in other arenas, so too are our sex lives far from static. A year after Henry e-mailed me to express his embarrassment over our interview, I contacted him again to ask for his permission to include his story in this book. This time, he was in a very different state of mind. "I did have sex, last Saturday, as it happens," he wrote. He thought it was great but said, "[N]othing really changed. It didn't make me a better person, or a different person for that matter." The real change was that Henry now understood that sex did not define him.

Sex Is Not
(the Only Form of) Freedom

Another avenue through which the Sex Myth derives its power is through the potent associations between sex, freedom, and oppression. These connections are not without reason. The special importance attributed to sex means that historically, people whose sexual experiences and desires have deviated from the ideal have been punished with ostracism, imprisonment, and even death—and in many parts of the world, this is still the case.

The fight for people to be able to pursue love and pleasure without fear of harm or intimidation is an important one, and it is not over. In 2011, two Cameroonian men were sentenced to five years in prison for the crime of "looking gay." At the time of this writing, homosexuality is illegal in seventy-eight countries, and in the United States, young lesbian, gay, and bisexual people are four times as likely to attempt suicide as their straight peers, due to risk factors such as rejection from family, lack of social support, and the stress of living with daily discrimination and prejudice.

Women's sexuality, too, continues to be fiercely regulated, both legally and through the use of physical brutality. According to data from the World Health Organization, more than one in three women worldwide have experienced sexual violence, and in the United States, nearly one in five women have been raped. In war zones, rape is employed as a weapon, with hundreds of thousands of women sexually assaulted during the conflicts in Rwanda, Sierra Leone, Liberia, Yugoslavia, and the Democratic Republic of the Congo. In the United States, reproductive rights remain a hot-button issue, with lawmakers in states including North Dakota, Texas, Ohio, Iowa, Arkansas, Oklahoma, Arizona, Kansas, and Virginia enacting 231 restrictions on abortion between 2011 and 2014 alone.

Under the old sexual ideal, the Sex Myth was most visible in what people were told *not* to do: in the message that if we had sex—outside of marriage, with someone of the same gender, or in a nonreproductive way—we were immoral, unnatural, or dirty. But today, the tension between control and freedom manifests in more complex ways. The Sex Myth is palpable not only in what we *cannot* do without fear of stigma or harm, but in what we feel we *must* do in order to avoid feelings of shame and inadequacy.

The Sex Myth teaches us that we are disgusting if we are attracted to people of the same sex, or if we have "too many" sexual partners, or if we are not monogamous. But it also tells us that we are failing if we are *not* sexually active, if we have too few partners, or if we are not sufficiently sexually "skilled." At first glance, these directives might appear to be opposites, but in fact they are two sides of the same regulatory system.

Under both sets of standards, sex is infused with the same otherworldly significance, a level of primacy that makes it difficult to pursue an authentic desire, whatever that might be. As Sarah, whom we met in chapter 1, puts it, "Everything in our culture tells you that if you're not having sex or on the hunt for it, you're missing out on something incredible. No one ever tells you not to worry about it."

The Sex Myth feeds upon two mutually reinforcing ideas: that our "true" sexual appetites are being suppressed by an external force, and that we will find the truth of who we are, both as a species and as individuals, through unrestricted sexual expression. It is the fear that sex is being quashed that infuses it with such liberatory potential, and the sense that we are engaging in something forbidden makes freedom all the sweeter.

But the belief that sex is an inherently liberatory force is founded on a view of power that is fundamentally flawed. Sex is no longer solely repressed in our society; it is also demanded of us. And with that shift in how power is exercised comes a demand for a new vision of sexual freedom.

The Sex Myth Is Reactionary

Today, the Sex Myth is sold through a mirage of liberalism, urging us to perform symbols of freedom such as casual sex, creative sexual experimentation, and passionate desire. But the Sex Myth is not inherently liberal, not even on the most superficial level. Nor is it inherently concerned with freedom. It is a regulatory force that shapes our sexual beliefs and behavior to reflect the preoccupations and ideals of the culture we live in. The Sex Myth can be—and still is—employed just as easily for conservative means as it is for progressive ones.

Both liberals and conservatives believe that sex is powerful. But the way in which they believe it to be powerful is often split down ideological lines. Where liberals tend to frame sex as a positive energy that has been unfairly repressed, conservatives are more likely to view sex as a dangerous force that needs to be contained. The liberal celebration of sex as the ultimate pleasure is mirrored by the conservative belief that in order for the specialness of sex to be preserved, it should be enjoyed only in the most intimate of relationships.

That is to say, the Sex Myth is not just responsible for performance anxiety, sexualized popular culture, and compulsory casual sex. It is also responsible for slut-shaming, homophobia, and abstinence education. It doesn't just teach us that sex is the best thing, the source of our liberation, but also that sex is the *worst* thing, something that threatens and degrades us.

We can see this reactionary side of the Sex Myth in the way that we respond to survivors of sexual assault: in the assumption that because sex is corrupting, the victim has been sullied, and that this act of violence and degradation is a reflection of the personal qualities of the person who was attacked. Following the rape of a sixteen-year-old high school student in Steubenville in the summer of 2012, the young woman's peers took to Twitter and YouTube with debasing comments such as "some people deserve to be peed on" and "you don't sleep through a wang in the butthole." The implication was that the girl was complicit in the crimes committed against her; that she would not have been assaulted if she were not already in some way compromised.

The reactionary side of the Sex Myth is also present in the negative portrayals of gay and lesbian people. In a 2012 interview with anti-gay lobby group Americans for Truth About Homosexuality, Christian minister and conservative politician E. W. Jackson asserted that same-sex attracted people had "perverted minds" and were "very sick people psychologically, mentally and emotionally." But gay sex didn't just corrupt the individual, according to Jackson; it was a force so powerful that it had the potential to corrupt all of society. "Homosexuality is a horrible sin," he said. "It poisons culture, it destroys families, it destroys societies."

The belief that sex is a perilous force is echoed too in the lessons taught in abstinence education. In programs deployed by Colorado-based abstinence advocates Education for a Lifetime, students are

taught that "sex is like fire . . . good when controlled, but dangerous otherwise." In another analogy, sexual intercourse is likened to
sticking together two pieces of duct tape—stick two pieces together
often enough, and soon you won't be able to stick to anyone else.

The extraordinary significance of sex under the Sex Myth has
made it a fixture of our conversations: in media, in popular culture,
and in day-to-day life. But the specialness of sex can also make it
more difficult to talk about, denying us the information we need to
lead happy, healthy emotional lives. It is because we believe that
sex matters more than other things that we are embarrassed to talk
about it with our children, that we warn teenagers away from it, and
that we find sex so difficult to address honestly in our own lives.

To achieve true sexual freedom, we need to do more than just
change the rules under which our sexual behavior is governed. We
must eradicate the Sex Myth altogether.

Conclusion:
Beyond the Sex Myth

L ooking back, the insecurities that plagued me in my early
twenties feel a bit absurd. It seems obvious now that the fact
that I wasn't sexually active didn't mean there was something terri-
bly wrong with me. Nor did my lack of a sex life negate any of the
good qualities I had in my possession. It didn't erase my connections with other people, my enthusiasm, my emotional generosity,
or my wicked sense of fun. It didn't make me ugly or unwanted. My
sexual history wasn't a window into the "truth" of who I was or what
others saw in me—rather, it was a series of events that made up one
part of my life story. The only thing that made me "defective" back
then was my belief that I was defective.

I did eventually have sex for the first time, in a manner that was
casual and loving and—dare I say it—"liberated" all at once, in the
sense that it was something *I* sought out and had control over. Once I
had done the deed, I realized that sex was not the transformative force
I had believed it to be. It didn't render me suddenly experienced, any
more than not having had a penis inside of that particular part of my

body the day before had made me "pure." I was pleased and relieved that I had finally done it, but it did not metamorphize me.

My sex life was not the only one that changed shape over the course of my researching the Sex Myth. I spoke with Cara, the sexually circumspect Seattleite who thought she might be asexual, over the phone two years after I first interviewed her, as she nursed a hangover one Sunday morning. She was living with a boyfriend now, a man she had met at the grocery store around the corner from her office, shortly after we had met. He had first struck up a conversation with her about a book she was reading for the feminist book club she had joined—although it took him almost a year after that to work up the courage to ask her out. When they started dating, he was sensitive to her fears and reservations, and happy to wait until she was ready to have sex.

"It wasn't that a magical man came around, it was that I was finally comfortable with myself," Cara said when we talked. "When you and I met, I was in a really bad place. I had friends, but they weren't connected to each other. I was just kind of lonely." Through her book club and other activities, Cara has made new friends, "women who are super comfortable with themselves and with their bodies. It made me realize that, okay, I am a worthy person"— however "normal" or otherwise her sex life might be.

When I first met Henry, he was a virgin who was overwhelmed with anxiety about his self-perceived unattractiveness. Less than a year and a half later, he was a star of his local BDSM scene, sought after for his skills in Japanese bondage. Monica, my friend who inspired me to write this book, went through another two years of semi-involuntary celibacy before finally having sex again. As I wrote this chapter, she was hanging out with her Dutch anthropologist lover on a beach in the South China Sea, and as I edited it, she asked me to let you know that she was single and celibate once again.

For me, these stories serve as reminders that nothing in life is permanent, least of all during the period of rapid personal change that takes place in our twenties. Our sexual histories are not unblemished mirrors of our souls but an ever-changing and unpredictable series of events that, while they may have meaning in our lives at any particular moment, do not define us. As one commenter on the feminist website Jezebel put it: "Getting laid is mostly a matter of luck, opportunity and sex drive, not desirability."

I still don't feel like my own sexual history accurately reflects the person that I am inside. It feels less gregarious than I am, less inclined to take risks—like it belongs to someone more meticulously virtuous and self-contained. But it is not the source of insecurity it used to be, either. I don't feel like my sex life *needs* to define me the way I once did.

Of course, it's easy not to worry about your sex life when it fits the ideal that has been set out for you by your culture. The Sex Myth fades into the background when we are secure in our choices. It is when our footing is less solid that it is most powerful. That I am no longer haunted by those feelings of inadequacy is a small personal victory. But it would be a greater victory still if no one was consumed by those feelings. And that requires more than individuals changing their behavior to fit the established norms, or even denouncing the terms upon which those norms are set. It means challenging the centrality of sex in our society and reframing what it means to be sexually "free."

There are signs that the way our culture speaks about sex is starting to change—that we are starting to question the standards that have been laid out for us, and even beginning to question the Sex Myth itself.

The major force driving this shift is the Internet, which with its plurality of voices and lower barriers to publishing has allowed a greater variety of sexual stories to be heard than ever before. New websites such as Jezebel, Role Reboot, the Good Men Project, the Hairpin, and Feministing have carved a niche for themselves as myth busters that question received wisdom and challenge our perceptions of what it means to be "normal" in the process. The crowd-sourced Tumblr site Do Tell collates anonymous sex stories from women that look nothing like the confessions typically aired in women's media. Instead of stories about public sex or bikini waxes gone wrong, the accounts on Do Tell are tales of profound triumph and shame. "If I let him spend more than three minutes—one minute—between my legs, I feel greedy, defective, and somehow less like a woman," confesses one contributor, while another writes, "I've always been lucky in love/sex. . . . I'm happily having casual sex right now and feeling great about it."

These changes in the dialogue have begun to trickle down to popular culture, too. When Lena Dunham's cult HBO series *Girls* first hit screens in 2012, it was praised for its unglamorous, "awkward" depictions of young people's sex lives. "I feel like I was cruelly duped by much of the television I saw," Dunham told the *New York Times*. With her show, she said, she aspired to create a more realistic picture of twentysomething sex.

And the sex on *Girls* is certainly less romanticized than the sex portrayed in other television comedies. In one scene in the first season of the show, Dunham's character, Hannah, is hooking up with her sometime boyfriend Adam when he shifts them into a role play, with her as a preteen prostitute and him as her pimp. In another scene, he pees on her in the shower, not as an act of kink or titillation, but to make her laugh. In the second season, Hannah has sex with her friend's teenage stepbrother in a graveyard. The sex on *Girls* is less aspirational than it is uncomfortable, both physically and emotionally.

But what is even more radical about the show—and what sets *Girls* apart from previous "gritty" or confronting depictions of young people and sex, such as *Skins* or *Gossip Girl*—is the relatively tangential role that sex plays in its characters' lives. The young women on *Girls* have sex—in some cases quite a lot of it—but sex isn't what keeps them up at night or what they grill each other about, *Sex and the City*-style, over brunch. On *Girls*, sex is just an ordinary part of life, something that happens (or doesn't happen) between eating a cupcake, going to the bathroom, and ruminating on the state of your creative and economic prospects. Sometimes it is great, sometimes it is terrible, but most of the time it is just a *thing*.

There are signs, too, that we are beginning to grow tired of the Sex Myth and its mystical elevation of sex as the most powerful and profound act known to humankind. When third-wave feminist author Naomi Wolf published her book *Vagina* in 2012, she was criticized by *New Yorker* journalist Ariel Levy for "situating the essence of the female" in the body, and specifically, in one particular part of it: the vagina. Where Wolf believed that the vagina was "a gateway to a woman's happiness and to her creative life" and even the source of her connection to "the Goddess," Levy argued it was just another body part like any other—and certainly no substitute for a woman's brain.

Levy's essay did not name the Sex Myth explicitly, but it did circle and dismantle some of its core tenets. Levy critiqued the notion that, as she put it, "sex is the solution to every problem and the source of everything worth anything." She was also critical of the idea that sex was intrinsically liberating. "Orgasms are swell," she quipped, "but they are not the remedy to every injustice."

There are rumblings too of a reemergence of what some young women are calling "sex negative" feminism, suggesting that we may be headed for a break from an idea that has dominated popular feminism for the past twenty years: that in a world where women's sexuality is repressed, a woman being sexual is an inherently powerful act. In 2013, xoJane.com published an opinion piece by young radical feminist Jillian Horowitz, arguing that "the way you fuck is not 'private,' apolitical, or outside the realm of critique." In 2014, in an article for the Toast, asexual writer Julie Decker argued that one unintended consequence of the sexual revolution had been that people now assumed that "everyone who doesn't celebrate sex or include it liberally in their lives is suffering from internalized oppression."

Decker wrote: "Until women's sexual agency includes acceptance of those who abstain, we'll continue to see it celebrated only if it manifests along normative lines to serve dudekind." The same might be said of men's sexual agency, or the agency of people whose gender identity doesn't neatly fit into the male/female binary.

I have trouble getting behind the idea of a "sex negative" future. As you and I know by now, sex is neither inherently good nor bad, neither intrinsically empowering nor oppressive. We don't need to bottle it up and restrict its use in order to keep ourselves safe, but nor do we need to worship it in order to set ourselves free. And just as attempts to reframe sex as a transcendent, emancipating force haven't made it free from cultural regulation, nor will problematizing it as a "negative" force eliminate the pressure to be sexual in particular, socially desirable ways.

Dismantling the Sex Myth means seeking a previously unarticulated middle ground, one that is neither blindly affirming nor formidably fearful. It means embracing sex not as a source of transcendence or transformation, but as sociologist Stevi Jackson puts it, "as part of the fabric of routine day-to-day social life," an act like any other.

At first glance, the Sex Myth appears to make our relationship with sex richer, infusing it with meaning, imagination, and pleasure. But in practice, our cultural investment in sex—and its status as an act unlike any other—limits the ways in which we allow ourselves and other people to be sexual. It is not just the content of our current media discourses and popular culture that produce our sexual malaise, but the special importance that we invest in sexuality itself.

Making sex the key to our selfhood renders it more emotionally powerful, particularly in the early stages of our sexual lives when we are still figuring out how we want to engage with sex and what role we want it to play in our lives and relationships. It positions sexuality as something that is fixed and unchangeable, rather than as something to be played with and explored.

As we grow a little older and more secure in ourselves and our experiences, this anxiety starts to dissolve. Anecdotal evidence, at least, suggests that there are fewer sexual neurotics at the age of thirty-five than there are at twenty. But as the example of Pamela Haag, the "marital misfit" in chapter 3, shows, sexual disquiet can raise its head at any time we feel uncertain or otherwise off balance in our lives.

We need an alternative way of speaking about sex, one that appreciates the role it plays in our lives without overhyping it as *the* most important thing. The next iteration of the sexual revolution needs to challenge the root of sexual power in our culture. And that will mean confronting the Sex Myth.

It is time to forge a new brand of sexual freedom, a freedom that incorporates the right *not* to do as much as the right to do. A freedom in which our sexual choices and histories are not burdened with such an excess of significance, in which there is no stigma attached to the gay, the transgendered, or the sexually audacious, but in which there is equally no stigma attached to the asexual, the vanilla, or the carnally prudent.

And then there is the ultimate freedom: the freedom in which these desires and experiences can be just one small part of the puzzle of who each of us is, instead of the load that defines us.

It is we who are responsible for creating the future. We are creating it already, in the things we say, do, and choose to believe. The Sex Myth may be powerful, but we have the ability to dismantle it. You just need to cast off the stories and the symbolism, and let yourself be.

Acknowledgments

Thank you to everyone who reached out to me to be interviewed for this book: for your honesty, your hospitality, and your perfect turns of phrase that alternate between incisive, heartfelt, and hilarious. After spending years mulling over your words, many of you feel like friends to me. And it was your enthusiasm for the ideas in this book that buoyed me when writing it was tough.

Thank you to Rebecca Friedman, for being the first person I met whose dreams for *The Sex Myth* were as big as my own. To Karyn Marcus, for seeing its potential, and to Sydney Tanigawa, whose expert guidance helped me to achieve that potential. To Brooke Warner, who put me through the wringer to create a "bulletproof" proposal, and to Kate Crawford, for teaching me to HTFU. Each one of you has made me a clearer thinker and a better writer.

Thank you to all the friends, family, and colleagues who gave feedback on early drafts, brainstormed ideas, listened to me vent, or provided support in some other way. Given that this book has spanned seven years from conception to completion, there are a lot of you! Thanks to Akshay Shanker, Anna Rose, Anna Samson, Anna Sussman, Autumn Whitefield-Madrano, Bethany Peterson, BJ Jackson, Cate Blake, Catharine Lumby, Charles McPhederan, Chloe Angyal, Elena Rossini, Elisha London, Emerald Fitzgerald, Eric Anderson,

215

Feona Attwood, Fiona Cox, Hannah Tattersall, Jeanne Ellard, Jordan Hewson, Judith Rowland, Julia Baird, Kate Fridkis, Kirsten Albrecht, Kylie Stott, Larissa Brown, Lauren Sams, Lena Chen, Lisa Wade, Matti Navellou, Monica Tan, Nicola Slawson, Nicole Comforto, Nina Funnell, Penny Crossley, Penny Sullivan, Rachel Rabbit White, Rosalind Gill, Samantha Rea, Sara Fagir, Sarah Christie, Sarah Jansen, Sarah Oakes, Sarah Tarca, Scarlett Harris, Symmie Swil, Tim Andrews, Tony Moore, Zach Alexopoulos, and more.

Thank you to the writers and thinkers whose work has influenced and inspired my own: Ariel Levy, Gail Hawkes, Gayle Rubin, Ken Plummer, John Gagnon, Leonore Tiefer, Michael Kimmel, Michel Foucault, Naomi Wolf, Paula England, Stevi Jackson, and William Simon. What I have written is only possible because of what you have written before me.

Thank you to my family for believing that "writer" was a viable career, and for being so unruffled by the topic I chose to write about.

And finally, thank you to Simon. Without your love, generosity, and support in all ways, this book might never have happened. To the ideas that we will pursue together for many years to come.

Questions for Readers

To discuss with your friends, students, or book club,
or to consider by yourself.

Do you believe that sex is "an act unlike any other" in your culture? Why/why not? Is this status deserved?

Which people, groups, or institutions do you think play the biggest role in perpetuating the Sex Myth?

In what ways have you been affected by the Sex Myth? In what ways have you perpetuated it?

How have you seen the Sex Myth play out among people you know?

What role does sex play in shaping how you feel about yourself?

Which sexual behaviors do you think are embraced as "normal" today? Which are treated as abnormal or problematic?

Have you ever thought you were abnormal when it comes to your sex life? When? Why? How did it make you feel?

How do the conversations we have about sex help to shape our ideas of how we should be sexually?

How does the Sex Myth play out differently for men and for women? For gay people and straight people? For people of different races, economic classes, or religious backgrounds?

How are our experiences of sex shaped by social and cultural factors? How are they shaped by biology?

How is sex connected to our ideas about what it means to be successful?

What is the relationship between the Sex Myth and consumer culture?

What are the differences in the ways that conservatives and progressives talk about sex? What are the similarities?

In chapter 1, Rachel argues that "sex doesn't need to be actively suppressed in order to be controlled." Do you agree? How is sex regulated today?

What actions can you take in your own life to combat the Sex Myth?

Notes

Epigraph

vii *"The most toxic formulas"*: Remarks by Junot Díaz at Word Up Community Bookshop, 2012.

vii *"My point is not that everything is bad"*: Michel Foucault, "On the Genealogy of Ethics: An Overview of Work in Progress," in Hubert L. Dreyfus and Paul Rabinow, *Michel Foucault: Beyond Structuralism and Hermeneutics*, 2nd ed. (Chicago: The University of Chicago Press, 1983), 231–32.

Introduction

3 *The second-century theologian*: Gail Hawkes, *Sex and Pleasure in Western Culture* (Cambridge, UK: Polity, 2004), 50.

4 *The average answer*: Michael Kimmel, *Guyland: The Perilous World in Which Boys Become Men* (New York: HarperCollins, 2008), 209.

4 *80 percent is the proportion*: Ibid.

4 *"The actual percentage"*: Ibid.

4 *assumed that other young people*: Kathleen Bogle, *Hooking Up: Sex, Dating, and Relationships on Campus* (New York: New York University Press, 2008), 88.

6 *broad-scale quantitative surveys*: Such as Paula England's Online College Social Life Survey, which commenced in 2005.

1 This Is Not What Liberation Looks Like

11 *"We go to a party"*: Bryan Elsley, "Tony," *Skins*, season 1, episode 1, aired January 25, 2007.

11 *"the most dangerous show for children"*: Brett Berk, "Is *Skins* Really 'the Most Dangerous Television Show for Children Ever'?" VanityFair.com, January 13, 2011. http://www.vanityfair.com/online/daily/2011/01

/is-skins-really-the-most-dangerous-television-show-for-children-ever. Accessed November 21, 2014.

12 *"[made] light of lying to parents"*: Morgan Jeffrey, "Parents' group slams MTV's *Skins*," DigitalSpy.co.uk, January 14, 2011. http://www.digitalspy .co.uk/ustv/s89/skins/news/a297965/parents-group-slams-mtvs-skins .html. Accessed November 21, 2014.

14 *Beyoncé*: "Girls of Maxim: Beyoncé Knowles," Maxim.com. http://www .maxim.com/girls-of-maxim/beyonce-knowles. Accessed October 3, 2014.

14 *Amanda Beard*: "Amanda Beard in FHM," SheKnows.com. http://www .sheknows.com/health-and-wellness/top-female-athletes-gallery/aman- da-beard/amanda-beard-in-fhm. Accessed October 3, 2014.

14 *would-be lawyers*: Veronika Belenkaya, "It's Juris-Imprudence," *Daily News* (NY), April 10, 2007. http://www.nydailynews.com/news/juris-impru dence-article-1.208599. Accessed October 3, 2014.

14 *"What we once regarded"*: Ariel Levy, *Female Chauvinist Pigs: Women and the Rise of Raunch Culture* (New York: Free Press, 2005), 5.

14 *On NPR*: Brenda Wilson, "Sex Without Intimacy: No Dating, No Relation- ships," NPR, June 8, 2009. http://www.npr.org/templates/story/story .php?storyId=105008712. Accessed October 3, 2014.

14 *"sexual economics"*: Mark Regnerus, "Sex Is Cheap: Why Young Men Have the Upper Hand in Bed, Even When They're Failing in Life," *Slate*, February 25, 2011. http://www.slate.com/articles/double_x/doublex/2011/02 /sex_is_cheap.html. Accessed October 3, 2014.

14 *"deeply disturbing . . . generation SEX"*: Olivia Lichtenstein, "How the face- less and immoral world of cyberspace has created a deeply disturbing . . . generation SEX," *Daily Mail*, January 28, 2009. http://www.dailymail.co.uk /femail/article-1129978/How-faceless-amoral-world-cyberspace-created- deeply-disturbing—generation-SEX.html. Accessed October 3, 2014.

14 *"like G-stringed baboons in oestrus"*: Fenella Souter, "Generation Sex," *Good Weekend, Sydney Morning Herald*, February 11, 2006.

14 *"They're here, they're mostly bare"*: Richard Jinman, "Generation Sex," *Syd- ney Morning Herald Spectrum*, October 8, 2005.

15 *"how casually their daughters were accustomed"*: F. Scott Fitzgerald, *This Side of Paradise* (Scribner: New York, 1920).

15 *"lead to sexual anarchy"*: Nancy Gibbs, "The Pill at 50: Sex, Freedom and Para- dox," *Time*, April 22, 2010. http://content.time.com/time/magazine/article/ 0,9171,1983884,00.html#ixzz2pM7f5NaO. Accessed October 3, 2014.

15 *"champagne parties for teenagers"*: "Morals: The Second Sexual Revolution," *Time*, January 24, 1964. http://content.time.com/time/subscriber/article/ 0,33009,875692-1,00.html. Accessed October 3, 2014.

15 *"one big Orgone Box"*: Ibid.

15 *28 percent of American adults had never married*: "The Fraying Knot," *Economist*, January 12, 2013. http://www.economist.com/news/united-states/21569433-americas-marriage-rate-falling-and-its-out-wedlock-birth-rate-soaring-fraying. Accessed October 3, 2014.

16 *"[m]any teenagers and young adults"*: Debra Jopson and Elicia Murray, "'Generation sex' as norms shift," *Age*, May 17, 2009. http://www.theage.com.au/national/generation-sex-as-norms-shift-20090516-b6tn.html. Accessed October 3, 2014.

17 *72 percent of college students*: Paula England, Online College Social Life Survey. Correspondence with author, November 21, 2014.

17 *40 percent of those surveyed*: Elizabeth A. Armstrong, Laura Hamilton, and Paula England, "Is hooking up bad for young women?" *Contexts*, Summer 2010. http://contexts.org/articles/summer-2010/is-hooking-up-bad-for-young-women/. Accessed October 3, 2014.

17 *Only one-third of students*: Ibid.

17 *one in five students*: Ibid.

21 *medical innovations such as penicillin*: Andrew M. Francis, "The wages of sin: how the discovery of penicillin reshaped modern sexuality," *Archives of Sexual Behavior* 42 (November 2013), 5–13.

21 *the Pill*: Gibbs, "The Pill at 50."

21 *"At the time"*: Linda Grant, *Sexing the Millennium: A Political History of the Sexual Revolution* (London: HarperCollins, 1993), 130.

22 *"What sustains our eagerness"*: Michel Foucault, *The History of Sexuality*, vol. 1, *The Will to Knowledge* (New York: Penguin, 1998), 7.

24 *British cultural theorist Mark Jancovich*: Mark Jancovich, "Naked Ambitions: Pornography, Taste, and the Problem of the Middlebrow," *Scope: An Online Journal of Film Studies* (June 2001). URL not available.

24 *developing their own set of ethics*: Erin Connell and Alan Hunt, "Sexual ideology and sexual physiology in the discourses of sex advice literature," *Canadian Journal of Human Sexuality* 15 (March 2006), 28.

25 *"respectability and restraint"*: Jancovich, "Naked Ambitions."

25 *"an ethic of fun"*: Ibid.

26 *"Young New Yorkers"*: Nate Freeman, "Sexless and the City: Web Warps Libidos of Coked-Up Careerists," *New York Observer*, March 15, 2011. http://observer.com/2011/03/sexless-and-the-city-web-warps-libidos-of-cokedup-careerists/. Accessed October 6, 2014.

26 *"day laborers in film"*: Ibid.

26 *"Sex is antithetical"*: Ibid.

26 *"It's harder to go home"*: Ibid.

31 *through heated discussions*: Foucault, *History of Sexuality*, 25.

31 *sexual attitudes in Finland*: Osmo Kontula and Elina Haavio Mannila, *Seksin Trendit Meilla Ja Naapureissa* (Helsinki: WSOY, 2001). Cited in Kaarina Nikunen, "Cosmo Girls Talk: Blurring Boundaries of Porn and Sex," in *Pornification: Sex and Sexuality in Media Culture*, ed. Susanna Paasonen, Kaarina Nikunen, and Laura Saarenmaa (Oxford: Berg, 2007), 73–85.

32 *"It used to be that sex was so secret"*: Leonore Tiefer, *Sex Is Not a Natural Act and Other Essays* (Boulder, CO: Westview, 2004), 102.

2 Sex: An Act Unlike Any Other

35 *"the most fun you can have without laughing"*: Martin Chilton, "Woody Allen's 30 best one-liners," Telegraph.co.uk. http://www.telegraph.co.uk /culture/culturepicturegalleries/10196567/Woody-Allens-30-best-one -liners.html?frame=2624765. Accessed October 13, 2014.

35 *"has become the Big Story"*: Ken Plummer, *Telling Sexual Stories: Power, Change and Social Worlds* (London: Routledge, 1995), 4.

38 *forced to publicly atone*: Hawkes, *Sex and Pleasure in Western Culture*, 64–65.

38 *dangers of unrestrained reproduction*: Connell and Hunt, "Sexual ideology and sexual physiology," 26.

38 *"to be brought under conscious control"*: Ibid.

38 *corrupting influence of pornography*: Katherine Marrone, "Sex: Excessive pornographic exposure can screw you in the sack," DailyEmerald.com, June 6, 2013. http://dailyemerald.com/2013/06/06/sex-the-dark-side -of-pornography/. Accessed October 29, 2014.

38 *"gender and sexuality disorders"*: Family Research Council, "Ten Arguments From Social Science Against Same-Sex Marriage." http://www.frc.org/get .cfm?i=if04g01. Accessed October 6, 2014.

39 *"allowed many people to flirt openly"*: Natasha Vargas-Cooper, "Hard Core," *Atlantic*, January/February 2011. http://www.theatlantic.com/magazine /archive/2011/01/hard-core/308327/. Accessed October 6, 2014.

39 *"first date doggy-style encounters"*: Ibid.

39 *"an unvarnished (albeit partial) view"*: Ibid.

40 *the most profound act of intimacy*: Stevi Jackson and Sue Scott, "Sexual antinomies in late modernity," *Sexualities* 7 (May 2004), 243.

40 *"low modality" images*: David Machin and Joanna Thornborrow, "Branding and discourse: The case of *Cosmopolitan*," *Discourse & Society* 14 (July 2003), 459.

40 *"not only melancholy but also a boring life"*: Ela Przybylo, "Crisis and safety: The asexual in sexusociety," *Sexualities* 14 (August 2011), 446.

40 *the desire for sex is weaker*: John H. Gagnon and William Simon, *Sexual Conduct: The Social Sources of Human Sexuality* (Chicago: Aldine Publishing Company, 1973), 17.

40 *"sex is a relatively docile beast"*: Ibid., 103–4.

40 *we have exaggerated its importance*: Ibid., 17.

41 *"It may well be"*: Foucault, *History of Sexuality*, 33.

41 *releasing a cocktail of happy hormones*: Natasha Turner, ND, "5 unexpected health benefits of orgasms," Chatelaine.com, December 31, 2014. http://www.chatelaine.com/health/sex-and-relationships/five-unexpected-health-benefits-of-orgasms/. Accessed January 19, 2015.

42 *"cavegirlbrains"*: Korin Miller, "Why Taken Guys Seem Sexier," Cosmopolitan.com, May 4, 2010. http://www.cosmopolitan.com/sex-love/relationship-advice/why-taken-guys-are-sexier. Accessed October 6, 2014.

42 *because they are more fertile*: Christopher Ryan, "On Older Men, Younger Women, and Moralistic Claptrap," *Psychology Today*, June 14, 2013. http://www.psychologytoday.com/blog/sex-dawn/201306/older-men-younger-women-and-moralistic-claptrap. Accessed October 15, 2014.

42 *"a 'scientific' account"*: Stevi Jackson and Amanda Rees, "The Appalling Appeal of Nature: The Popular Influence of Evolutionary Psychology as a Problem for Sociology," *Sociology* 41 (October 2007), 921.

42 *"in a world where many still take 'scientific'"*: Ibid.

42 *central to achieving mainstream legitimacy*: Lisa Leff, "Actress' claim to be gay by choice riles activists," Yahoo! News, January 27, 2012. http://news.yahoo.com/actress-claim-gay-choice-riles-activists-201717513.html. Accessed October 29, 2014.

43 *prenatal hormonal*: Jacques Balthazart, "Minireview: Hormones and human sexual orientation," *Endocrinology* 152 (August 2011), 2937–47.

43 *genetic factors*: Alvaro Rodriguez-Larralde and Irene Paradisi, "Influence of genetic factors on human sexual orientation," *Journal of Clinical Investigation* 50 (September 2009), 377–91.

43 *45.2 percent of men and 36.9 percent of women*: Christian C. Joyal, Amelie Cossette, and Vanessa Lapierre, "What Exactly Is an Unusual Sexual Fantasy?" *Journal of Sexual Medicine*, published online October 30, 2014.

43 *only 2.3 percent of Americans*: Jan Hoffman, "How Many Americans Are Lesbian, Gay or Bisexual?" *New York Times*, July 21, 2014. http://well.blogs.nytimes.com/2014/07/21/how-many-americans-are-lesbian-gay-or-bisexual/?_r=1. Accessed November 21, 2014.

43 *"highly intimate and erotic"*: Tiefer, *Sex Is Not a Natural Act*, 80.

44 *"dirty, dangerous, and disgusting"*: Ibid.

45 *a new interdependence and awareness of the self*: Gail Hawkes, *A Sociology of*

Sex and Sexuality (Philadelphia: Open University Press, 1996), 20.

45 *"in order to be really courteous"*: Norbert Elias, *The Civilizing Process*, vol. 1, *The History of Manners* (Oxford: Blackwell, 1982), 78.

46 *It was not uncommon to share a bed*: Hawkes, *A Sociology of Sex and Sexuality*, 22.

46 *sex began to take on a new importance*: Ibid., 23.

47 *our ability to create a cohesive story*: Anthony Giddens, *Modernity and Self-Identity: Self and Society in the Late Modern Age* (Cambridge: Polity Press, 1991), 54.

49 *not just through what we do*: David Machin and Joanna Thornborrow, "Lifestyle and the Depoliticisation of Agency: Sex as Power in Women's Magazines," *Social Semiotics* 16, no. 1 (2006), 173.

50 *consumer sex*: Hawkes, *A Sociology of Sex and Sexuality*, 117.

50 *"the girls you hook up with"*: Kimmel, *Guyland*, 206.

52 *"beautiful twenty-nine-year-old"*: Levy, *Female Chauvinist Pigs*, 188.

52 *"pretty fucking lame"*: Ibid., 187.

52 *"The thing about when you start accumulating sex"*: Ibid., 188.

52 *"constrain severely the powerful sexual impulse"*: Gagnon and Simon, *Sexual Conduct*, 17.

53 *valued at $33 billion*: Lucia Moses, "Millennial Guys Are Turning to Makeup: Survey Finds Masculinity Isn't What It Used to Be," AdWeek.com, June 19, 2013. http://www.adweek.com/news/advertising-branding/millennial-guys-are-turning-makeup-150313. Accessed October 7, 2014.

53 *France*: Molly Moore, "As Europe Grows Grayer, France Devises a Baby Boom," *Washington Post*, October 18, 2006. http://www.washingtonpost.com/wp-dyn/content/article/2006/10/17/AR2006101701652.html. Accessed October 7, 2014.

53 *Germany*: Suzanne Daley and Nicholas Kulish, "Germany Fights Population Drop," *New York Times*, August 13, 2013. http://www.nytimes.com/2013/08/14/world/europe/germany-fights-population-drop.html?pagewanted=all&_r=0. Accessed October 7, 2014.

53 *Estonia*: Marcus Walker, "In Estonia, paying women to have babies pays off," *Pittsburgh Post-Gazette*, October 20, 2006. http://www.post-gazette.com/life/lifestyle/2006/10/20/In-Estonia-paying-women-to-have-babies-pays-off/stories/200610200166. Accessed October 7, 2014.

53 *Australia*: Nick Parr, "The baby bonus failed to increase fertility, but we should still keep it," The Conversation, December 4, 2011. https://theconversation.com/the-baby-bonus-failed-to-increase-fertility-but-we-should-still-keep-it-4528. Accessed October 7, 2014.

3 Freaks and Geeks: The Trouble with "Normal"

60 *earliest known tales of premature ejaculation*: Otto F. Ehrentheil, "A case of premature ejaculation in Greek Mythology," *Journal of Sex Research* 10 (May 1974), 128.

60 *it wasn't until the 1960s*: Lawrence K. Hong, "Survival of the fastest: On the origin of premature ejaculation," *Journal of Sex Research* 20 (May 1984), 119.

60 *"seemed to regard the quick ejaculator"*: Ehrentheil, "A case of premature ejaculation," 129.

60 *75 percent of American men*: Alfred Kinsey, Wardell Pomeroy, and Clyde Martin, *Sexual Behavior in the Human Male* (Philadelphia: W. B. Saunders, 1948), 580.

60 *between 5.4 and 7.5 minutes*: Marcel D. Waldinger et al., "Ejaculation Disorders: A Multinational Population Survey of Intravaginal Ejaculation Latency Time," *Journal of Sexual Medicine* 2 (July 2005), 492–97.

60 *7.5 minutes*: Donald L. Patrick et al., "Premature Ejaculation: An Observational Study of Men and Their Partners," *Journal of Sexual Medicine* 2 (May 2005), 358–67.

61 *Nineteenth-century medical circles*: J. S. Haller, "Spermatic Economy: A 19th Century View of Male Impotence," *Southern Medical Journal* 82 (August 1989), 1010.

61 *"total and sometimes permanent impotence"*: Ibid.

61 *"Marriage alone is sufficient"*: Joseph W. Howe, "On the etiology, pathology, and treatment of spermatorrhoea and impotence," *Medical Record* 12 (October 27, 1877), 698.

65 *"Someone who is incapable"*: Dan Savage, "Asexuality for Beginners," *Stranger*, September 1, 2009. http://slog.thestranger.com/slog/archives/2009/09/01/asexuality-for-beginners. Accessed October 10, 2014.

66 *young Republicans were distancing themselves*: Susan Saulny, "Young in G.O.P. Erase the Lines on Social Issues," *New York Times*, August 8, 2012. http://www.nytimes.com/2012/08/09/us/politics/young-republicans-erase-lines-on-social-issues.html?hp&_r=0. Accessed October 10, 2014.

67 *"rationalize the well-being"*: Gayle Rubin, "Thinking Sex: Notes for a Radical Theory of the Politics of Sexuality," in *Pleasure and Danger: Exploring Female Sexuality*, ed. Carole S. Vance (London, UK: Routledge, 1984), 280.

68 *When the word "heterosexual"*: Jonathan Katz, *The Invention of Heterosexuality* (New York: Dutton, 1995), 12.

69 *68 percent of Americans born after 1981*: Pew Research Center, "Changing Attitudes on Gay Marriage," March 2014. http://features.pewforum.org/ same-sex-marriage-attitudes/slide2.php. Accessed October 10, 2014.

69 *"gay couples should have exactly the same rights"*: Populus, "Gay Couples' Rights Survey," March 2012. http://www.populus.co.uk/wp-content/ uploads/OmGay_Rights.pdf. Accessed October 10, 2014.

71 *"At one time, I genuinely considered 'looking gayer'"*: Ariana Barreto, "'Too Pretty to Be a Lesbian': A Conversation with a Bigot," *In Our Words*, January 5, 2012. https://inourwordsblog.wordpress.com/2012/01/05/ looking-gayer-a-conversation-with-a-bigot/. Accessed October 10, 2014.

74 *produced a YouTube video*: GetUp! Australia, "It's Time," YouTube, November 24, 2011. http://www.youtube.com/watch?v=_TBd-UCwVAY. Accessed October 10, 2014.

78 *four times more likely*: Jaime M. Grant, Lisa A. Mottet, and Justin Tannis, "Injustice at Every Turn: A Report of the National Transgender Discrimination Survey," 2011. http://endtransdiscrimination.org/PDFs/NTDS_ Exec_Summary.pdf. Accessed October 10, 2014.

78 *forty-seven US states*: "11 Facts About Gay Rights," DoSomething.org. http://www.dosomething.org/tipsandtools/11-facts-about-gay-rights. Accessed October 10, 2014.

79 *"small[est] differences in value"*: Rubin, "Thinking Sex," 279.

79 *"Only when I fell out of step"*: Pamela Haag, "My Sex-Drought Marriage," *Times Magazine*, December 17, 2011.

80 *"'Preferring not to' [have sex]"*: Ibid.

4 Hot, Horny, and In Control:
The Importance of Desire

86 *less than a quarter of men*: Anjani Chandra et al., "Sexual Behavior, Sexual Attraction, and Sexual Identity in the United States: Data from the 2006–2008 National Survey of Family Growth," *National Health Statistics Report* 36 (March 3, 2011). http://www.cdc.gov/nchs/data/nhsr/nhsr036.pdf. Accessed October 10, 2014.

87 *"the halo effect"*: Catherine Hakim, *Honey Money: The Power of Erotic Capital* (London: Allen Lane, 2011), 111.

87 *years of positive social reception*: Ibid., 111.

93 *"the rating and dating complex"*: Willard Waller, "The Rating and Dating Complex," *American Sociological Review* 2 (October 1937), 727–34.

93 *Dating only emerged in the 1920s*: Peter Ling, "Sex and the Automobile in the Jazz Age," *History Today* 39 (November 1989). http://www.history

today.com/peter-ling/sex-and-automobile-jazz-age. Accessed October 10, 2014.

93 *"dalliance relationship"*: Waller, "Rating and Dating Complex," 729.

93 *fearing that "going steady"*: Coronet Instructional Films, *Going Steady?*, 1951. http://archive.org/details/GoingSte1951. Accessed October 10, 2014.

94 *"[In dating] as nowhere else"*: Waller, "Rating and Dating Complex," 730.

95 *"Pretty is a set of skills"*: Emily Armstrong, "Pretty Is a Set of Skills," Jezebel, September 2, 2013. http://jezebel.com/pretty-is-a-set-of-skills-1202247029. Accessed October 10, 2014.

100 *"compulsory carelessness"*: Lisa Wade and Caroline Heldman, "Hooking Up and Opting Out: Negotiating Sex in the First Year of College," in *Sex for Life: From Virginity to Viagra, How Sex Changes Throughout Our Lives*, ed. Laura M. Carpenter and John DeLamater (New York: New York University Press, 2012), 128.

101 *she only had one or two sexual partners each year*: Mark Regnerus and Jeremy Uecker, *Premarital Sex in America: How Young Americans Meet, Mate, and Think About Marriage* (New York: Oxford University Press, 2011), 25.

103 *a means of deflecting from their own emotional needs*: Wendy Hollway, "Gender difference and the production of subjectivity," in *Changing the Subject: Psychology, Social Regulation and Subjectivity*, J. Henriques et al. (London: Methuen, 1984), 227–63. http://www.brown.uk.com/brownlibrary/WEN2.htm. Accessed October 10, 2014.

103 *"A sober hookup indicates [you are] serious"*: Wade and Heldman, "Hooking Up and Opting Out," 139.

106 *Research by American sociologists*: Elizabeth A. Armstrong, Paula England, and Alison C. K. Fogarty, "Orgasm in College Hookups and Relationships," in *Families as They Really Are*, ed. Barbara Risman (New York: Norton, 2009), 367.

106 *"Sex in relationships tends to be better"*: Ibid., 366.

5 Masculinity: Inside the Boys' Club

110 *a new breed of frat*: Eric Anderson, "Inclusive Masculinity in a Fraternal Setting," *Men and Masculinities* 10 (August 2008), 604–20.

110 *a more inclusive brand of masculinity*: Eric Anderson, "'Being Masculine Is Not About Who You Sleep With . . .': Heterosexual Athletes Contesting Masculinity and the One-time Rule of Homosexuality," *Sex Roles* 58 (2008), 106.

110 *fraternity men are three times more likely*: John D. Foubert, Johnathan T. Newberry, and Jerry L. Tatum, "Behavior differences seven months later:

Effects of a rape prevention program," *NASPA Journal* 44, no. 4 (2007), 728–49.

113 *the vagaries of popular culture*: Katie Roiphe, "Spanking Goes Mainstream," *Newsweek*, April 16, 2012. http://mag.newsweek.com/2012/04/15/working-women-s-fantasies.html. Accessed October 11, 2014.

113 *emotion*: Alexandra Simotas, "Female Sex Drive Linked to Emotions," *Houston Chronicle*, September 6, 2006. http://blog.chron.com/herhealth/2006/09/female-sex-drive-linked-to-emotions/. Accessed October 11, 2014.

113 *how much housework they've done*: Adele Horin, "Men who share the load clean up in the bedroom," *Sydney Morning Herald*, January 8, 2010. http://www.smh.com.au/lifestyle/life/men-who-share-the-load-clean-up-in-the-bedroom-20100106-lude.html. Accessed October 11, 2014.

114 *"has no memory and no conscience"*: Vic Kaplan (Producer) and Bruce Gowers (Director), *Robin Williams: Live at the Met*, Mr. Happy Productions, August 9, 1986.

114 *by having sex they don't want*: Jennie Curtin, "What Makes a Happy Marriage? Sex!" *Sydney Morning Herald*, February 28, 2009. http://www.smh.com.au/articles/2009/02/27/1235237920126.html. Accessed October 11, 2014.

114 *being more sexually inventive*: Panteá Farvid and Virginia Braun, " 'Most of us guys are raring to go anytime, anyplace, anywhere': Male and female sexuality in *Cleo* and *Cosmo*," *Sex Roles* 55 (September 2006), 301.

114 *changing their clothes*: Raymond Kwan, "Don't Dress Like a Slut: Toronto Cop," *Excalibur*, April 23, 2011. http://www.excal.on.ca/news/dont-dress-like-a-slut-toronto-cop/. Accessed October 11, 2014.

114 *to avoid unwanted sexual advances*: Emily Yoffe, "College Women: Stop Getting Drunk," *Slate*, October 15, 2013. http://www.slate.com/articles/double_x/doublex/2013/10/sexual_assault_and_drinking_teach_women_the_connection.html. Accessed October 11, 2014.

115 *A 2004 study*: Deborah L. Tolman, Renee Spencer, Tricia Harmon, Myra Rosen-Reynoso, and Meg Striepe, "Getting Close, Staying Cool: Early Adolescent Boys' Experiences with Romantic Relationships," in *Adolescent Boys: Exploring Diverse Cultures of Boyhood*, ed. Niobe Way and Judy Chu (New York: New York University Press, 2004), 235–55.

116 *"I don't know what it was"*: Ibid., 247–48.

116 *"it was kind of a rip-off"*: Ibid., 246.

116 *A 2010 survey*: National Campaign to Prevent Teen and Unplanned Pregnancy, *That's What He Said: What Guys Think About Sex, Love, Contraception and Relationships*, January 2010. https://thenationalcampaign.org/resource/thats-what-he-said. Accessed October 11, 2014.

116 *pressure from other boys*: Shelley Walker, "Sexting: Young Women's and Men's Views on Its Nature and Origins," *Journal of Adolescent Health* 52 (June 2013), 697–701.

116 *more likely than girls to share*: Melissa Fleschler Peskin et al., "Prevalence and Patterns of Sexting Among Ethnic Minority Urban High School Students," *Cyberpsychology, Behavior, and Social Networking* 16 (June 2013), 456.

118 *young women so much expected*: Elizabeth M. Morgan and Eileen L. Zurbriggen, "Wanting sex and wanting to wait: Young adults' accounts of sexual messages from first significant dating partners," *Feminism & Psychology* 17 (November 2007), 515–41.

118 *"I was really surprised"*: Ibid., 524.

118 *"He didn't want to force anything"*: Ibid., 526.

118 *"[Guys] think that they have to ask"*: Ibid., 523.

118 *Just over half of the female college students*: Ibid., 524 and 525.

119 *"Most of us guys are raring to go anytime"*: Farvid and Braun, "'Most of us guys,'" 301.

119 *"[B]eing male, I find that sometimes your groin can take over"*: Ibid.

119 *depicting their readers as insatiable*: Laramie D. Taylor, "All for Him: Articles About Sex in American Lad Magazines," *Sex Roles* 52 (February 2005), 153–63.

120 *"an alpha male idiot"*: "Bro," UrbanDictionary.com. http://www.urban dictionary.com/define.php?term=bro. Accessed October 11, 2014.

120 *the top 2 percent of men*: Kathleen Mullan Harris et al., *The National Longitudinal Study of Adolescent to Adult Health*, referenced in *Premarital Sex in America: How Young Americans Meet, Mate, and Think About Marrying*, by Mark Regnerus and Jeremy Uecker (New York: Oxford University Press, 2011), 25.

122 *"girl hunt"*: David Grazian, "The Girl Hunt: Urban Nightlife and the Performance of Masculinity as Collective Activity," *Symbolic Interaction* 30 (Spring 2007), 221–43.

125 *a 2008 paper*: Michael Flood, "Men, Sex and Homosociality: How Bonds Between Men Shape Their Sexual Relations with Women," *Men and Masculinities* 10 (April 2008), 339–59.

126 *found guilty of using Skype*: Michael Inman, "Guilty Verdict in ADFA Skype Sex Case," *Canberra Times*, August 23, 2013. http://www.canberratimes .com.au/act-news/guilty-verdict-in-adfa-skype-sex-case-20130828-2sq7v .html?rand=1382489144939. Accessed October 11, 2014.

127 *"The fact is that too many young male athletes"*: Dave Zirin, "How Jock Culture Supports Rape Culture, from Maryville to Steubenville," *Nation*,

October 25, 2013. http://www.thenation.com/blog/176846/how-jock-culture-supports-rape-culture-maryville-steubenville#. Accessed October 11, 2014.

127 *two reports on "lad culture"*: NUS, *That's What She Said: Women Students' Experiences of "Lad Culture" in Higher Education* (London: NUS, 2013).

127 *one in five American women*: Roni Caryn Rabin, "Nearly 1 in 5 Women in US Survey Say They Have Been Sexually Assaulted," *New York Times*, December 14, 2011. http://www.nytimes.com/2011/12/15/health/nearly-1-in-5-women-in-us-survey-report-sexual-assault.html. Accessed October 11, 2014.

127 *the vast majority of offenses*: David Lisak and Paul M. Miller, "Repeat Rape and Multiple Offending Among Undetected Rapists," *Violence and Victims* 17 (February 2002), 73–84.

127 *only a quarter of guys*: Andrew P. Smiler, *Challenging Casanova: Beyond the Stereotype of the Promiscuous Young Male* (San Francisco: Jossey-Bass, 2013), 65.

127 *"being funny, nice, outgoing"*: Ibid., 58.

127 *only one-fifth of the students*: Grazian, "Girl Hunt," 226.

130 *whether they were the penetrator or the penetrated*: Michel Foucault, *The History of Sexuality: The Use of Pleasure* (London: Penguin, 1998).

130 *men walk down the streets holding hands*: Alecia Simmonds, "When did it stop being OK for men to hold hands?" *Daily Life*, March 13, 2013. http://www.dailylife.com.au/news-and-views/dl-opinion/when-did-it-stop-being-ok-for-men-to-hold-hands-20130313-2g098.html. Accessed October 11, 2014.

131 *"flamboyantly feminine"*: John Stossel and Gena Binkley, "Gay Stereotypes: Are They True?" ABC News, September 15, 2006. http://abcnews.go.com/2020/story?id=2449185. Accessed October 11, 2014.

131 *"homohysteria"*: Eric Anderson, *Inclusive Masculinity: The Changing Nature of Masculinities* (London: Routledge, 2009).

132 *"They have worked hard for those muscles"*: Ibid., 85.

132 *"one-time rule of homosexuality"*: Anderson, "'Being Masculine,'" 102–15.

132 *89 percent of young British men*: Eric Anderson, Adi Adams, and Ian Rivers, "'I Kiss Them Because I Love Them': The Emergence of Heterosexual Men Kissing in British Institutes of Education," *Archives of Sexual Behavior* 41 (April 2012), 421–30.

133 *"The only way you can kiss another guy"*: Clifton Evers, interview with author, November 11, 2010.

135 *"While it is not necessarily acceptable to be gay"*: C. J. Pascoe, "'Dude, You're

a Fag': Adolescent Masculinity and the Fag Discourse," *Sexualities* 8 (July 2005), 338.

136 *"The choice of a man as a sexual object"*: Raewyn Connell, "A Very Straight Gay: Masculinity, Homosexual Experience and the Dynamics of Gender," *American Sociological Review* 57 (December 1992), 746.

137 *men actually have a narrower spectrum*: Todd G. Morrison, Travis A. Ryan, Lisa Fox, Daragh T. McDermott, and Melanie A. Morrison, "Canadian university students' perceptions of the practices that constitute 'normal' sexuality for men and women," *Canadian Journal of Human Sexuality* 17, no. 4 (2008), 161–71.

138 *"more like girls"*: Amy T. Schalet, "Caring, Romantic, American Boys," *New York Times*, April 6, 2012. http://www.nytimes.com/2012/04/07/opinion/caring-romantic-american-boys.html. Accessed October 11, 2014.

138 *data from the Centers for Disease Control*: G. Martinez, C. E. Copen, and J. C. Abma, "Teenagers in the United States: Sexual activity, contraceptive use, and childbearing, 2006–2010 National Survey of Family Growth," *Vital and Health Statistics* 23, no. 31 (October 2011). http://www.cdc.gov/nchs/data/series/sr_23/sr23_031.pdf. Accessed October 11, 2014.

6 Femininity: The Madonna/Gaga Complex

140 *"one is not born, but rather becomes, a woman"*: Simone de Beauvoir, *The Second Sex* (New York: Vintage, 1989), 267.

140 *the inevitably heterosexual happily-ever-afters*: Karin Martin and Emily Kazyak, "Hetero-romantic love and heterosexiness in children's G-rated films," *Gender & Society* 23 (June 2009), 315–36.

143 *two Illinois sociologists*: Kristen Myers and Laura Raymond, "Elementary School Girls and Heteronormativity: The Girl Project," *Gender & Society* 24 (April 2010), 167–88.

143 *"I want to talk about crushes"*: Ibid., 174.

143 *"If a boy really likes you"*: Ibid.

144 *A 2009 study*: Martin and Kazyak, "Hetero-romantic love," 315–36.

144 *"magical," "exceptional," and "transformative"*: Ibid., 323.

144 *"The primary account of heterosexuality"*: Ibid., 322.

146 *make them more licentious*: Hawkes, *Sex and Pleasure in Western Culture*, 32.

146 *up to fifty times per day*: Mary Jane Sherfey, "The evolution and nature of female sexuality in relation to psychoanalytic theory," *Journal of the American Psychoanalytic Association* 14 (January 1966), 28–128.

146 *repositioned as enforcers of virtue*: Carol Groneman, "Nymphomania: The Historical Construction of Female Sexuality," *Signs* 19 (1994), 345.

146 *"nymphomaniac"*: Ibid., 337–67.

146 *"the virginity movement"*: Jessica Valenti, *The Purity Myth: How America's Obsession with Virginity Is Hurting Young Women* (Berkeley: Seal Press, 2009), 23.

151 *like many lapsed abstinence pledgers*: Janet Elise Rosenbaum, "Patient Teenagers? A Comparison of the Sexual Behavior of Virginity Pledgers and Matched Nonpledgers," *Pediatrics* 123 (January 2009), 110–20. The study found that "unmarried pledgers were less likely to report using birth control and condoms in the last year, and birth control at last sex."

151 *"The sex organ of a man is simple"*: de Beauvoir, *The Second Sex*, 386.

152 *doing sex and relationships on men's terms*: Regnerus, "Sex Is Cheap," February 25, 2011.

152 *"fragile" and "easily distracted"*: Curtin, "What Makes a Happy Marriage? Sex!" February 28, 2009.

152 *"Was there anyone more starved than I"*: Nancy Friday, *The Power of Beauty* (London: Hutchinson, 1996), 203.

152 *"Until [a girl] discovers that her own hand"*: Ibid.

152 *"We can start your training tonight"*: E. L. James, *Fifty Shades of Grey* (London: Arrow Books, 2012), 110.

152 *"woken and tamed by him"*: Ibid., 288.

153 *"If boys and men tend to take in messages"*: Daniel Bergner, "Unexcited? There May Be a Pill for That," *New York Times*, May 22, 2013. http://www.nytimes.com/2013/05/26/magazine/unexcited-there-may-be-a-pill-for-that.html?pagewanted=1&_r=3&ref=magazine. Accessed October 13, 2014.

156 *"embodies ambition, passion, and a confidence"*: "Life Planner: Fun Fearless Female." http://www.cosmopolitan.co.za/career-money/AwesomeWomen/Archive. Accessed August 1, 2014.

158 *"an engine of female progress"*: Hanna Rosin, "Boys on the Side," *Atlantic*, August 22, 2012. http://www.theatlantic.com/magazine/archive/2012/09/boys-on-the-side/309062/. Accessed October 13, 2014.

158 *consciously delaying committed relationships*: Laura Hamilton and Elizabeth A. Armstrong, "Gendered Sexuality in Young Adulthood: Double Binds and Flawed Options," *Gender & Sexuality* 23 (October 2009), 589–616.

158 *"To put it crudely"*: Rosin, "Boys on the Side."

159 *"There's this hypothetical"*: Kate Taylor, "Sex on Campus: She Can Play That Game Too," *New York Times*, July 12, 2013. http://www.nytimes.com/2013/07/14/fashion/sex-on-campus-she-can-play-that-game-too.html. Accessed October 13, 2014.

159 *"I definitely wouldn't say I've regretted"*: Ibid.

159 *"Guys were texting and calling me"*: Rosin, "Boys on the Side."

159 *today women are viewed as sexual* subjects: Rosalind Gill, "From sexual objectification to sexual subjectification: The resexualisation of women's bodies in the media," *Feminist Media Studies* 3 (2003), 100–106.

160 *"subjectification"*: Ibid.

160 *"the secondary empowerment"*: Kaye Mitchell, "Raunch vs prude: contemporary sex blogs and erotic memoirs by women," *Psychology and Sexuality* 3 (January 2012), 21.

160 *"Let's be honest"*: Brooke Magnanti, *The Intimate Adventures of a London Call Girl* (London: Orion, 2005), 94.

161 *"has for women increasingly become"*: Ibid., 23.

161 *"Where's the pudgy-faced liquid semen and sadness?"*: Lena Dunham and Jennifer Konner, "On All Fours," *Girls*, season 2, episode 9, aired March 10, 2013.

162 *a bigger aspirational "lifestyle" package*: David Machin and Joanna Thornborrow, "Branding and Discourse," 451–71.

163 *released a commercial*: Harvey Nichols, "A Harvey Nichols Christmas 2011—Ever Faced the Walk of Shame?" YouTube, December 3, 2011. http://www.youtube.com/watch?v=kwxTf7NGVXg&feature=player _embedded. Accessed October 13, 2014.

163 *"Avoid the walk of shame this season"*: Ibid.

163 *A 2014 study*: Elizabeth A. Armstrong and Laura T. Hamilton, "'Good Girls': Gender, Social Class, and Slut Discourse on Campus," *Social Psychology Quarterly* 77 (June 2014), 100–122.

163 *"failure to successfully perform"*: Ibid., 112.

164 *"She has some issues"*: Ibid., 113.

7 Use It or Lose It: The Performance Premium

167 *"thrusts per minute"*: Spreadsheets app website, http://spreadsheetsapp .com/. Accessed October 15, 2014.

167 *Users can earn points*: Ibid.

168 *more than eight hundred sex acts*: Kindu app website, http://www.kindu .us/. Accessed October 15, 2014.

168 *sends users push notifications*: Julie Zeilinger, "Kahnoodle App Makes Reigniting Your Relationship into a Game," *Huffington Post*, August 9, 2013. http://www.huffingtonpost.com/2013/08/09/kahnoodle-app-makes -reigniting-your-relationship-into-a-game_n_3732916.html. Accessed October 15, 2014.

168 *the ability to watch themselves having sex*: Alex Hern, "How to make sex 'more awesome' using Google Glass," *Guardian*, January 21, 2014. http:// www.theguardian.com/technology/2014/jan/21/how-to-make-sex -more-awesome-using-google-glass. Accessed October 15, 2014.

168 *"possibly the least sexy app we've ever heard of"*: Huffington Post UK, "Sex App That Measures Your Performance in a Spreadsheet Is Surely the Least Sexiest Thing?" *Huffington Post*, August 13, 2013. http://www.huffington post.co.uk/2013/08/13/sex-app-performance-spreadsheet_n_3748999 .html. Accessed October 15, 2014.

168 *"if you need an app to figure this out"*: Jessica Roy, " 'Spreadsheets' App Measures How Loud You Moan to Determine If You're Good at Sex," *Betabeat*, August 12, 2013.http://betabeat.com/2013/08/spreadsheets-app-measures-how-loud-you-moan-to-determine-if-youre-good-at-sex/. Accessed October 15, 2014.

169 *"[T]o be bad at sex"*: Jackson and Scott, "Sexual antinomies," 241.

169 *young men who pop a Viagra*: S. Anderson, "Meet His New Saturday Night Wingman," *Cleo*, June 2008, 64–65.

169 *when they believed their partners were*: Gayle Brewer and Colin A. Hendrie, "Evidence to Suggest that Copulatory Vocalizations in Women Are Not a Reflexive Consequence of Orgasm," *Archives of Sexual Behavior* 40 (June 2010), 559–64.

169 *28 percent of sexually active men*: Charlene L. Muehlenhard and Sheena K. Shippee, "Men's and Women's Reports of Pretending Orgasm," *Journal of Sex Research* 47, no. 6 (2010), 552–67.

170 *"reap the blissful benefits"*: Jane Katz, "Yes, You Have a G-Spot," Cosmopolitan .com, May 21, 2009. http://www.cosmopolitan.com/sex-love/advice/ a2923/yes-you-have-a-g-spot-0409/. Accessed January 19, 2015.

170 *if you want sex with the same person*: Natasha Burton, "Keep 'em begging for more," *Maxim*, March 2013, 78.

170 *fills an important gap*: Carmel Siebold, "Factors Influencing Young Women's Sexual and Reproductive Health," *Contemporary Nurse* 37 (February 2011), 124–36.

171 *"the easiest—and most fun—way"*: Em and Lo, "The Summer Sex Plan," *Glamour* (UK), June 2012, 82–86.

171 *"less stress, more intimacy, improved mood"*: Ibid.

171 *"Using a plan is great"*: Ibid.

172 *"power, endurance, and control"*: Alex Harris, "Taking a Stand," *Men's Health*, March 2013, 125.

172 *"summer sex bucket list"*: Julia Naughton, "The Summer (Sex) Bucket List," *Cosmopolitan* (Australia), December 2012, 31.

172 *"if you're going to be having lots of sex"*: Ibid.

172 *"how to close the deal with beautiful women"*: Christian Hudson, Felix Economakis, and Daniel Sloss, "How to Close the Deal with Beautiful Women," *FHM* (UK), March 2013, 84–91.

172 *"taste culture"*: Kaarina Nikunen, "Cosmo girls talk: Blurring boundaries of porn and sex," in *Pornification: Sex and Sexuality in Media Culture*, ed. Susanna Paasonen, Kaarina Nikunen, and Laura Saarenmaa (Oxford: Berg, 2007), 73–85.

173 *"good, giving, and game"*: "GGG," UrbanDictionary.com. http://www.urbandictionary.com/define.php?term=GGG. Accessed October 15, 2014.

173 *"Instead of playing it safe and boring"*: Burton, "Keep 'em begging."

173 *"mix it up a bit and be adventurous"*: "Confessions . . ." *Zoo Weekly*, July 13, 2009, 79.

174 *"Tender sex can be intense"*: Siski Green, "You are 5 questions away from great sex," *Glamour* (UK), March 2013, 92–97.

174 *A 2012 study*: Tricia J. Burke and Valerie J. Young, "Sexual Transformations and Intimate Behaviors in Romantic Relationships," *Journal of Sex Research* 49, no. 5 (2012), 454–63.

174 *"a byword for 'sexually pedestrian'"*: Catherine Scott, "Thinking Kink: Is Vanilla Sex Boring? Who Gets to Decide?" *Bitch*, July 16, 2012. http://bitchmagazine.org/post/thinking-kink-vanilla-sex-bdsm-feminist-magazine-sexuality. Accessed October 15, 2014.

174 *an early episode of the sitcom* Friends: Jeffrey Astrof and Mike Sikowitz, "The One with the Blackout," *Friends*, season 1, episode 7, aired November 3, 1994.

174 *"the foot of the bed"*: Ibid.

175 *"I just never had a relationship"*: Ibid.

175 *"And you didn't marry him because . . . ?"*: Ibid.

175 *"It just seems a little wild"*: Shana Goldberg-Meehan and Scott Silveri, "The One with Rachel's Big Kiss," *Friends*, season 7, episode 20, aired April 26, 2001.

177 *"personal pleasure hunt"*: Anna Davies, "My Summer of Try-It-All Sex," *Glamour* (UK), April 2013, 79–86.

177 *"connection to climax"*: Ibid.

177 *"When I thought about what had gone on"*: Ibid.

178 *"I realized I'd never have wanted to do it"*: Tracey Cox, "What happens when you act out your sex fantasies?" *Cosmopolitan* (UK), May 2013, 194–98.

178 *"Fantasies about you and your partner"*: Ibid.

180 *"Sometimes your vagina dies"*: Jenni Avins, "Olivia Wilde Said a Great Many Things About Her Vagina Last Night," *Vulture*, October 9, 2012. http://

www.vulture.com/2012/10/olivia-wilde-has-a-lot-to-say-about-her
-vagina.html. Accessed October 15, 2014.

181 *less than ten times in the past twelve months*: Kathleen Deveny, "No Sex,
Please, We're Married," *Newsweek*, June 30, 2003.

181 *"lesbian bed death"*: Philip Blumstein and Pepper Schwartz, *American Couples: Money, Work, Sex* (New York: William Morrow & Co, 1983).

185 *"response anxiety"*: Tiefer, *Sex Is Not a Natural Act*, 101–2.

186 *boost your immune system*: Alan Farnham, "Is Sex Necessary?" *Forbes*, October 8, 2003. http://www.forbes.com/2003/10/08/cz_af_1008health
.html. Accessed October 15, 2014.

186 *releasing endorphins into the brain*: Vanessa Luis, "Emotional and Mental
Health Benefits of Sex," Health Me Up, July 15, 2014. http://healthmeup
.com/news-healthy-living/emotional-and-mental-health-benefits-of
-sex/29015. Accessed October 15, 2014.

186 *a satisfactory orgasm*: Christopher Turner, "Wilhelm Reich: The Man Who
Invented Free Love," *Guardian*, July 9, 2011. http://www.theguardian.com/
books/2011/jul/08/wilhelm-reich-free-love-orgasmatron. Accessed October 15, 2014.

186 *"the Sex-Crazy Nympho Dream Girl"*: Clarisse Thorn, "The Myth of the
Sex-Crazy Nympho Dream Girl," The Good Men Project, May 20, 2011.
http://goodmenproject.com/sex-relationships/myth-sex-crazy-nympho-
dream-girl/. Accessed October 15, 2014.

186 *"Before I had any actual sexual partners"*: Ibid.

186 *"I just got rewarded for it so much"*: Clarisse Thorn, interview with author,
February 12, 2014.

187 *"ultimate meeting with our true (sexual) selves"*: Annie Potts, *The Science/Fiction of Sex: Feminist Deconstruction and the Vocabularies of Heterosex* (Sussex: Routledge, 2002), 76.

187 *to be alienated from an essential aspect of yourself*: Ibid., 80.

188 *"infantile" clitoral*: Faye Flam, "Female orgasm: From Freud to Lloyd,"
Seattle Times, October 26, 2005. http://seattletimes.com/html
/living/2002583270_carnalknowledge26.html. Accessed October 15,
2014.

188 *75 percent of women*: Michael Castleman, "The Most Important Sexual Statistic," *Psychology Today*, March 16, 2009. http://www.psychologytoday
.com/blog/all-about-sex/200903/the-most-important-sexual-statistic.
Accessed October 15, 2014.

189 *"Not only am I not normal"*: Astrea Media/Chicken and Egg Pictures, *Orgasm Inc.*, directed by Elizabeth Canner, 2011.

189 *"That's wonderful"*: Ibid.

190 *"generate healthier and more functional tissue"*: Lauren Streicher, "Pain for Pleasure? The O-Shot," Oz Blog, March 19, 2014. http://blog.doctoroz .com/oz-experts/pain-for-pleasure-the-o-shot. Accessed October 15, 2014.

190 *"superhuman erection"*: Manuel Hung, "Daddy's Little Helpers," *Next Magazine*, September 7, 2012. http://www.nextmagazine.com/content /daddy's-little-helpers. Accessed October 15, 2014.

190 *"corporate sponsored"*: Ray Moynihan, "The Making of a Disease: Female Sexual Dysfunction," *British Medical Journal* 326 (January 4, 2003), 45–47.

191 *any sort of sexual difficulty for two months or more*: Ibid., 46.

191 *"perfectly normal"*: Ibid.

8 You Aren't What You Do: Why We've Got It Wrong

196 *The British sociologist Anthony Giddens*: Giddens, *Modernity and Self-Identity*, 54.

197 *"integrity of the self"*: Ibid., 65.

198 *the more important a belief or ideal was*: G. M. Breakwell and L. J. Millward, "Sexual Self-Concept and Sexual Risk-Taking," *Journal of Adolescence* 20 (February 1997), 31.

199 *the panopticon*: Michel Foucault, *Discipline and Punish: The Birth of the Prison* (New York: Vintage, 1995).

199 *a tool not of liberation but of regulation and control*: Michel Foucault, Bob Gallagher, and Alexander Wilson, "Sex, power, and the politics of identity," in *Michel Foucault: Ethics, Subjectivity and Truth*, vol. 1, ed. Paul Rabinow (New York: The New Press, 1994).

200 *"If the perennial question [people] ask"*: Ibid., 166.

201 *for the crime of "looking gay"*: Faith Karimi, "Cameroon court acquits 2 men imprisoned for 'looking gay,' " CNN, January 10, 2013. http://edition.cnn .com/2013/01/09/world/africa/cameroon-gay-men-freed. Accessed October 28, 2014.

201 *illegal in seventy-eight countries*: "78 countries where homosexuality is illegal," http://76crimes.com/76-countries-where-homosexuality-is-illegal/. Accessed October 28, 2014.

201 *four times as likely to attempt suicide*: The Trevor Project, "Suicide Prevention Resources: Facts About Suicide," http://www.thetrevorproject.org/ pages/facts-about-suicide. Accessed January 19, 2015.

201 *living with daily discrimination and prejudice*: National Action Alliance for Suicide Prevention, "National Action Alliance for Suicide Prevention Tackles LGBT Suicide," http://actionallianceforsuicideprevention.blogspot

.com/2012/04/national-action-alliance-for-suicide.html. Accessed January 19, 2015.

201   *one in three women worldwide*: World Health Organization, "Violence against women," fact sheet no. 239. http://www.who.int/mediacentre/factsheets/fs239/en/. Accessed October 28, 2014.

201   *one in five women has been raped*: National Center for Injury Prevention and Control, Division of Violence Prevention, "Sexual Violence: Facts at a Glance," 2012. http://www.cdc.gov/ViolencePrevention/pdf/SV-Data-Sheet-a.pdf. Accessed October 28, 2014.

201   *hundreds of thousands of women sexually assaulted*: Outreach Programme on the Rwanda Genocide and the United Nations, "Background Information on Sexual Violence Used as a Tool of War." http://www.un.org/en/preventgenocide/rwanda/about/bgsexualviolence.shtml. Accessed October 28, 2014.

202   *North Dakota*: John Eligon and Erik Eckholm, "New Laws Ban Most Abortions in North Dakota," *New York Times*, March 26, 2013. http://www.nytimes.com/2013/03/27/us/north-dakota-governor-signs-strict-abortion-limits.html?pagewanted=all. Accessed October 28, 2014.

202   *Texas*: Lindsay Beyerstein, "Texas anti-abortion law forces women to make tough choices," Al Jazeera America, January 5, 2014. http://america.aljazeera.com/articles/2014/1/5/in-texas-abortionclinicsclose.html. Accessed October 28, 2014.

202   *Ohio*: Tara Culp-Ressler, "Ohio's New Abortion Ban Forces Women to Continue Doomed Pregnancies Against Their Doctors' Wishes," ThinkProgress, February 11, 2014. http://thinkprogress.org/health/2014/02/11/3277111/ohio-abortion-doctors-ban/. Accessed October 28, 2014.

202   *Iowa*: Tara Culp-Ressler, "Iowa Governor Must Personally Decide Whether Each Poor Woman on Medicaid Deserves Abortion Coverage," ThinkProgress, June 25, 2013. http://thinkprogress.org/health/2013/06/25/2210571/iowa-governor-medicaid-abortion-coverage/. Accessed October 28, 2014.

202   *Arkansas*: Joseph Serna, "Federal judge rules Arkansas abortion law unconstitutional," *Los Angeles Times*, March 14, 2014. http://articles.latimes.com/2014/mar/14/nation/la-na-nn-arkansas-abortion-law-unconstitutional-20140314. Accessed October 28, 2014.

202   *Oklahoma*: Tara Culp-Ressler, "Oklahoma Considers Enacting Texas-Style Abortion Restrictions," ThinkProgress, February 12, 2014. http://thinkprogress.org/health/2014/02/12/3281841/oklahoma-texas-abortion-restrictions/. Accessed October 28, 2014.

202   *Arizona*: Alia Beard Rau, "Appeals Court to continue blocking Arizona abortion law," AZCentral, June 4, 2014. http://www.azcentral.com/story/

news/arizona/politics/2014/06/03/arizona-abortion-law-blocked -appeals-court/9917647/. Accessed October 28, 2014.

202 *Kansas*: Kevin Murphy, "Kansas set to enact life-starts-'at fertilization' abortion law," Reuters, April 6, 2013. http://www.reuters.com/article/ 2013/04/06/us-usa-kansas-abortion-idUSBRE93501220130406. Accessed October 28, 2014.

202 *Virginia*: Dahlia Lithwick, "Virginia's Proposed Ultrasound Law Is an Abomination," *Slate*, February 16, 2012. http://www.slate.com/articles/ double_x/doublex/2012/02/virginia_ultrasound_law_women_who _want_an_abortion_will_be_forcibly_penetrated_for_no_medical _reason.html. Accessed October 28, 2014.

202 *231 restrictions on abortion*: Guttmacher Institute, "In Just the Last Four Years, States Have Enacted 231 Abortion Restrictions," January 5, 2015. http://www.guttmacher.org/media/inthenews/2015/01/05/index.html. Accessed January 19, 2015.

204 *"some people deserve to be peed on"*: Alexandria Goddard, "Some people deserve to be peed on #whoareyou," Prinniefied.com, August 28, 2012. http://prinniefied.com/wp/some-people-deserve-to-be-peed-on-whoare you-2/. Accessed October 28, 2014.

204 *"you don't sleep through"*: Kristen Gwynne, "How Anonymous Hacking Exposed Steubenville Rape Case," Alternet.org, January 4, 2013. http:// www.alternet.org/how-anonymous-hacking-exposed-steubenville-high -school-rape-case. Accessed October 28, 2014.

204 *"pervertedminds"*: Brian Tashman, "E.W. Jackson: Gays and Lesbians are 'Very Sick People Psychologically, Mentally and Emotionally,'" Right Wing Watch, October 25, 2012. http://www.rightwingwatch.org/content/jackson- gays-lesbians-very-sick-people-psychologically-mentally-emotionally. Accessed October 28, 2014.

204 *"Homosexuality is a horrible sin"*: Ibid.

205 *"sex is like fire"*: Anthony Lane, "Sex, lies and duct tape: Science and morality make for strange bedfellows in D-11," *Colorado Springs Independent*, April 8, 2010. http://www.csindy.com/coloradosprings/sex-lies-and -duct-tape-science-and-morality-make-for-strange-bedfellows-in-d-11/ Content?oid=1672302. Accessed October 28, 2014.

205 *two pieces of duct tape*: Ibid.

Conclusion: Beyond the Sex Myth

209 *"getting laid is mostly a matter of luck"*: Tracy Moore, "Happiness Is Not Just Getting Laid, It's Getting the MOST Laid," Jezebel, April 20, 2013.

http://jezebel.com/happiness-is-not-just-getting-laid-its-getting-the-mos-476483024. Accessed October 28, 2014.

210 *"If I let him spend more than three minutes"*: Anonymous, "Last night and this morning . . . ," Do Tell. http://dotellstories.tumblr.com/post/90296261541/anonymous. Accessed October 28, 2014.

210 *"I've always been lucky in love/sex"*: E., 24, Argentina, "I've always been lucky...," Do Tell. http://dotellstories.tumblr.com/post/91888644517/e-24-argentina. Accessed October 28, 2014.

210 *"I feel like I was cruelly duped"*: Frank Bruni, "Naked in New York," *New York Times*, March 31, 2012. http://bruni.blogs.nytimes.com/2012/03/31/naked-in-new-york/. Accessed October 28, 2014.

211 *"situating the essence of the female"*: Ariel Levy, "The Space in Between," *New Yorker*, September 10, 2012. http://www.newyorker.com/magazine/2012/09/10/the-space-in-between. Accessed October 28, 2014.

211 *"a gateway to a woman's happiness"*: Ibid.

212 *"sex is the solution"*: Ibid.

212 *"the way you fuck is not 'private' "*: Jillian Horowitz, "Unpopular opinion: I'm a sex-negative feminist," xoJane.com, July 10, 2013. http://www.xojane.com/issues/im-a-sex-negative-feminist. Accessed October 28, 2014.

212 *"everyone who doesn't celebrate sex"*: Julie Decker, " 'Enjoy Your Houseful of Cats': On Being an Asexual Woman," The Toast, July 1, 2014. http://the-toast.net/2014/07/01/enjoy-houseful-cats-asexual-woman/. Accessed October 28, 2014.

213 *"as part of the fabric of routine day-to-day social life"*: Stevi Jackson, "Ordinary Sex," *Sexualities* 11 (February 2008), 35.

Bibliography

Anderson, Eric. *Inclusive Masculinity: The Changing Nature of Masculinities.* London: Routledge, 2009.

———. "Inclusive Masculinity in a Fraternal Setting." *Men and Masculinities* 10 (August 2008), 604–20.

———. "'Being Masculine Is Not About Who You Sleep with...': Heterosexual Athletes Contesting Masculinity and the One-time Rule of Homosexuality." *Sex Roles* 58 (2008), 105–15.

Anderson, Eric, Adi Adams, and Ian Rivers. "'I Kiss Them Because I Love Them': The Emergence of Heterosexual Men Kissing in British Institutes of Education." *Archives of Sexual Behavior* 41 (April 2012), 421–30.

Anderson, S. "Meet His New Saturday Night Wingman." *Cleo*, June 2008, 64–65.

Anonymous. "Last night and this morning..." Do Tell. http://dotellstories.tumblr.com/post/90296261541/anonymous. Accessed October 28, 2014.

Armstrong, Elizabeth A., Paula England, and Alison C. K. Fogarty. "Orgasm in College Hookups and Relationships." In *Families as They Really Are*, ed. Barbara Risman, 362–77. New York: Norton, 2009.

Armstrong, Elizabeth A., and Laura T. Hamilton, "'Good Girls': Gender, Social Class, and Slut Discourse on Campus." *Social Psychology Quarterly* 77 (June 2014), 100–122.

Armstrong, Elizabeth A., Laura Hamilton, and Paula England. "Is hooking up bad for young women?" *Contexts*, Summer 2010. http://contexts.org/articles/summer-2010/is-hooking-up-bad-for-young-women/. Accessed October 3, 2014.

Armstrong, Emily. "Pretty Is a Set of Skills." Jezebel, September 2, 2013. http://jezebel.com/pretty-is-a-set-of-skills-1202247029. Accessed October 10, 2014.

Astrea Media/Chicken and Egg Pictures. *Orgasm Inc.* Directed by Elizabeth Canner. 2011.

Astrof, Jeffrey, and Mike Sikowitz. "The One with the Blackout." *Friends*, season 1, episode 7, aired November 3, 1994.

Avins, Jenni. "Olivia Wilde Said a Great Many Things About Her Vagina Last Night." *Vulture*, October 9, 2012. http://www.vulture.com/2012/10/olivia-wilde-has-a-lot-to-say-about-her-vagina.html. Accessed October 15, 2014.

Balthazart, Jacques. "Minireview: Hormones and human sexual orientation." *Endocrinology* 152 (August 2011), 2937–47.

Barreto, Ariana. " 'Too Pretty to Be a Lesbian': A Conversation with a Bigot." In Our Words, January 5, 2012. http://inourwordsblog.com/2012/01/05/looking-gayer-a-conversation-with-a-bigot/. Accessed October 10, 2014.

Beard Rau, Alia. "Appeals Court to continue blocking Arizona abortion law." AZCentral, June 4, 2014. http://www.azcentral.com/story/news/arizona/politics/2014/06/03/arizona-abortion-law-blocked-appeals-court/9917647/. Accessed October 28, 2014.

Beauvoir, Simone de. *The Second Sex.* New York: Vintage, 1989.

Belenkaya, Veronika. "It's Juris-Imprudence." *Daily News* (NY), April 10, 2007. http://www.nydailynews.com/news/juris-imprudence-article-1.208599. Accessed October 3, 2014.

Bergner, Daniel. "Unexcited? There May Be a Pill for That." *New York Times*, May 22, 2013. http://www.nytimes.com/2013/05/26/magazine/unexcited-there-may-be-a-pill-for-that.html?pagewanted=1&_r=3&ref=magazine. Accessed October 13, 2014.

Berk, Brett. "Is *Skins* Really 'the Most Dangerous Television Show for Children Ever'?" VanityFair.com, January 13, 2011. http://www.vanityfair.com/online/daily/2011/01/is-skins-really-the-most-dangerous-television-show-for-children-ever. Accessed November 21, 2014.

Beyerstein, Lindsay. "Texas anti-abortion law forces women to make tough choices." Al Jazeera America, January 5, 2014. http://america.aljazeera.com/articles/2014/1/5/in-texas-abortionclinicsclose.html. Accessed October 28, 2014.

Blumstein, Philip, and Pepper Schwartz. *American Couples: Money, Work, Sex.* New York: William Morrow & Co, 1983.

Bogle, Kathleen. *Hooking Up: Sex, Dating, and Relationships on Campus.* New York: New York University Press, 2008.

Breakwell, G. M., and L. J. Millward. "Sexual Self-Concept and Sexual Risk-Taking." *Journal of Adolescence* 20 (February 1997), 29–41.

Brewer, Gayle, and Colin A. Hendrie. "Evidence to Suggest that Copulatory Vocalizations in Women Are Not a Reflexive Consequence of Orgasm." *Archives of Sexual Behavior* 40 (June 2010), 559–64.

"Bro." UrbanDictionary.com. http://www.urbandictionary.com/define .php?term=bro. Accessed October 11, 2014.

Bruni, Frank. "Naked in New York." *New York Times,* March 31, 2012. http:// bruni.blogs.nytimes.com/2012/03/31/naked-in-new-york/. Accessed October 28, 2014.

Burke, Tricia J., and Valerie J. Young. "Sexual Transformations and Intimate Behaviors in Romantic Relationships." *Journal of Sex Research* 49, no. 5 (2012), 454–63.

Burton, Natasha. "Keep 'em begging for more." *Maxim,* March 2013, 78.

Castleman, Michael. "The Most Important Sexual Statistic." *Psychology Today,* March 16, 2009. http://www.psychologytoday.com/blog/all-about -sex/200903/the-most-important-sexual-statistic. Accessed October 15, 2014.

Chandra, Anjani, et al. "Sexual Behavior, Sexual Attraction, and Sexual Identity in the United States: Data from the 2006–2008 National Survey of Family Growth." *National Health Statistics Report* 36 (March 3, 2011). http://www.cdc.gov/nchs/data/nhsr/nhsr036.pdf. Accessed October 10, 2014.

Chilton, Martin. "Woody Allen's 30 best one-liners." Telegraph.co.uk. http:// www.telegraph.co.uk/culture/culturepicturegalleries/10196567/Woody -Allens-30-best-one-liners.html?frame=2624765. Accessed October 13, 2014.

Connell, Erin, and Alan Hunt. "Sexual ideology and sexual physiology in the discourses of sex advice literature." *Canadian Journal of Human Sexuality* 15 (March 2006), 23–45.

Connell, Raewyn. "A Very Straight Gay: Masculinity, Homosexual Experience and the Dynamics of Gender." *American Sociological Review* 57 (December 1992), 735–51.

Coronet Instructional Films. *Going Steady?,* 1951. http://archive.org/details/ GoingSte1951. Accessed October 10, 2014.

Cox, Tracey. "What happens when you act out your sex fantasies?" *Cosmopolitan* (UK), May 2013, 194–98.

Culp-Ressler, Tara. "Oklahoma Considers Enacting Texas-Style Abortion Re-

strictions." ThinkProgress, February 12, 2014. http://thinkprogress.org/
health/2014/02/12/3281841/oklahoma-texas-abortion-restrictions/.
Accessed October 28, 2014.

———. "Ohio's New Abortion Ban Forces Women to Continue Doomed
Pregnancies Against Their Doctors' Wishes." ThinkProgress, February
11, 2014. http://thinkprogress.org/health/2014/02/11/3277111/ohio-
abortion-doctors-ban/. Accessed October 28, 2014.

———. "Iowa Governor Must Personally Decide Whether Each Poor Woman
on Medicaid Deserves Abortion Coverage." ThinkProgress, June 25, 2013.
http://thinkprogress.org/health/2013/06/25/2210571/iowa-gover
nor-medicaid-abortion-coverage/. Accessed October 28, 2014.

Curtin, Jennie. "What Makes a Happy Marriage? Sex!" *Sydney Morning Herald*, February 28, 2009. http://www.smh.com.au/articles/2009/02/27/
1235237920126.html. Accessed October 11, 2014.

Daley, Suzanne, and Nicholas Kulish. "Germany Fights Population Drop." *New
York Times*, August 13, 2013. http://www.nytimes.com/2013/08/14/
world/europe/germany-fights-population-drop.html?pagewanted=all&
_r=0. Accessed October 7, 2014.

Davies, Anna. "My Summer of Try-It-All Sex." *Glamour* (UK), April 2013,
79–86.

Decker, Julie. " 'Enjoy Your Houseful of Cats': On Being an Asexual Woman."
The Toast, July 1, 2014. http://the-toast.net/2014/07/01/enjoy-house
ful-cats-asexual-woman/. Accessed October 28, 2014.

Deveny, Kathleen. "No Sex, Please, We're Married." *Newsweek*, June 30, 2003.

Dreyfus, Hubert L., and Paul Rabinow. *Michel Foucault: Beyond Structuralism
and Hermeneutics.* 2nd ed. Chicago: The University of Chicago Press, 1983.

E., 24, Argentina. "I've always been lucky . . ." Do Tell. http://dotellstories
.tumblr.com/post/91888644517/e-24-argentina. Accessed October 28, 2014.

Ehrentheil, Otto F. "A case of premature ejaculation in Greek Mythology."
Journal of Sex Research 10 (May 1974), 128–31.

Elias, Norbert. *The Civilizing Process.* Vol. 1, *The History of Manners.* Oxford:
Blackwell, 1982.

"11 Facts About Gay Rights," DoSomething.org. http://www.dosomething
.org/tipsandtools/11-facts-about-gay-rights. Accessed October 10, 2014.

Eligon, John, and Erik Eckholm. "New Laws Ban Most Abortions in
North Dakota." *New York Times*, March 26, 2013. http://www.nytimes
.com/2013/03/27/us/north-dakota-governor-signs-strict-abortion-lim
its.html?pagewanted=all. Accessed October 28, 2014.

Elsley, Bryan. "Tony." *Skins*, season 1, episode 1, aired January 25, 2007.

Em & Lo. "The Summer Sex Plan." *Glamour* (UK), June 2012, 82–86.

Family Research Council. "Ten Arguments from Social Science Against Same-Sex Marriage." http://www.frc.org/get.cfm?i=if04g01. Accessed October 6, 2014.

Farnham, Alan. "Is Sex Necessary?" *Forbes*, October 8, 2003. http://www.forbes.com/2003/10/08/cz_af_1008health.html. Accessed October 15, 2014.

Farvid, Panteá, and Virginia Braun. " 'Most of us guys are raring to go anytime, anyplace, anywhere': Male and female sexuality in *Cleo* and *Cosmo*." *Sex Roles* 55 (September 2006), 295–310.

Fitzgerald, F. Scott. *This Side of Paradise*. Scribner: New York, 1920.

Flam, Faye. "Female orgasm: From Freud to Lloyd." *Seattle Times*, October 26, 2005. http://seattletimes.com/html/living/2002583270_carnalknowledge26.html. Accessed October 15, 2014.

Fleschler Peskin, Melissa, et al. "Prevalence and Patterns of Sexting Among Ethnic Minority Urban High School Students." *Cyberpsychology, Behavior, and Social Networking* 16 (June 2013), 454–59.

Flood, Michael. "Men, Sex and Homosociality: How Bonds Between Men Shape Their Sexual Relations with Women." *Men and Masculinities* 10 (April 2008), 339–59.

Foubert, John D., Johnathan T. Newberry, and Jerry L. Tatum, "Behavior differences seven months later: Effects of a rape prevention program." *NASPA Journal* 44, no. 4 (2007), 728–49.

Foucault, Michel. *The History of Sexuality*. Vol. 1, *The Will to Knowledge*. New York: Penguin, 1998.

———. *Discipline and Punish: The Birth of the Prison*. New York: Vintage, 1995.

Foucault, Michel, Bob Gallagher, and Alexander Wilson. "Sex, power, and the politics of identity." In *Michel Foucault: Ethics, Subjectivity and Truth*, ed. Paul Rabinow. New York: The New Press, 1994, 1:163–73.

Francis, Andrew M. "The wages of sin: How the discovery of penicillin reshaped modern sexuality." *Archives of Sexual Behavior* 42 (November 2013), 5–13.

"The Fraying Knot," *Economist*, January 12, 2013. http://www.economist.com/news/united-states/21569433-americas-marriage-rate-falling-and-its-out-wedlock-birth-rate-soaring-fraying. Accessed October 3, 2014.

Freeman, Nate. "Sexless and the City: Web Warps Libidos of Coked-Up Careerists." *New York Observer*, March 15, 2011. http://observer.com/2011/03/sexless-and-the-city-web-warps-libidos-of-cokedup-careerists/. Accessed October 6, 2014.

Friday, Nancy. *The Power of Beauty*. London: Hutchinson, 1996.

Gagnon, John H., and William Simon. *Sexual Conduct: The Social Sources of Human Sexuality*. Chicago: Aldine Publishing Company, 1973.

GetUp! Australia. "It's Time." YouTube, November 24, 2011. http://www .youtube.com/watch?v=_TBd-UCwVAY. Accessed October 10, 2014.

"GGG." UrbanDictionary.com. http://www.urbandictionary.com/define .php?term=GGG. Accessed October 15, 2014.

Gibbs, Nancy. "The Pill at 50: Sex, Freedom and Paradox." *Time*, April 22, 2010. http://content.time.com/time/magazine/article/0,9171,1983884,00 .html#ixzz2pM7f5NaO. Accessed October 3, 2014.

Giddens, Anthony. *Modernity and Self-Identity: Self and Society in the Late Modern Age*. Cambridge: Polity Press, 1991.

Gill, Rosalind. "From sexual objectification to sexual subjectification: The resexualisation of women's bodies in the media." *Feminist Media Studies* 3 (2003), 100–106.

Goddard, Alexandria. "Some people deserve to be peed on #whoareyou." Prinniefied.com, August 28, 2012. http://prinniefied.com/wp/some -people-deserve-to-be-peed-on-whoareyou-2/. Accessed October 28, 2014.

Goldberg-Meehan, Shana, and Scott Silveri. "The One with Rachel's Big Kiss." *Friends*, season 7, episode 20, aired April 26, 2001.

Grant, Jaime M., Lisa A. Mottet, and Justin Tannis. "Injustice at Every Turn: A Report of the National Transgender Discrimination Survey," 2011. http:// endtransdiscrimination.org/PDFs/NTDS_Exec_Summary.pdf. Accessed October 10, 2014.

Grant, Linda. *Sexing the Millennium: A Political History of the Sexual Revolution*. London: HarperCollins, 1993.

Grazian, David. "The Girl Hunt: Urban Nightlife and the Performance of Masculinity as Collective Activity." *Symbolic Interaction* 30 (Spring 2007), 221–43.

Green, Siski. "You are 5 questions away from great sex." *Glamour* (UK), March 2013, 92–97.

Griffin, Christine, Agnes Nairn, Patricia Gaya Wicks, Anne Phoenix, and Janine Hunter. "Girly Girls, Tomboys and Micro-waving Barbie: Child and Youth Consumption and the Disavowal of Femininity." *Eighth ACR Conference on Gender, Marketing and Consumer Behavior*, June 29–July 1, 2006, Edinburgh. http://www.acrwebsite.org/volumes/gmcb_v08/CP%20paper%20 1C%20Griffin.pdf. Accessed October 10, 2014.

Groneman, Carol. "Nymphomania: The Historical Construction of Female Sexuality." *Signs* 19 (1994), 337–67.

Gwynne, Kristen. "How Anonymous Hacking Exposed Steubenville Rape Case." Alternet.org, January 4, 2013. http://www.alternet.org/how-anony mous-hacking-exposed-steubenville-high-school-rape-case. Accessed October 28, 2014.

Haag, Pamela. "My Sex-Drought Marriage." *Times Magazine*, December 17, 2011.

Haller, J. S. "Spermatic Economy: A 19th Century View of Male Impotence." *Southern Medical Journal* 82 (August 1989), 1010–16.

Hamilton, Laura, and Elizabeth A. Armstrong. "Gendered Sexuality in Young Adulthood: Double Binds and Flawed Options." *Gender & Sexuality* 23 (October 2009), 589–616.

Harris, Alex. "Taking a Stand." *Men's Health*, March 2013, 125.

Harvey Nichols. "A Harvey Nichols Christmas 2011. Ever Faced the Walk of Shame?" YouTube, December 3, 2011. http://www.youtube.com/watch?v=kwxTf7NGVXg&feature=player_embedded. Accessed October 13, 2014.

Hawkes, Gail. *Sex and Pleasure in Western Culture*. Cambridge: Polity, 2004.

———. *A Sociology of Sex and Sexuality*. Philadelphia: Open University Press, 1996.

Hern, Alex. "How to make sex 'more awesome' using Google Glass." *Guardian*, January 21, 2014. http://www.theguardian.com/technology/2014/jan/21/how-to-make-sex-more-awesome-using-google-glass. Accessed October 15, 2014.

Hoffman, Jan. "How Many Americans Are Lesbian, Gay or Bisexual?" *New York Times*, July 21, 2014. http://well.blogs.nytimes.com/2014/07/21/how-many-americans-are-lesbian-gay-or-bisexual/?_r=1. Accessed November 21, 2014.

Hollway, Wendy. "Gender difference and the production of subjectivity." In *Changing the Subject: Psychology, Social Regulation and Subjectivity*, J. Henriques et al. London: Methuen, 1984, 227–63. http://www.brown.uk.com/brownlibrary/WEN2.htm. Accessed October 10, 2014.

Hong, Lawrence K. "Survival of the fastest: On the origin of premature ejaculation." *Journal of Sex Research* 20 (May 1984), 119.

Horin, Adele. "Men who share the load clean up in the bedroom." *Sydney Morning Herald*, January 8, 2010. http://www.smh.com.au/lifestyle/life/men-who-share-the-load-clean-up-in-the-bedroom-20100106-lude.html. Accessed October 11, 2014.

Horowitz, Jillian. "Unpopular opinion: I'm a sex-negative feminist." xoJane.com, July 10, 2013. http://www.xojane.com/issues/im-a-sex-negative-feminist. Accessed October 28, 2014.

Howe, Joseph W. "On the etiology, pathology, and treatment of spermator-rhoea and impotence." *Medical Record* 12 (October 27, 1877), 698.

Hudson, Christian, Felix Economakis, and Daniel Sloss. "How to Close the Deal with Beautiful Women." *FHM* (UK), March 2013, 84–91.

Hung, Manuel. "Daddy's Little Helpers." *Next Magazine*, September 7, 2012. http://www.nextmagazine.com/content/daddy's-little-helpers. Accessed October 15, 2014.

Inman, Michael. "Guilty Verdict in ADFA Skype Sex Case." *Sydney Morning Herald*, August 23, 2013. http://www.canberratimes.com.au/act-news/guilty-verdict-in-adfa-skype-sex-case-20130828-2sq7v.html?rand=1382489144939. Accessed October 11, 2014.

Jackson, Stevi. "Ordinary Sex." *Sexualities* 11 (February 2008), 33–37.

Jackson, Stevi, and Amanda Rees. "The Appalling Appeal of Nature: The Popular Influence of Evolutionary Psychology as a Problem for Sociology," *Sociology* 41 (October 2007), 917–30.

Jackson, Stevi, and Sue Scott. "Sexual antinomies in late modernity." *Sexualities* 7 (May 2004), 233–48.

James, E. L. *Fifty Shades of Grey*. London: Arrow Books, 2012.

Jancovich, Mark. "Naked Ambitions: Pornography, Taste, and the Problem of the Middlebrow." *Scope: An Online Journal of Film Studies* (June 2001). URL not available.

Jeffrey, Morgan. "Parents' group slams MTV's *Skins*." DigitalSpy.co.uk, January 14, 2011. http://www.digitalspy.co.uk/ustv/s89/skins/news/a297965/parents-group-slams-mtvs-skins.html. Accessed November 21, 2014.

Jinman, Richard. "Generation Sex." *Sydney Morning Herald Spectrum*, October 8, 2005.

Jopson, Debra, and Elicia Murray. " 'Generation sex' as norms shift." *The Age*, May 17, 2009. http://www.theage.com.au/national/generation-sex-as-norms-shift-20090516-b6tn.html. Accessed October 3, 2014.

Joyal, Christian C., Amelie Cossette, and Vanessa Lapierre. "What Exactly Is an Unusual Sexual Fantasy?" *Journal of Sexual Medicine*, published online October 30, 2014.

Kaplan, Vic (Producer) and Bruce Gowers (Director). *Robin Williams: Live at the Met*. Mr. Happy Productions, August 9, 1986.

Karimi, Faith. "Cameroon court acquits 2 men imprisoned for 'looking gay.'" CNN, January 10, 2013. http://edition.cnn.com/2013/01/09/world/africa/cameroon-gay-men-freed. Accessed October 28, 2014.

Katz, Jane. "Yes, You Have a G-Spot," Cosmopolitan.com, May 21, 2009. http://www.cosmopolitan.com/sex-love/advice/a2923/yes-you-have-a-g-spot-0409/. Accessed January 19, 2015.

Katz, Jonathan. *The Invention of Heterosexuality.* New York: Dutton, 1995.

Kimmel, Michael. *Guyland: The Perilous World in Which Boys Become Men.* New York: HarperCollins, 2008.

Kinsey, Alfred, Wardell Pomeroy, and Clyde Martin. *Sexual Behavior in the Human Male.* Philadelphia: W. B. Saunders, 1948.

Kwan, Raymond. "Don't Dress Like a Slut: Toronto Cop." *Excalibur,* April 23, 2011. http://www.excal.on.ca/news/dont-dress-like-a-slut-toronto-cop/. Accessed October 11, 2014.

Lane, Anthony. "Sex, lies and duct tape: Science and morality make for strange bedfellows in D-11." *Colorado Springs Independent,* April 8, 2010. http://www.csindy.com/coloradosprings/sex-lies-and-duct-tape-science-and-morality-make-for-strange-bedfellows-in-d-11/Content?oid=1672302. Accessed October 28, 2014.

Leff, Lisa. "Actress' claim to be gay by choice riles activists." Yahoo! News, January 27, 2012. http://news.yahoo.com/actress-claim-gay-choice-riles-activists-201717513.html. Accessed October 29, 2014.

Levy, Ariel. "The Space in Between." *New Yorker,* September 10, 2012. http://www.newyorker.com/magazine/2012/09/10/the-space-in-between. Accessed October 28, 2014.

———. *Female Chauvinist Pigs: Women and the Rise of Raunch Culture.* New York: Free Press, 2005.

Lichtenstein, Olivia. "How the faceless and immoral world of cyberspace has created a deeply disturbing . . . generation SEX." *Daily Mail,* January 28, 2009. · http://www.dailymail.co.uk/femail/article-1129978/How-faceless-amoral-world-cyberspace-created-deeply-disturbing—generation-SEX.html. Accessed October 3, 2014.

"Life Planner: Fun Fearless Female." http://www.cosmopolitan.co.za/career-money/AwesomeWomen/Archive. Accessed August 1, 2014.

Ling, Peter. "Sex and the Automobile in the Jazz Age." *History Today* 39 (November 1989). http://www.historytoday.com/peter-ling/sex-and-automobile-jazz-age. Accessed October 10, 2014.

Lisak, David, and Paul M. Miller. "Repeat Rape and Multiple Offending Among Undetected Rapists." *Violence and Victims* 17 (February 2002), 73–84.

Lithwick, Dahlia. "Virginia's Proposed Ultrasound Law Is an Abomination." *Slate*, February 16, 2012. http://www.slate.com/articles/double_x/doublex/2012/02/virginia_ultrasound_law_women_who_want_an_abortion_will_be_forcibly_penetrated_for_no_medical_reason.html. Accessed October 28, 2014.

Luis, Vanessa. "Emotional and Mental Health Benefits of Sex." Health Me Up, July 15, 2014. http://healthmeup.com/news-healthy-living/emotional-and-mental-health-benefits-of-sex/29015. Accessed October 15, 2014.

Machin, David, and Joanna Thornborrow. "Lifestyle and the Depoliticisation of Agency: Sex as Power in Women's Magazines." *Social Semiotics* 16, no. 1 (2006), 173–88.

———. "Branding and discourse: the case of *Cosmopolitan*." *Discourse & Society* 14 (July 2003), 443–71.

Marrone, Katherine. "Sex: Excessive pornographic exposure can screw you in the sack." DailyEmerald.com, June 6, 2013. http://dailyemerald.com/2013/06/06/sex-the-dark-side-of-pornography/. Accessed October 29, 2014.

Martin, Karin, and Emily Kazyak. "Hetero-romantic love and heterosexiness in children's G-rated films." *Gender & Society* 23 (June 2009), 315–36.

Martinez, G., C. E. Copen, and J. C. Abma. "Teenagers in the United States: Sexual activity, contraceptive use, and childbearing, 2006–2010 National Survey of Family Growth." *Vital and Health Statistics* 23, no. 31 (October 2011). http://www.cdc.gov/nchs/data/series/sr_23/sr23_031.pdf. Accessed October 11, 2014.

Miller, Korin. "Why Taken Guys Seem Sexier." Cosmopolitan.com, May 4, 2010. http://www.cosmopolitan.com/sex-love/relationship-advice/why-taken-guys-are-sexier. Accessed October 6, 2014.

Mitchell, Kaye. "Raunch versus prude: Contemporary sex blogs and erotic memoirs by women." *Psychology and Sexuality* 3 (January 2012), 12–25.

Moore, Molly. "As Europe Grows Grayer, France Devises a Baby Boom." *Washington Post*, October 18, 2006. http://www.washingtonpost.com/wp-dyn/content/article/2006/10/17/AR2006101701652.html. Accessed October 7, 2014.

Moore, Tracy. "Happiness Is Not Just Getting Laid, It's Getting the MOST

Laid." Jezebel, April 20, 2013. http://jezebel.com/happiness-is-not-just-getting-laid-its-getting-the-mos-476483024. Accessed October 28, 2014.

"Morals: The Second Sexual Revolution." *Time*, January 24, 1964. http://content.time.com/time/subscriber/article/0,33009,875692-1,00.html. Accessed October 3, 2014.

Morgan, Elizabeth M., and Eileen L. Zurbriggen. "Wanting sex and wanting to wait: young adults' accounts of sexual messages from first significant dating partners." *Feminism & Psychology* 17 (November 2007), 515–41.

Morrison, Todd G., Travis A. Ryan, Lisa Fox, Daragh T. McDermott, and Melanie A. Morrison. "Canadian university students' perceptions of the practices that constitute 'normal' sexuality for men and women." *Canadian Journal of Human Sexuality* 17, no. 4 (2008), 161–71.

Moses, Lucia. "Millennial Guys Are Turning to Makeup: Survey Finds Masculinity Isn't What It Used to Be." AdWeek.com, June 19, 2013. http://www.adweek.com/news/advertising-branding/millennial-guys-are-turning-makeup-150313. Accessed October 7, 2014.

Moynihan, Ray. "The Making of a Disease: Female Sexual Dysfunction." *British Medical Journal* 326 (January 4, 2003), 45–47.

Muehlenhard, Charlene L., and Sheena K. Shippee. "Men's and Women's Reports of Pretending Orgasm." *Journal of Sex Research* 47, no. 6 (2010), 552–67.

Murphy, Kevin. "Kansas set to enact life-starts-'at fertilization' abortion law." Reuters, April 6, 2013. http://www.reuters.com/article/2013/04/06/us-usa-kansas-abortion-idUSBRE93501220130406. Accessed October 28, 2014.

Myers, Kristen, and Laura Raymond. "Elementary School Girls and Heteronormativity: The Girl Project." *Gender & Society* 24 (April 2010), 167–88.

National Campaign to Prevent Teen and Unplanned Pregnancy. *That's What He Said: What Guys Think About Sex, Love, Contraception and Relationships.* January 2010. https://thenationalcampaign.org/resource/thats-what-he-said. Accessed October 11, 2014.

National Center for Injury Prevention and Control, Division of Violence Prevention. "Sexual Violence: Facts at a Glance." 2012. http://www.cdc.gov/ViolencePrevention/pdf/SV-DataSheet-a.pdf. Accessed October 28, 2014.

Naughton, Julia. "The Summer (Sex) Bucket List." *Cosmopolitan* (Australia), December 2012, 31.

Nikunen, Kaarina. "Cosmo Girls Talk: Blurring Boundaries of Porn and Sex."

In *Pornification: Sex and Sexuality in Media Culture*, ed. Susanna Paasonen, Kaarina Nikunen, and Laura Saarenmaa. Oxford: Berg, 2007, 73–85.

NUS. *That's What She Said: Women Students' Experiences of "Lad Culture" in Higher Education* (London: NUS, 2013).

Outreach Programme on the Rwanda Genocide and the United Nations. "Background Information on Sexual Violence Used as a Tool of War." http://www.un.org/en/preventgenocide/rwanda/about/bgsexualvio lence.shtml. Accessed October 28, 2014.

Parr, Nick. "The baby bonus failed to increase fertility, but we should still keep it." The Conversation, December 4, 2011. https://theconversation .com/the-baby-bonus-failed-to-increase-fertility-but-we-should-still -keep-it-4528. Accessed October 7, 2014.

Pascoe, C. J. "'Dude, You're a Fag': Adolescent Masculinity and the Fag Discourse." *Sexualities* 8 (July 2005), 326–48.

Patrick, Donald L., et al. "Premature Ejaculation: An Observational Study of Men and Their Partners." *Journal of Sexual Medicine* 2 (May 2005), 358–67.

Pew Research Center. "Changing Attitudes on Gay Marriage." March 2014. http://features.pewforum.org/same-sex-marriage-attitudes/slide2.php. Accessed October 10, 2014.

Plummer, Ken. *Telling Sexual Stories: Power, Change and Social Worlds*. London: Routledge, 1995.

Populus. "Gay Couples' Rights Survey." March 2012. http://www.populus.co.uk/ wp-content/uploads/OmGay_Rights.pdf. Accessed October 10, 2014.

Potts, Annie. *The Science/Fiction of Sex: Feminist Deconstruction and the Vocabularies of Heterosex*. Sussex: Routledge, 2002.

Przybylo, Ela. "Crisis and safety: The asexual in sexusociety." *Sexualities* 14 (August 2011), 446.

Rabin, Roni Caryn. "Nearly 1 in 5 Women in US Survey Say They Have Been Sexually Assaulted." *New York Times*, December 14, 2011. http://www .nytimes.com/2011/12/15/health/nearly-1-in-5-women-in-us-survey -report-sexual-assault.html. Accessed October 11, 2014.

Regnerus, Mark. "Sex Is Cheap: Why Young Men Have the Upper Hand in Bed, Even When They're Failing in Life." *Slate*, February 25, 2011. http:// www.slate.com/articles/double_x/doublex/2011/02/sex_is_cheap .html. Accessed October 3, 2014.

Regnerus, Mark, and Jeremy Uecker. *Premarital Sex in America: How Young Americans Meet, Mate, and Think About Marriage*. New York: Oxford University Press, 2011.

Rodriguez-Larralde, Alvaro, and Irene Paradisi. "Influence of genetic factors on human sexual orientation." *Journal of Clinical Investigation* 50 (September 2009), 377–91.

Roiphe, Katie. "Spanking Goes Mainstream." *Newsweek,* April 16, 2012. http://mag.newsweek.com/2012/04/15/working-women-s-fantasies .html. Accessed October 11, 2014.

Rosenbaum, Janet Elise. "Patient Teenagers? A Comparison of the Sexual Behavior of Virginity Pledgers and Matched Nonpledgers." *Pediatrics* 123 (January 2009), 110–20.

Rosin, Hanna. "Boys on the Side." *Atlantic,* August 22, 2012. http://www .theatlantic.com/magazine/archive/2012/09/boys-on-the-side/ 309062/. Accessed October 13, 2014.

Roy, Jessica. " 'Spreadsheets' App Measures How Loud You Moan to Determine If You're Good at Sex." *Betabeat,* August 12, 2013. http://betabeat .com/2013/08/spreadsheets-app-measures-how-loud-you-moan-to-de termine-if-youre-good-at-sex/. Accessed October 15, 2014.

Rubin, Gayle. "Thinking Sex: Notes for a Radical Theory of the Politics of Sexuality." In *Pleasure and Danger: Exploring Female Sexuality,* ed. Carole S. Vance, 267–319. London, UK: Routledge, 1984.

Ryan, Christopher. "On Older Men, Younger Women, and Moralistic Claptrap." *Psychology Today,* June 14, 2013. http://www.psychologytoday .com/blog/sex-dawn/201306/older-men-younger-women-and-moralis tic-claptrap. Accessed October 15, 2014.

Sanders, Stephanie A., et al. "Misclassification bias: Diversity in conceptualizations about having 'had sex.' " *Sexual Health* 7 (March 2010), 31–34.

Saulny, Susan. "Young in G.O.P. Erase the Lines on Social Issues." *New York Times,* August 8, 2012. http://www.nytimes.com/2012/08/09/us/ politics/young-republicans-erase-lines-on-social-issues.html?hp&_r=0. Accessed October 10, 2014.

Savage, Dan. "Asexuality for Beginners." *Stranger,* September 1, 2009. http:// slog.thestranger.com/slog/archives/2009/09/01/asexuality-for-begin ners. Accessed October 10, 2014.

Schalet, Amy T. "Caring, Romantic, American Boys." *New York Times,* April 6, 2012. http://www.nytimes.com/2012/04/07/opinion/caring-roman tic-american-boys.html. Accessed October 11, 2014.

Scott, Catherine. "Thinking Kink: Is Vanilla Sex Boring? Who Gets to Decide?" *Bitch,* July 16, 2012. http://bitchmagazine.org/post/thinking-kink -vanilla-sex-bdsm-feminist-magazine-sexuality. Accessed October 15, 2014.

Serna, Joseph. "Federal judge rules Arkansas abortion law unconstitutional." *Los Angeles Times*, March 14, 2014. http://articles.latimes.com/2014/mar/14/nation/la-na-nn-arkansas-abortion-law-unconstitutional-20140314. Accessed October 28, 2014.

"78 countries where homosexuality is illegal." Erasing 76 Crimes. http://76crimes.com/76-countries-where-homosexuality-is-illegal/. Accessed October 28, 2014.

"Sex App That Measures Your Performance in a Spreadsheet Is Surely the Least Sexiest Thing?" *Huffington Post UK*, August 13 2013. http://www.huffingtonpost.co.uk/2013/08/13/sex-app-performance-spreadsheet_n_3748999.html. Accessed October 15, 2014.

Sherfey, Mary Jane. "The evolution and nature of female sexuality in relation to psychoanalytic theory." *Journal of the American Psychoanalytic Association* 14 (January 1966), 28–128.

Siebold, Carmel. "Factors Influencing Young Women's Sexual and Reproductive Health." *Contemporary Nurse* 37 (February 2011), 124–36.

Simmonds, Alecia. "When did it stop being OK for men to hold hands?" *Daily Life*, March 13, 2013. http://www.dailylife.com.au/news-and-views/dl-opinion/when-did-it-stop-being-ok-for-men-to-hold-hands-20130313-2g098.html. Accessed October 11, 2014.

Simotas, Alexandra. "Female Sex Drive Linked to Emotions." *Houston Chronicle*, September 6, 2006. http://blog.chron.com/herhealth/2006/09/female-sex-drive-linked-to-emotions/. Accessed October 11, 2014.

Smiler, Andrew P. *Challenging Casanova: Beyond the Stereotype of the Promiscuous Young Male*. San Francisco: Jossey-Bass, 2013.

Souter, Fenella. "Generation Sex." *Good Weekend, Sydney Morning Herald*, February, 11, 2006.

Stossel, John, and Gena Binkley. "Gay Stereotypes: Are They True?" ABC News, September 15, 2006. http://abcnews.go.com/2020/story?id=2449185. Accessed October 11, 2014.

Streicher, Lauren. "Pain for Pleasure? The O-Shot." The Oz Blog, March 19, 2014. http://blog.doctoroz.com/oz-experts/pain-for-pleasure-the-o-shot. Accessed October 15, 2014.

Tashman, Brian. "E. W. Jackson: Gays and Lesbians Are 'Very Sick People Psychologically, Mentally and Emotionally.'" Right Wing Watch, October 25, 2012. http://www.rightwingwatch.org/content/jackson-gays-lesbians-very-sick-people-psychologically-mentally-emotionally. Accessed October 28, 2014.

Taylor, Kate. "Sex on Campus: She Can Play That Game Too." *New York Times,* July 12, 2013. http://www.nytimes.com/2013/07/14/fashion/sex-on -campus-she-can-play-that-game-too.html. Accessed October 13, 2014.

Taylor, Laramie D. "All for Him: Articles About Sex in American Lad Magazines." *Sex Roles* 52 (February 2005), 153–63.

Thorn, Clarisse. "The Myth of the Sex-Crazy Nympho Dream Girl." The Good Men Project, May 20, 2011. http://goodmenproject.com/sex-relation ships/myth-sex-crazy-nympho-dream-girl/. Accessed October 15, 2014.

Tiefer, Leonore. *Sex Is Not a Natural Act and Other Essays.* Boulder, CO: Westview, 2004.

Tolman, Deborah L., Renee Spencer, Tricia Harmon, Myra Rosen-Reynoso, and Meg Striepe. "Getting Close, Staying Cool: Early Adolescent Boys' Experiences with Romantic Relationships." In *Adolescent Boys: Exploring Diverse Cultures of Boyhood,* ed. Niobe Way and Judy Chu. New York: New York University Press, 2004, 235–55.

Turner, Christopher. "Wilhelm Reich: The Man Who Invented Free Love." *Guardian,* July 9, 2011. http://www.theguardian.com/books/2011/ jul/08/wilhelm-reich-free-love-orgasmatron. Accessed October 15, 2014.

Turner, Natasha, ND. "5 unexpected health benefits of orgasms," Chatelaine .com, December 31, 2014. http://www.chatelaine.com/health/sex-and -relationships/five-unexpected-health-benefits-of-orgasms/. Accessed January 19, 2015.

Valenti, Jessica. *The Purity Myth: How America's Obsession with Virginity Is Hurting Young Women.* Berkeley: Seal Press, 2009.

Vargas-Cooper, Natasha. "Hard Core." *Atlantic,* January/February 2011. http://www.theatlantic.com/magazine/archive/2011/01/hard -core/308327/. Accessed October 6, 2014.

Wade, Lisa. "College, Fun, and Pluralistic Ignorance." *Sociological Images,* September 6, 2012. http://thesocietypages.org/socimages/2012/09/06/ college-fun-and-pluralistic-ignorance/. Accessed October 3, 2014.

Wade, Lisa, and Caroline Heldman. "Hooking Up and Opting Out: Negotiating Sex in the First Year of College." In *Sex for Life: From Virginity to Viagra, How Sex Changes Throughout Our Lives,* ed. Laura M. Carpenter and John DeLamater, 128–45. New York University Press: New York, 2012.

Waldinger, Marcel D., et al. "Ejaculation Disorders: A Multinational Population Survey of Intravaginal Ejaculation Latency Time." *Journal of Sexual Medicine* 2 (July 2005), 492–97.

Walker, Marcus. "In Estonia, paying women to have babies pays off." *Pittsburgh Post-Gazette,* October 20, 2006. http://www.post-gazette.com/life/life style/2006/10/20/In-Estonia-paying-women-to-have-babies-pays-off/ stories/200610200166. Accessed October 7, 2014.

Walker, Shelley. "Sexting: Young Women's and Men's Views on Its Nature and Origins." *Journal of Adolescent Health* 52 (June 2013), 697–701.

Waller, Willard. "The Rating and Dating Complex." *American Sociological Review* 2 (October 1937), 727–34.

Wilson, Brenda. "Sex Without Intimacy: No Dating, No Relationships." NPR, June 8, 2009. http://www.npr.org/templates/story/story.php?sto ryId=105008712. Accessed October 3, 2014.

World Health Organization. "Violence against women," fact sheet no. 239. http://www.who.int/mediacentre/factsheets/fs239/en/. Accessed October 28, 2014.

Yew, Lee Kuan. "Warning Bell for Developed Countries: Declining Birth Rates." *Forbes,* April 25, 2012. http://www.forbes.com/global/2012/0507/ current-events-population-declining-birth-rates-lee-kuan-yew.html. Accessed October 14, 2014.

Yoffe, Emily. "College Women: Stop Getting Drunk." *Slate,* October 15, 2013. http://www.slate.com/articles/double_x/doublex/2013/10/sexual _assault_and_drinking_teach_women_the_connection.html. Accessed October 11, 2014.

Zeilinger, Julie. "Kahnoodle App Makes Reigniting Your Relationship into a Game." *Huffington Post,* August 9, 2013. http://www.huffingtonpost .com/2013/08/09/kahnoodle-app-makes-reigniting-your-relationship -into-a-game_n_3732916.html. Accessed October 15, 2014.

Zirin, Dave. "How Jock Culture Supports Rape Culture, from Maryville to Steubenville." *Nation,* October 25, 2013. http://www.thenation.com/ blog/176846/how-jock-culture-supports-rape-culture-maryville-steu benville#. Accessed October 11, 2014.

Index

About the Author

Rachel Hills is an Australian journalist living in New York City. As in *The Sex Myth*, her writing deals with big ideas in gender, sociology, and popular culture in ways that are accessible and relatable. Her work has been published widely both in print and online, in publications including *Vogue, Cosmopolitan,* the *Atlantic, Time,* the *New Republic, New York,* the *Sydney Morning Herald,* and many others.

Rachel's blog, Musings of an Inappropriate Woman (RachelHills.tumblr.com), has more than one hundred thousand subscribers spanning the globe. You can connect with her on Twitter at @rachelhills, on Facebook at www.facebook.com/rachelhillswriter, or sign up to receive occasional letters from her at www.tinyletter.com/rachelhills.

Index

The New Nietzsche, ed. D. Allison (New York: Delta, 1977). An insight into contemporary French readings by Derrida, Deleuze and others. Difficult but provocative.

Nietzsche, by Michael Tanner (Oxford: Oxford University Press, 1994). Irascible, humorous and full of insights. The best modern short commentary.

Biographies

The Tragic Philosopher, by F. Lea (London: Athlone Press, 1993). Highly stylized and biased, but containing much interesting detail.

Nietzsche on Tragedy, by M. Silk and J. Stern (Cambridge: Cambridge University Press, 1981). A biographical commentary, full of useful insights.

Acknowledgements

Laurence Gane would like to thank Chris Horrocks, Michael Tanner, Richard Appignanesi and the ghost of Michel Foucault. Supreme gratitude to Gabrielle for her undying provocation and Nietzschean fortitude.

The artist would like to thank Richard Appignanesi (it was a pleasure to work with him), and dedicate this book to Osvaldo, Amanda, Car, Ro, Mori, Roci, El Barba, Dora, Mono, Papo, Yeyo, Lili, Chancho, Cacho, Fer, Lu, Meme and of course Silvina.

Laurence Gane read Philosophy at University College London and Kings College, London. He teaches at the Royal College of Art and lives in Snowdonia, Wales.

Piero is an illustrator, artist and graphic designer. He earned his degree at the Art University of La Plata, Buenos Aires, and his work has twice been included in the Royal College of Art in London. He is also the illustrator of *Introducing Shakespeare*, *Introducing Anthropology* and *Introducing Psychiatry*.